THE IDEA OF MODERN JI

The Reference Library of Jewish Intellectual History

ACADEMIC
STUDIES
PRESS

The Idea of Modern Jewish Culture

ELIEZER SCHWEID

Translated by Amnon HADARY
edited by Leonard LEVIN

BOSTON
2010

ISBN 978-1-936235-09-4

On the cover: David Tartakover, Proclamation of Independence, 1988 (Detail)
Book design by Yuri Alexandrov

Published by Academic Studies Press in 2010
28 Montfern Avenue
Brighton, MA 02135, USA
press@academicstudiespress.com
www.academicstudiespress.com

Contents

Editor's Preface

The Idea of Modern Jewish Culture is the keystone of the intellectual-historical and theoretical thought of Eliezer Schweid. In it, he articulates his own personal formulation of the "spiritual-Zionist" vision of Ahad Ha-Am, Bialik, and A. D. Gordon, of which he is one of the leading contemporary proponents and spokesmen.

Eliezer Schweid was a child of pioneer Zionism. Born in Jerusalem in 1929, he was educated in the secular Zionist schools and youth movement, and was a member of a kibbutz-forming *"gar'in."* At 19, he was a soldier in the Israeli War of Independence. His spiritual crises, growing out of that experience, led him to explore the legacy of Jewish thought in all its manifestations — religious and secular, ancient, medieval and modern. As Professor of Jewish Thought at Hebrew University, educator and intellectual, and author of 40 books on Jewish thought of all periods, he has taught and mentored generations of Israelis to mine the spiritual, intellectual and moral legacy of Jewish thought for the formation of their own identities and to provide the experiential background and moral compass to guide them in the present.

The current work addresses the questions: (1) How did Jews, from the Enlightenment to the present, come to perceive their Jewish existence as "culture"? (2) How has that perception shaped nearly all the forms — religious and secular, academic, Zionist, Yiddishist and general-political — that Jewish life has taken in the modern age? (3) Has the dream to create an authentic Jewish culture ever been fully realized? Is it being realized now?

This book is "prophetic," not in the prognostic sense but in the spiritual-critical sense that Ahad Ha-Am articulated in his essays "Priest and Prophet" and "Moses." It is designed to arouse discomfort in every reader, whether Jewish or non-Jewish, Israeli or Diaspora, secular or religious, political or apolitical in orientation. The discomfort is aroused by calling attention to ideals that were only partly fulfilled in their heyday, but refuse to be relegated to the dust-bin of history, because they still have the power to stand as a beacon and basis of critique of current reality.

The ideal central to this book is simple and powerful: that Judaism, conceived as a humanly-created culture on religious foundations, distilled from over three millennia of Israelite-and-Jewish history, life and thought, should stand as a beacon and guide to the formation of a distinctive Jewish group-life today, in dialogue with contemporary world culture but not overpowered by and subordinate to it.

The ideal is clear and powerful. The critique that issues from it is equally powerful, for hardly anywhere in the world today — not in the disco-clubs of secular Tel Aviv or the yeshivot of ultra-Orthodox Mea Shearim, not in the Bar Mitzvah parties of American Jews or (except now and then) in the halls of Jewish academia, and only haltingly and imperfectly in the best communal foci of Jewish group-life, religious or secular throughout the world — is this vision taken to heart and turned into flesh-and-blood reality.

It is easy to disqualify this vision-statement and critique. The ultra-religious may disqualify it because it does not recognize the unqualified divine origin of Judaism. Diaspora Jews may disqualify it because it depicts typical Diaspora institutions — liberal Jewish religion, Western-style academic Jewish scholarship, the early-20th-century Yiddish literary flourishing and more recent Yiddish revival — as less potently "Jewish" and more assimilationist in tendency than the Hebrew-based cultural revival. Politically-minded Israelis may disqualify it because the call to Jewish culture seems utopian and does not provide a ready practical answer to Israel's current pressing realities. Academic scholars may disqualify it because Schweid admittedly does not aim at producing the most detailed, footnoted empirically-based factual research for its own sake but has instead made another objective the central focus of his attention — namely, how the fruits of historical scholarship can be enlisted in addressing the existential spiritual concerns of the Jewish people, redefining its identity and guiding its life-decisions in the present age as in previous ages. There may be some validity in each of the critiques, from their respective standpoints. But each critic should examine his own soul and ask, whether the critique may perhaps arise partly from defensive motives, to avoid taking seriously the prophetic challenge implicit in Schweid's vision.

Apart from its value as visionary-critical statement, *The Idea of Modern Jewish Culture* provides two other valuable services, analytical and histo-rical-pedagogic. As an analytical essay-monograph, it provides a compre-hensive overview of the impact of the notion of "culture" on many phases of modern Jewish life — liberal Jewish religion, academic historical Jewish scholarship, the Jewish nationalist and socialist movements, and even Jewish assimilationism — that are not normally studied together. The value of such an analytical approach for generating insight should be self-evident. In the heat of debate between polar opposite positions — the religious-versus-secular, the Diaspora-versus-Zionist — it is important to stress the common denominator between them. It is not intuitively obvious, for instance, to view a modern religious movement as having a secular-cultural dimension, or a secular movement as responding to religious questions, but once we learn to appreciate these subtleties, our understanding of each of the phenomena is enriched, as well as their place in the total sweep of modern Jewish history.

Ultimately, it is to the understanding of Jewish intellectual history that this work — as well as the vast majority of Schweid's oeuvre — is devoted. In that larger enterprise, this work stands as a monograph devoted to a specific topic: the role of "the idea of Jewish culture" in the unfolding of alternative programs for Jewish existence in the modern period. Specific in focus, it addresses one facet of a complex reality. On the axis of the religious-secular dichotomy, this inquiry focuses predominantly — though not exclusively — on the secular side. The reader of Schweid's larger oeuvre will easily find other works, written from different perspectives, to complement the specificity of this focus. To name three:

1. In *The Classic Jewish Philosophers* (*Ha-Filosofim ha-Gedolim Shelanu*), Schweid offers a general historical narrative of medieval Jewish philosophy, in which however his overarching cultural-analytical perspective is clearly noticeable beneath the surface. The intellectual problems of medieval philosophy are thus presented as varied exercises in cultural mediation: how to present a unified outlook that does justice to the contradictory methods and views of pagan Greek philosophy and the monotheistic Jewish traditional religious teaching. Schweid also gives notice there how the diverse intellectual stances of such thinkers as Halevi, Maimonides and Crescas will provide precedents and intellectual tools for modern thinkers to capitalize on — a promissory note that is fully redeemed in his studies in modern Jewish intellectual history (as note the close comparison of Krochmal with Maimonides in the current volume).

2. In *Philosophy of the Bible as Foundation for Jewish Culture*, Schweid offers his personal reading of the Bible, based on those of modern Jewish thinkers whom he analyzes elsewhere (Spinoza, Cohen, Buber, Heschel), that is rich in implied lessons for contemporary Jewish existence. That book is an object-lesson and demonstration of the theory of Jewish culture articulated in the present volume: how to reinterpret the classic foundational works of the Jewish tradition in a way that bridges ancient and modern experience, weaving the diverse materials of ancient memory and present-day life into an integral whole, and building contemporary existence on the template of the old.

3. In *The History of Modern Jewish Religious Philosophy*, Schweid provides balance to the current volume in two ways: (a) Whereas the emphasis in the current volume is tilted toward secular themes, in *The History of Modern Jewish Religious Philosophy* Schweid focuses on the religious — for instance,

by giving major treatment to thinkers such as Hermann Cohen and Franz Rosenzweig who are not treated in this volume. (b) Whereas the current volume is selective in the service of a single idea, the other study is more comprehensive, treating the unfolding of modern Jewish thought from a multitude of perspectives.

Thus the self-imposed limitations of this work are fully compensated elsewhere in Schweid's output. Still, the importance of this book should not be underrated. Though specific in focus, the current work is central to Schweid's overall project, both in addressing the strands of thought (especially, but not exclusively, the history of modern spiritual Zionism) most basic to his own outlook, and for its systematic exploration of the concept of "Jewish culture" that is fundamental to his methodology throughout all his writings.

May this book find a wide audience and help stimulate a continuation of the renaissance of Jewish culture whose progress up to the present day it chronicles.

Leonard Levin
New York, December, 2007

Foreword

Perhaps the most important and characteristic feature of modern culture generally — and of modern Judaism in particular — is the centrality of the notion of "culture" itself (rather than "God's will," eternal verities, or unchanging natural law) to its many impressive philosophical and scholarly self-understandings. But this notion of culture — pervasive in our philosophical and scholarly self-understandings — suffers from a plethora of meanings. We cannot employ this term precisely and systematically without first defining the aspects and contexts intended.

In the most general sense, which is trivial but is pre-assumed by the more precise theoretical usages, culture is the totality of material and intellectual creations (including their interdependencies) that are produced and preserved by a human society. The etymology of the Hebrew term *tarbut* points to its source: its root meaning is "increase," and it comprises the value added by humans to those resources found originally in a pristine state. Every alteration of those natural resources — whether quantitative, qualitative, or formal, by way of reworking, completion, or development with the aim of realizing objectives and purposes that a human society sets for itself — is a cultural process. We can extend this basic notion to include the infinite variety of human creations, goals, ends, means, and circumstances and their myriad interconnections. The generic notion of culture adds to these specific matters only the fundamental presupposition that is the basis of all inquiries and research on this topic, namely that in all its domains we are dealing with practical human activity on the raw materials of nature — or of nature and human spirit* — in interaction with each other.

But when we come to deal with the meaning of the term "Jewish culture," the primary, trivial sense takes on a deliberate, non-trivial significance: it points to the polarizing confrontation that accompanied the emergence of this concept in public discourse. The debate was over whether "Judaism"

---

* The term "spirit" in the context of this book generally is synonymous with the German *Geist*, signifying the whole inner world of human intellectual and emotional life and creativity. (LL)

(another concept that was born at the time of the debate and was part and parcel of it) is a culture in the sense that the intellectual legacies of all other peoples or religions are cultures. Is "Judaism," regarded as a culture distinct from other cultures, a human creation, a product of the Jewish people? Ultra-orthodox Jews, who saw themselves entrusted with preserving a Judaism that they perceived to be unchanged for generations, opposed applying the term "culture" to Judaism. They considered the notion of Judaism as a culture to be tantamount to assimilation and idolatrous heresy. In their view Judaism was nothing less than the word of God. Admittedly, the law was entrusted into the hands of the Jewish people, interpreted and maintained by them, but even the interpretation and propagation were accomplished by revealed instruments and were a continuation of revelation itself.

The following inquiry will examine the spiritual and philosophical trajectory of several movements that arose in the modern period. These movements defined Judaism as essentially a culture. Understandably, these movements also regarded the creative output of their critics and opponents as a kind of culture, *a religious culture*. As creators of a new Jewish culture, they assumed that they had a need and a natural right to use the "tradition" (a term that both they and their opponents could accept since it does not specify who authored the tradition) that they received from prior generations as a cultural resource from which they could select and develop their culture as Jews.

By making such a claim, they knew of course that they were relating to their "tradition" just as their enlightened European contemporaries related to their own national traditions, and that such a consciousness of tradition and the ways in which it should be developed differed from the consciousness of their own ancestors and their Orthodox opponents. Still, they were sure that they were doing in effect just what their ancestors had done, and as their opponents continued to do, even though the latter did not acknowledge the fact.

Thus the term "Jewish culture" grew out of the attempt to develop an alternative to the traditional religious position, one that would be in keeping with the scientific, critical perception of the time. In the traditional view, the Jewish people are differentiated from other peoples by their beliefs and convictions, their way of life, their literary creativity, science and art. All of these are essentially a divine teaching which human beings may neither add to nor detract from, much less change, reform or develop with a view to *improving* them by the light of their judgment and needs. It bears emphasizing that the inventors of the new alternative — the *maskilim* (proponents of Jewish Enlightenment) and founders of historical Jewish scholarship (*Jüdische Wissenschaft*) who first coined the term "Judaism" in parallel with "Hellenism," "Christianity," "Germanism" or "Gallicism," in the broader European context of historical research of human cultures — saw Judaism as basically a culture like that of other peoples. They turned, indeed, to the same historical memory, to the same "literary sources," to the same languages, to which their ancestors, believing in literally revealed Torah, resorted. But they understood that there must be substantive differences between a religious culture formed in the consciousness that it is *all* the product of divine revelation, and a culture created in awareness of its human origins (even if some of them agreed that it contained a *response* to divine revelation). The same concepts, values, symbols and norms assume utterly different meanings if one takes them to be a human creation representing human authority.

If so, the new interpretation is more than an interpretation: there is indeed continuity between the source and its interpretation, but we are speaking of a deliberate transformation of an ancient culture into a modern culture.

What brought about such a far-reaching change? Since culture is a human life process that continues over time — that is, a historical process — a description of the change and the thought behind it ought to begin by taking the historical background into account: the impact of the secularization of European culture on the life-environment of the Jewish people in the second half of the 18th century.

From the political, economic, and social standpoints, the beginning of the change is rooted in the conflict over the Emancipation. Jews sought liberation from the ghetto, from laws that isolated, repressed and discriminated against them — a situation in which they had suffered for generations in all the lands of their dispersion and exile, particularly under Christian domination. The facts are well known and there is no need to repeat them here. What does bear emphasizing is the substantive connection between emancipation and political, social, and cultural secularization. The ghetto was originally instituted by the Jews themselves, but it was reimposed on them time and again by Christian authorities because of the competition and hatred that marked the relations between the persecuting and persecuted religions. So long as Christianity was directly involved in government, so long as it set the norms of social and cultural behavior through coercion, and so long as Jewish religion had an unmediated, authoritative, and absolute sway over the Jewish community's way of life, there was no chance that emancipation would come from the surrounding non-Jewish society or be sought by the Jewish community.

For both sides, secularization was a precondition. First and foremost, political secularization displaced the Church from its position of direct involvement in the regime. It turned the modern European state into a centralized secular-national entity whose main concerns were the temporal functioning of the regime. Spiritual and religious life were relegated to the free choice of the citizen. This development in non-Jewish society had immediate repercussions for the status of the rabbinic establishment whose internal coercive authority had relied on the backing of the non-Jewish authorities. The end of this coercive power signaled the end of internal restrictions: Jews who wanted to be free and to leave the ghetto could now "throw off the yoke." But the political process was only one practical expression of larger social, economic and cultural processes; hence, the Emancipation could not remain confined to the political arena. Precisely those parts of the surrounding society that were willing to absorb the Jews as citizens with equal rights (though with qualifications) had become secular in their overall functioning, values, and behavioral norms. Thus, Jews who wanted to integrate into the social and cultural life of their surroundings had to adopt the secular culture of their environment.

As for religion, for several generations (and to a large extent today as well) it continued to be a private factor shaping the life of European society and culture, though stripped of its former compulsory authority. The role that it played led in effect to a double standard. Though religious tolerance was a principle of the liberal, secular regime and a necessary component of its secular ethos, the social practice of tolerance was hampered because of the effects of religious teaching. In effect, secular enlightened European society recognized the theoretical right of Jews to live by their religion as private citizens but expected, even pressured them, to forsake their religion and preferably convert to Christianity as a condition of ultimate acceptance.

But for Jews seeking emancipation, their Jewish religion was the only legitimate expression of a separate and independent identity. Even this held true only so long as Judaism did not try to shape the overall social relationships, schooling, behavior and occupations of individual Jews. First and foremost, Jews who desired emancipation had to accept the assumptions of the secular culture around them. They had to relate to their religion in the way that secular Christians related to theirs — not as an authority above culture but as one component of their culture. Thus Jewish supporters of the Emancipation were expected and willingly agreed to develop their own "religious culture" alongside Christian culture as a unique strand within the fabric of modern, secular society. Thus was born the phenomenon that we examine here: the intellectual, scholarly, educational and literary-creative process whose agenda was the creation of Judaism as a new culture, distinctive in its historical roots, but integrated with the modern culture of the West.

Of course, this was only the beginning. Afterwards new vistas were revealed, new possibilities as well as formidable obstacles both internal and external. The process of exodus from the ghetto and the freedom to mix in the cultural arena of the West forced the Jewish people time and again to make choices and to come up with creative responses. As we shall see, this was a complex process that played out in several locales, against the backdrop of constant changes in historical circumstances and under the influences of nationalist movements that posed their own challenges, forcing them to choose repeatedly among the contradictory alternatives that presented themselves. In the coming chapters we shall describe in historical order the different theoretical models that were developed to realize the ideal of modern Jewish culture, beginning with the Enlightenment and continuing to the establishment of the State of Israel, and the attempts that were made to translate these models into historical reality.

THE IDEA OF
MODERN JEWISH CULTURE

Chapter One
CULTURE AS A CONCEPT AND CULTURE AS AN IDEAL

We said above that the concept of "Jewish culture" or "Judaism as a culture" developed against the background of the process of secularization through absorption and imitation of the modern, secular European culture that had opened the door to emancipation. It is fitting, then, that we should examine the specifics of this influential paradigm and refine our initial definition: What secular features of the European culture were the Jewish proponents of the Emancipation expected (indeed, wished) to imitate?

A key to the general orientation of a culture can be found by identifying the ideals the culture was meant to serve. When a society's activity is dominated by a religious establishment, the culture created is intended primarily to serve religious ideals. If religion is conceived of as a superhuman authority and thus supra-cultural, then culture itself is conceived as a means to a religious ideal but it is not itself considered an ideal sought out for its own sake. By contrast, a secular culture, even when it reserves a place in its domain for religion, carves out its ideals from within itself. More correctly, it becomes an ideal, for it embodies the human values through which are manifested the uniqueness of the human being in nature as a creature who is himself a creator, a being who shapes his environment and who fashions himself within that environment.

If so, according to the modern secular outlook that takes the place of the traditional religious outlook, human culture has no otherworldly or supra-human ideals whose realization must depend on a supernatural or supra-human authority. On the contrary, human culture is itself a creation that manifests the qualities, properties and values that are peculiar to man; it is its own ideal. Human culture seeks to exist, develop and maintain its independent identity while adapting itself to changing needs and striving towards perfection.

That being said, we should emphasize that culture comes about originally to satisfy the survival needs of human beings in nature. This is culture's original and primary "ideal." At the same time, culture incorporates

1

those ideals which express man's orientation to his surroundings, his aspirations, the goals he has set up for himself, and the meaning that he ascribes to his distinctive existence in nature. In other words, the ideal or ideals are structural, qualitative components of culture as an expression of man's (subjective) spiritual *superiority* over all other creatures. Man is unique among all the creatures of nature in many ways that focus on his creative intelligence: his reason, his power of imagination, his feelings and aspirations, and his ability to translate all these faculties into creative acts, whether directly or instrumentally. With the aid of tools he is able to develop a secondary environment that he creates for himself and superimposes on the natural infrastructure even as he develops himself within it.

Other living creatures, which from the standpoint of their physical and spiritual functions, are born nearly fully developed into an environment that they are mostly unable to change through their own initiative. In contradistinction, man is born as an animal meant to develop into a human being in a social environment that he creates through his own initiative; in other words, he becomes a human being only once outside the womb. Obviously his development is conditioned by circumstances and resources that he finds in his surroundings, but he is able to fashion his surroundings and adapt them to his aspirations. To be human implies striving to be human, to perpetuate that which is human, and to progress in the fulfillment of this goal from stage to stage. In this sense, the *human* is an ideal realized in society and embodied in its creations. This applies to all cultures, but every culture has its own particular ideals, and every culture is set apart from others by its natural resources, historic fate, and the notion of human perfection for which it strives.

The significance of this statement (that secular culture posited its ideals within itself and not beyond itself) becomes clear when one goes from the theoretical to the actual. This is the historic juncture which occurred in the transition from a religious culture (whether Christian or Jewish) to a secular western culture. Secular culture defined itself as aspiring to the perfectibility of man insofar as he is a natural, this-worldly creature with special spiritual/psychological qualities* that are part of his nature. The sought-for perfection was to be found through the creative application of man's superior characteristics.

---

* "Spiritual/psychological qualities" — *segulot ruaḥ*. The Hebrew *ruaḥ* (like the German *Geist*) is ambiguous as between "spiritual" in an otherworldly sense and in a psychological-intellectual-cultural sense. This ambiguity lends itself to the transformation in modernity of traditional religious values into this-worldly cultural values. The reader should not take "spiritual" to refer to otherworldly, but should be guided by context in each case. (LL)

Such a definition of human perfection was not entirely novel in the cultural heritage of Europe. Culture is a historic development and it relies on precedents. The first models of humanistic European culture were to be found in Europe's pagan legacy, especially the Greco-Roman. But the Jewish-Biblical legacy was not devoid of earthly ideals either. The secular Enlightenment formulated its humanistic ideals primarily through a return to these sources, especially the pagan sources. This is attested by the choice of the Latinate words that it adopted by way of self-definition: "culture" (and similarly "the cultural ideal"). The Jewish enlightenment movement, which paralleled the beginnings of European enlightenment, employed the same term in the same way that it was understood in Central Europe.

The Hebrew word *tarbut* appears only once in the Bible, with a decidedly negative connotation (*"breed* of sinful men" — Numbers 32:14). Yet this word was selected to translate the two terms common to European languages: "culture" and "civilization." This fact is symptomatic of the special difficulty faced by the development of modern secular Jewish culture when it drew on the paradigm of traditional religious culture for its terminology. Apparently Jewish culture lacks even the necessary linguistic tools for communicating the special meaning which culture holds in its modern context. The etymology of the Hebrew word *tarbut* was appropriate in conveying the notion of "increase" that is common to "culture" and "civilization," but it was inadequate in communicating the special meaning of each of these words:

"Civilization" refers to the material infrastructure of each human society — its tools, economy, technology, administration, and political organization, while the primary meaning of "culture" is cultivation, improvement, refinement.* This word thus comes to distinguish between what nature provides by natural growth and what human beings adduce by cultivation and improvement in order to realize their aspirations and satisfy their needs. Examples include domesticated animals that people have bred and trained, and agricultural crops that have been improved as distinct from wild varieties, etc. Similarly, human beings are born in a natural, wild state but become truly human through discipline, cultivation and refinement by a process of education and socialization that transcends nature.

"Culture" is therefore an expression of the attribute of humanity resulting from an intended and purposeful self-improvement and cultivation: broad-ranging and systematic knowledge, rich language that is precise and elegant, esthetic appearance and expression, refined artistic sensibility, moral and well considered behavior, fine manners. These are the hallmarks

---

* Though not familiar to English-speakers, the distinction between "civilization" and "culture" that Schweid draws here is a common one in German social thought. (LL)

of a refined and well-bred cultured individual who aspires to perfection, whose education distinguishes him from the natural, barbaric, primitive, or aboriginal person.

The ideal of a *cultured* person arose from this basic distinction: *natural man* acts as a creature in response to his instinctual drives, lives a primarily physical-sensual life, devoid of education from without or restraint from within. He is simple and lacking sophistication. His pleasures are crude, direct, without refinement or forethought. By contrast, the cultured man is intellectual, educated, self-aware, critical and restrained. He lives on the level of the mind, including cultivated imagination and emotions. He is refined and sophisticated in his conduct, his appearance and his sensory enjoyments. In all of these manifestations, there is a definite rejection of making do with a *necessary minimum* merely for purposes of function and survival. The cultured person aspires to pre-eminence; the cultured life is an aim in itself. Clearly, therefore, the more perfectly a person internalizes the values of such training, restraint, refinement and sophistication, and applies them in all spheres of his activity and relationships, the more noble and accomplished that person is — or with radical simplicity, the more *human*. One might say that the savage is only *potentially* human. Only one who has achieved a certain level of cultural accomplishment is truly human.

But for understanding the social meaning of this cultural ideal (which as we shall soon see had a fateful significance for Jews), we should emphasize that there followed from it not only a distinction between primitive peoples and cultured peoples (together with all the intermediate gradations by which one ranked the superiority of one national culture over another) but also a distinction within each people and within the framework of each multi-tiered national culture, between the popular culture that was considered "vulgar" — crude, unrefined, restrained only by external governmental authority — and the elite culture that was "aristocratic," expressing a high level of individual autonomy, the fruit of free internalization of social, ethical and esthetic values.

Clearly the distinction between "vulgar" and "aristocratic" belittles the humanity of the common person, who is sometimes depicted as worse than the savage. The primitive is considered an untutored child, while the man of the masses is thought to possess not merely a low culture but a corrupted culture, flawed or even malignant and degenerate, a culture that under certain circumstances deserves to be despised.

This distinction had a far-reaching importance for the development of the cultural ideal among Jews. Jews absorbed some of the implications of religious hatred and prejudices against themselves in social and cultural spheres, and despite the enlightened general European principle of religious tolerance vis à vis other religions, Jews went so far as to repeat and justify prejudices aimed at themselves. Enlightened European secular society regarded Jews who wished to leave the ghetto as representatives of a vulgar, inferior, and deformed culture. In order to integrate, Jews were expected to prove that they had overcome their cultural inferiority, rejected their "low" and "vulgar" culture, and internalized the lofty cultural ideals of their surroundings both outwardly (language, ethics, etiquette, dress and customs) and internally (education, refined thought, feelings and esthetics). Consequently, should the Jews wish to maintain their own unique culture and identify with it, they had to prove that it was high-minded, in no way inferior to the culture into which they sought to be integrated, a culture to which they had contributed in the past and could yet contribute something of value.

The ideal of the cultured person is an ideal of human perfection to which one aspires for its own sake. When one speaks of a secular culture, the goal is humanity for its own sake, without a higher metaphysical purpose. An instructive parallel — as well as a crucial distinction — between secular ideals and traditional religious ones was expressed in paradigmatic adjectives for the ideal Jewish human type, such as the *talmid ḥakham* (learned scholar), the *tzaddik* (righteous person), the *ḥasid* (pious person), the God-fearer. The ideal held in common by the secular view and the religious view it displaced was that man was born as a physical creature and required education in society in order to exist as a human being; furthermore, that this is not only a condition of survival in nature but the special purpose of man's humanity.

Another notion held in common was that being human means continually striving for a higher state beyond the limited bounds of achievement at each stage of development. A person must always strive to achieve more than s/he has yet achieved, i.e. s/he must strive for self-transcendence and even to ascend from the sphere of physical activity to that of intellectual-spiritual activity, and from a lower spiritual sphere to a higher one. Moreover, the two ideal frameworks agree in assuming a continual dialectical tension between the physical and the spiritual, and that realizing the human ideal requires constant struggle in order to give the spiritual preeminence over the physical, in order to restrain the physical drives and channel them in the desired direction.

It is important to stress the similarities between the modern humanistic cultural ideal and religious ideals. First, despite secular culture's rebellion against religious domination, one finds there is a direct influence of traditional religion on modern culture; indeed, there is proof of a certain continuity between them. Secondly, these similarities made possible various forms of synthesis between the secular cultural ideal and the traditional religious ideal.

In fact, the modern cultural ideal that Jews developed sought just such a synthesis; without it, it would have been impossible to preserve the distinctive original characteristics of a Jewish cultural ideal that was nourished by a religious culture.

But we must place equal emphasis on the differences that exist between secular ideals and religious-traditional ideals. Modern culture's view of human nature was substantially different from the religious view. The cultural ideal as an ideal of human perfection for its own sake was based on the assumption that despite the dialectic tension between them, there is a substantive, unbroken link between physical, psychological and spiritual life. In other words, according to this-worldly secular anthropology, the spirit is a natural, this-worldly function and not a supernatural ghost-like entity that was exiled and imprisoned in its bodily-earthly existence. On the contrary, the spirit was considered a perfecting and ennobling dimension of natural life. It develops by means of the refinement and inspiration of natural physical functions — senses, drives, feelings, imagination; under no circumstances does it repress those functions, as if that were necessary to give strength to the spiritual faculties. By contrast, religious morality, even when it refrained from extreme asceticism, tended always toward austerity. The intention was to liberate the spirit, an emanation of the divine sphere, from its physical prison. The goal was to make the human being a citizen of Heaven even before his death. Therefore religion could permit certain sensual pleasures, sciences, and esthetic creativity only as a means to an otherworldly goal. Sensory enjoyment for its own sake, or even knowledge of natural science for its own sake, were suspect in its eyes. By contrast, secular worldly ethics considered refined and fulfilled natural living to be a spiritual attainment, an elevation of human nature, and did not advocate subjugation of human nature or forsaking it for a higher goal. A cultured person's "eternity" would be found in the praise that his worldly accomplishments would enjoy for generations to come.

These cultural ideals were expressed in human paradigms. In contrast to the scholarly, righteous, pious and/or God-fearing man of tradition, modern secular temporal culture proposed the ideal of the *Maskil* (proponent of Enlightenment), the philosopher or the humanist as a different kind of hero of culture, devoted to the realization of humanist ideals. In the actual historical-social reality, the personalities who embodied these ideals functioned as the leadership elite in the political, quasi-governmental establishment and as models in the educational sphere. Once again it is important to emphasize that the integration of these two basic areas was another point of similarity between the religious and secular cultures. In place of a religious institution (ecclesiastical or rabbinic) that operated in a ruling capacity or as part of the ruling leadership, the modern period saw the rise of a secular educational elite which provided this vital service within the context of the political establishment. Instead of religious institutions such as the synagogue and the Beit Midrash, ḥeder, and yeshiva, a parallel and more diversified system of secular education and culture developed. It embraced educational institutions, particularly the gymnasia and the university, as well as the concert hall, museum, theater, and the "salon" in which culture was realized in an aristocratic lifestyle. These were instruments for transmitting the curriculum and values of the culture, but at the same time they served as symbols embodying the belief that cultural activity is a whole way of life, a goal in and of itself.

What were the principal values and content transmitted by the educational elites and institutions? In answering the question, it is necessary to keep in mind that we are speaking of a totality, a unified interrelationship of various components. Culture in its *cultural* sense is not a chance heap or random collection of items. Similarly, a school or university is not merely a marketplace containing wares sold by the ruler of the marketplace in response to the private demands of each buyer (as is in effect the practice today). According to the humanistic conception of enlightenment, culture must comprise a universe of human creativity, just as the world or nature is grasped as a unified cosmos. This outlook finds representative expression in the common name of that institution that stands at the highest level in unifying the culture, developing it and imparting it to the society — the "university." Here is an institution appointed to represent and unite within its walls all branches of knowledge and intellectual creativity into a comprehensive and unified schema. Furthermore, it was the intention that the university would not rest content with certifying experts in specified disciplines but would induct all who learned in it, stage by stage, into the totality of the culture. Also the program of studies of the classical humanistic gymnasia, which played a central role in the crystallization and transmission of the modern cultural ideal up to the start of the twentieth century, was a "curriculum" in the true sense, namely, an encompassing course* or "round" of study: each student engaged in a complete, comprehensive sequence of studies in order to enter into creative

---

* *Curriculum* (< Latin *curro*, to run: originally a circular racetrack). In the modern pedagogic sense, the original sense of "curriculum" is symbolic of the requirement that all students follow a prescribed path. *Course* derives from the same root (*curro, cursum*).

participation in the whole gamut of disciplines of the culture, to understand the relationship between them and to become a full partner in the cultural life of his family, his community, his people, and humanity.

Of course, professional training was an important factor in the high-school and university curriculum, but the minimal vocational course was reserved only for students who were not deemed fit, either from lack of talent or their parents' lowly socioeconomic background, to advance to the level of the representative elite. In any case, it never occurred to anyone that specialized professional training on no matter how high a level should be counted as entry to the general culture. The teacher, writer, political leader, judge, and artist, as well as the physician and lawyer and even the leading merchant and financier — all these must first be knowledgeable and upstanding citizens of their polity and society. But even more, they must be human beings, i.e. cultured individuals in the profoundest and most inclusive personal and social sense. Therefore they had to acquire and absorb an education aspiring to completeness. If one did not reach the level of the classical "Renaissance man," at least one sought broad and general knowledge and understanding in those disciplines regarded as essential. Only thus would one be regarded as an educated person, generally knowledgeable with a well-considered view of the world and a proper way of life.

Cultured education met the expectations of what was meant by an educated man on three levels: (1) comportment, or those ethical values and manners shaping personal conduct and their study; (2) systematic knowledge (enlightenment in its most basic sense); (3) a world view that provides an overall orientation to life. The training of a cultured or enlightened person began with instilling values that define personality and shape behavior. Personal habits came first, and this was followed by a study of morals. One was expected not to be simply law abiding, adhering to external manners, but also strictly ethical in personal and social responsibility, sense of justice and honor, nobility of action marked by generosity, refinement and sensitivity to others. Such were the higher virtues emphasized by the Enlightenment.

Two characteristics of the Enlightenment's cultural ideal deserve special emphasis. First, higher education was linked unambivalently with ethics and manners. It was assumed that appropriate behavior properly internalized and willingly acted out was not only a function of outward, mechanistic behavior but an outcome of judgment based on knowledge and true understanding. An unethical personality — that is, one that suffered from a dissonance between passions and reason — could not possibly reach the higher planes of knowledge. That meant that morality and manners depended on broad-ranging knowledge, and that this broad knowledge was in turn dependent on morality. Second, the ethical virtue that is most typical of the whole array of virtues characterizing the Enlightenment ideal of the secular-worldly individual is "dignity." This expresses the self-worth of the human individual, his value in his own eyes and in the eyes of his society. The virtue of dignity combines broad knowledge and profound understanding with ethical character and nobility that provide a person with worth, status, and authority as an independent, autonomous person.

Still, the most strongly-emphasized value was the value of knowledge and learning, i.e. the never-ending effort to advance the horizon of knowledge. Even the moral character of the enlightened individual was conceived as fundamentally a morality based on knowledge and learning: attachment to the value of truth, of objective rational judgment, and to the heartfelt, enthusiastic devotion to the value of truth as human perfection. This value system defined the Enlightenment's ideal of knowledge. To reiterate: more than an aggregate of information from various sources, knowledge is the profound understanding of the quintessence of knowledge; more than correct and relevant from the standpoint of usefulness, knowledge ought to be true to the supreme ideal of objectivity. This means that the advance of knowledge must be guided by the value of truth as such, embodied in a critical, systematic method of inquiry that is intrinsic to it. Of course, from here follows the demand that knowledge be "scientific," that it should constitute a totality systematic in scope, critical from the standpoint of methodological exactness, and profound in its continual uncovering of the connections between different domains of thought. The axis of the totality is man himself, the knower, who strives to know himself from the network of his relationships with his environment, and to know his environment by knowing himself more fully. This is the fulfillment of the value-statement, that striving for objective knowledge is the supreme subjective value of the person of culture. This is knowledge for its own sake in which the human essence is realized.

The third level: the orientation expressed in a world-outlook crystallized as a discipline in a philosophical system constructed as the highest integrative layer over all the previous learning. In the hierarchy of morality and knowledge of secular-worldly culture at the start of the modern age, philosophy took the place of religion. This was given clear institutional expression in the curricular framework of the classical gymnasia and the university. Indeed, two comprehensive and complementary disciplines were singled out for special status: history in the modern sense, and modern philosophy. But the intention was to enthrone both of them together to the status of the culture's self-consciousness: philosophy gave the outlook that articulated and arranged the totality of knowledge, while history reviewed the process of becoming and comprehensive development of the culture according to its intrinsic laws. If this is the case, the philosophy of history is the philosophy of culture. As such it lays the groundwork for values, sets out the direction for progress, and orients the creative processes in all spheres.

Of course we have been dealing with the themes and ideals of the culture of an elite, of the upper social strata at the time of the Enlightenment. It bears emphasizing that the Jews who wanted to leave the ghetto sought to become integrated into these social classes and to adopt their culture; not until several historical transformations took place did the cultural strata of the common classes become a focus of attention for Jews. The starting point was an affinity to humanistic, aristocratic culture. It was this culture that set the standard.

Chapter Two
TENSIONS AND CONTRADICTION

The cultural paradigm described in the last chapter expressed the outlook of a social class that was politically, socially and culturally dominant. The model, which was creatively applied and institutionalized in the educational, cultural and scientific systems, was a philosophic model, however, and, as such, utopian. The ideals were presented at the level of cultural creativity without considering the contradictions and tensions manifest in political, economic and social life. Over time, critics of the model claimed that, in effect, the elites used it hypocritically to cloak their own desire for domination. Behind the exalted humanistic values expressed on the plane of "culture" were other motivations, material values that sprang from the plane of industrial civilization and generated intermittent waves of upheavals. In the end, high culture also had to come to terms with this, to reflect and respond to it.

The Jews who yearned for emancipation, who wished to join the "progressive" dominant class — i.e., members of the middle class and haute bourgeoisie with whom the intellectuals were allied, would later take the measure of these tensions and contradictions by their impressive achievements, but also by the obstacles of anti-Semitic hatred which they encountered. The dilemmas arose most sharply among the creators of the culture: the writers, artists, philosophers, scientists and educators. They came to light in four specific planes of the paradigm: (1) in the tension between its national-democratic and its elitist-universal aspects; (2) between its social-national and its individualistic tendencies; (3) between the process of "culture" striving for an ideal intellectual life and that of "civilization" drawn to material values; and finally (4) that between nationalism and universalism. We will show later that even the theoretical thought-systems that guided the creation of the models of modern Jewish culture wrestled with these three axes of tension in the effort to offer positive solutions that would release the Jewish people from its difficulties. The details will become clear when we present those doctrines. In this prefatory exploration of the basic concepts we shall content ourselves with pointing out the substance of the dilemmas.

1. *On the political plane:* The elitist and universal character of the paradigm described earlier followed from the theory of human nature that it assumed and from the ideal of unattainable perfectionism for which it strove. The dichotomy between "cultured man" on the one hand and "natural man" or "plebian man" on the other exposed its aristocratic bias, which shied away not only from the vulgarity of the masses but also from popular culture with its affinity to nature. But at the same time the cultural paradigm was based on the values of nationalism and democracy. In that respect it required a connection to the vernacular language and popular culture. Only by invoking the notion of popular sovereignty was it possible to rattle the foundations of the *ancien régime* and lay the foundations of the modern centralized state; and only on the basis of democratic nationalism could they enlist a society of citizens.

It should be emphasized that the secular, temporal idea was substantively bound up with ideas of nationality and democracy. These notions were rooted in a natural, this-worldly infrastructure of human society and its natural goal. At the political level this required a constitutional agreement that all persons are equal in their humanity, and that the natural rights of man are safeguarded for all citizens by the state. Again it must be stressed that the notion of a democratic social contract was the sole basis for the legitimacy of a regime which would derive from independent, autonomous human authority rather than from divine right. On a cultural level, if one rejects the assumption that culture develops by means of supernatural revelation and by ancient traditions that are based on it, only literary and linguistic sources and the natural folkways of the people are left as starting points for a this-worldy culture.

2. *On the plane of the social ethos:* The innovative elitist character of a cultural model based on man's nature rather than on a supernal authority leads towards an individualistic ethos in which human value is found in every individual. Each individual is not only equal in humanity to his/her fellow, but unique in it. Each individual — a world unto him/herself. S/he has the right to his/her autonomous development. And yet the human potential of each individual is manifested and realized only in society. There is no humanity outside of society. If this is the case, what takes precedence — the individual or society? Does the individual's development and his welfare take precedence over the development of the group? Is it the yardstick for the good of the group? Or is the opposite true?

3. *On the plane of productive activity in a stratified society:* We recalled earlier the distinction between "civilization" and "culture." "Civilization"

refers to the technological-industrial, organizational, administrative and material framework of the society, whereas "culture" refers to the totality of its self-expression, the external articulation of inner human experience. Clearly the dichotomy between these two concepts is relative, not absolute. The development of material civilization is a condition and basis for development of higher culture ("if there is no bread, there is no Torah"). But at the same time, without a clearly articulated culture (linguistic, scientific, artistic), it is unlikely that material civilization can develop. Consequently in the ideal, theoretical sense these are two separate levels, or two different ways of manifesting the very same powers, the one objective and external, the other subjective and internal. This is especially prominent in the case of language, which serves as the basis of development of both culture and civilization, as well as for the sciences which are the acme of their advancement. Language is wholly culture; nonetheless, tools can serve as a means of communication between man and nature and between man and man, and without language they could not be made or used. As for the sciences, they are at the same time a human expression in response to the natural environment, including mankind, and also the most effective means for exercising human control over nature — including human nature.

It follows from all this that the distinction between "culture" and "civilization" is only a matter of choosing the directions of expression of those same spiritual forces found in humanity, and the balance between them. Still, there is a polarity, and when activated consistently in the effort to achieve a given effect, they express different and contradictory human motivations. We can easily see that the "cultural ideal" was originally constructed on the basis of a clear preference for culture as the highest goal, over "civilization" which is the means that must be harnessed in service of the goal. But in retrospect one cannot ignore the Marxist critique that discovered the ruling material interest of a new ruling power and a new dominant class behind the cultural paradigm that prides itself on its exalted ethical character. In that case, we will find that the relative success in developing the cultural paradigm effected, or uncovered, the forces of material civilization that threatened to destroy the paradigm from within: beyond a certain stage of cultural development it became clear that industrial civilization exploited cultural progress, especially in science, to create a mass society with a materialistic culture that tended toward a tyrannical collectivism, thus bringing on the process called "the crisis of humanism" by way of social struggles, revolutions and wars that increased steadily in their inclusiveness and cruelty, within and among the "enlightened" peoples of Europe.

4. The fourth dilemma arose *on the international level*, parallel to the domestic social dilemma, in the inter-relationships that existed between national European cultures. On one hand, the aspiration to uphold the independent cultures played into the political desire to strengthen the sovereignty of their national entities. On the other hand was the counter-vailing pull of the pan-human and universal tendencies which guided humanism. This tension generated conflicts between nationalist and uni-versalist trends in European culture. It is a historical irony that both sprang from the same source.

As modern Jewish culture developed, Jewish movements launched dif-ferent and competing paradigms which wrestled with all these dilemmas. They provided the backdrop for the tragic fate of the Jewish people in modern times. The search was on for comprehensive solutions that could enable an independent, self-identifying Jewish existence, unified in itself yet coexisting harmoniously with its surroundings.

Chapter Three
INTERNALIZING THE CULTURAL IDEAL

The task of internalizing the secular-modern cultural ideal in the major centers of the Jewish people in Europe ran up against special obstacles, some internal and some external. We saw that the Emancipation was a powerful factor for transmitting the paradigm: it was facilitated by the leading social-political class that manifested it, and by the spread of liberal-secular values. This was strikingly apparent in daily practice. So long as the Christian Church was successful in shaping European values and lifestyles, emancipation was held at bay in the social sphere even when it prevailed in the political arena. The spread of secular values paved the way to full social integration, and any one who wanted to integrate was expected to accept these values and internalize them.

Still, adoption of secular ideals demanded greater concessions from Jews than it did from Christians. Secular culture had a separate existence in Europe alongside the culture of religion even when the church was directly and officially involved in the state. It was based on the one hand on the legacy of Greece and Rome, and on the other hand on national languages and popular cultures. Therefore secularization did not depend on abnegation of one's national identity. On the contrary, it strengthened it. Modern culture developed in the guise of a liberating renaissance of national identities that had been suppressed in the Middle Ages.

Ultimately, the development of this cultural paradigm was sustained by victorious nationalist movements based in the state. This fact is important in its own right. It explains among other things the stringent demands made on the Jews: they had to achieve complete cultural and national assimilation as a condition of emancipation. In the fever stage of their establishment and self-validation, national movements are zealous of their identifying uniqueness and intolerant of any cultural or national pluralism in their midst. To bolster their own identity, they suppress the identity of minorities. Consequently, the Jewish people were expected to surrender in advance the same national cultural prerogative that their host-nations sought and established for themselves. In any case, Jews did not have an uninterrupted national, secular, cultural heritage on which to base a secularized, culturally unique identity. In the Diaspora, their national identity was primarily religious.

This is a well-worn familiar fact, even uncontested. But it needs qualification. The argument advanced by Orthodox thinkers, that the Jewish people had no individual culture other than its religious expression, is exaggerated. Even in the Diaspora, there was always a folk Jewish culture that was not regarded as part of normative rabbinic Judaism. In centers of higher secular learning (such as Egypt, medieval Spain and Italy) non-rabbinic culture did interact with the surroundings. This was particularly true in philosophy and the sciences, and in the realm of poetry, scientific-philosophic writings, and literary-linguistic works. In consequence, there developed a scientific-philosophical and a literary culture which engaged in knowledge and secular literature for their own sake.

In other words, there was a cultural sphere which mirrored religious and traditional values, yet was not considered part of them. At the same time, the cultural effects of Diaspora life undoubtedly reflected an ongoing process of acculturation that verged on assimilation. Jews consciously engaged in a competitive imitation of the seductive cultural achievements of the non-Jewish environment. Indeed, in the Middle Ages, there is no clear-cut differentiation between the popular or philosophic, scientific culture of the Jews and the surrounding Moslem and Christian cultures. The fact that one can speak of separate Jewish, Christian or Moslem cultures reflects rather the identities of their creators than the qualities of their culture. Even the national language played no special role in this respect: in their extra-religious cultural ventures, Jews generally employed the language of their environment or, in the area of popular culture, several jargons such as Judismo (Judeo-Arabic), Ladino or Yiddish.

From this description one might deduce that in Diaspora the culture that Jews required above and beyond their religious activity and expression was identical with the culture they had in common with their non-Jewish surroundings. They accommodated themselves to it, and it was in every sense their culture as well. It was not simply imitated or borrowed but a culture to which they contributed together with non-Jews. In every way possible, the Jews resembled their environment. To legitimate their accelerated acculturation into modern society they could rely on precedents drawn from the fullness of Jewish culture. But traditional culture could not provide them with an authentic model that was *secularly* unique because its Jewish distinctiveness derived solely from the authority of normative religion. Omitting religious values merely obscured or erased uniqueness.

The implication was that full secularization called for a total suspension of belief and the religious way of life. Secularization meant unconditional acceptance of the Emancipation's demand that Jews fully identify with the renewed national culture of the host people. This was tantamount to a denial of their own singularity — namely, it meant assimilation.

Consequently, in principle there remained only two alternatives to all but total dissolution: (1) Rejecting emancipation by freezing the traditional model; that is, a complete halt to the process of acculturation at the levels of both popular and higher culture. With the advent of modernity, any conscious accommodation to the surroundings was perceived as a grave threat to Jewish religious identity. This was the road followed by ultra-Orthodox Jewry, and it created a clearly sectarian Jewish religious culture, a fortress closed off to the outside. (2) Adaptation of Jewish religion to the surrounding culture by means of a new secularized conception of religion, designed to bring it into modern culture as one constituent of that culture, or by adapting essential elements of the surrounding modern culture into Judaism through selection, qualification and interpretation.

The latter was the method followed by Catholics and Protestants in modern culture. To cope with the process of secularization and survive, they sought ways to exercise influence on secular culture and to moderate it by joining it and functioning as a part of it. Jews were able to follow the same path that had achieved legitimacy around them. They could imitate modern Christian movements and, as exponents of the general culture, live as full participants who retained their private religious identity. But even this alternative raised a special problem for Jews: they had to change the traditional Jewish concept of religion so that it would be parallel to the Christian conception. In particular, it was necessary to forgo the aspiration, characteristic of halakhic Jewish religion, to provide a global religious way of life. In place of this traditional objective, it had to rest content with articulating a faith-based world-outlook expressed in symbolic and ceremonial forms. Even this had to be done cautiously to prevent formation of a hermetic social barrier between Jews and their neighbors.

This far-reaching form of assimilation stopped just short of total disappearance into the society. In any case, within such a partial and loose setting, it was difficult to create a distinctive and substantive Jewish culture. Nonetheless, modern religious movements (Reform, Conservative and Modern Orthodox) that were outgrowths of the Enlightenment movement opted for this path, and paid its price. The opposite option developed only later: the emergence of a secular, national, modern Jewish culture that could stand completely on its own.

Chapter Four
THE UNDERLYING PHILOSOPHY OF JEWISH ENLIGHTENMENT

From its inception, the movement for Jewish enlightenment was pragmatic and educational. The intent was to create and establish "Jewish" or "Hebrew" enlightenment as an institutionalized reality. (The distinction between the national and the cultural significances of these two orientations became clear only towards the end of the enlightenment process.) The Haskalah movement sought to propagate an ethical, scientific, linguistic and literary enlightenment among Jews which would be institutionalized through publication and propagation of appropriate media — books, journals, and school curricula. Initially there seemed to be no need to develop, rationalize or devise a theoretical basis for the movement. Perhaps the opposite was true. There were practical educational reasons for preferring pragmatic activity that stressed the immediate advantages of spreading knowledge itself, while pointing out the practical advantages it afforded its masters, and overlooking the severity of the problems it unleashed. A frontal theoretical and critical confrontation raising difficult issues of principle appeared unnecessary, even counterproductive.

At the outset, Jewish enlightenment (which lagged behind European enlightenment) imitated existing models. If there was a need to buttress his case, the *maskil* (exponent of Jewish enlightenment) could find philosophic theories in the work of the great philosophers of European enlightenment in Holland, Germany, England, and France. Experience proved, however, that presenting a general, theoretical plan immediately raised zealous opposition by the ultra-Orthodox Jewish establishment which, not without reason, regarded it as a sweeping threat to their embattled fortress. It was preferable to call attention to the vital reforms needed by traditional religious culture rather than to present the Enlightenment as a cultural alternative to religion, or as a proposal aimed at the general transformation of religious culture.

The course taken by the philosopher Moses Mendelssohn (1729–1786), who was considered to be the father of the Jewish Enlightenment movement, typified this. Mendelssohn's modest original contribution to the thought of his time was integrated into German and general European philosophy. He personified the individual Jew's ability to internalize the modern cultural ideal of his non-Jewish surroundings; he contributed to it and was integrated into it, even as he remained religiously fully Jewish.

As the father of the Haskalah (Jewish Enlightenment), in effect, Mendelssohn was the first "Jew of culture" in modern Europe. His almost archetypal influence, spanning more than two hundred years, derives from this. Although his message was a meaningful one, directed at both non-Jewish and Jewish society, it was restricted to the educational-pragmatic level. All of Mendelssohn's direct contributions to the development of modern Jewish culture, including the limited philosophic contribution he ultimately formulated in his book, *Jerusalem*, were solely intended to explain practical applications.

Mendelssohn began as a Hebrew *maskil* struggling to create Hebrew culture in a modest periodical entitled *Kohelet Musar* ("Tribune of Morals"). The publication did not last long but deserves pioneering recognition as the first Hebrew periodical to be published. Its contents were meant to propagate the Enlightenment by writing in Hebrew about literary topics that stressed the importance of ethics and the glory of nature and esthetics. Mendelssohn wanted to propose and emphasize both these decidedly cosmopolitan cultural ideals to his readers; to show that these values, for all their worldliness, did not come into conflict with Jewish religious values but were actually proper ethical, pious religious values, exhibiting piety toward God and the promise of otherworldly reward no less for their expression of enlightened integration into the life of the mundane world.

The modest hint was well taken, nonetheless it appeared too coarse to the magnates of Mendelssohn's Jewish community. The periodical was terminated. Mendelssohn's next contributions, both to the general education of Jews and to Hebrew culture, were a new translation of the Torah into German, together with the *Be'ur*, a Hebrew commentary that Mendelssohn edited in its entirety and part of which he himself wrote. Although the *Be'ur* was written in pure, simple and grammatical Hebrew it was still far from employing a modern critical scientific approach; rather it strictly followed Jewish law and tradition. In that case, how did it contribute to general enlightenment and Hebrew culture? By offering Jewish students a rich resource to learn German, to improve and refine their Hebrew. Thus it emancipated Jewish scholars from Yiddish which Mendelssohn, the cultivated proponent of culture, saw as an irritating expression of the vulgarity of the masses and the cultural degeneration that enlightened non-Jews imputed to Jews (a description with which Mendelssohn agreed).

Furthermore, Mendelssohn's recourse to the tradition of plain-sense interpretation and his highlighting of literary-esthetic and ethical motifs in Scripture tended again to emphasize the worldly values of the Enlightenment. In and of themselves, these elements were not religiously objectionable. On the contrary, emphasizing them was merely a corrective to what had become distorted and damaged in the culture of the Jews (through no fault of their own) because of a life of isolation and suppression in the ghetto.

This implied — in practical, not theoretical terms — that Jews should integrate into the surrounding culture (learn German, and through it attain a general education in the sciences and philosophy) and thereby develop their own culture: a Hebrew language capable of creating a distinctive literature, replete with worldly ethical and esthetic values. In Mendelssohn's view, these were two aspects of the same creative process: integration into the surrounding enlightened cultural milieu, and development of an independent cultural identity in the religious sphere.

Ultimately Mendelssohn was forced (in his book *Jerusalem*) to participate directly in the debate about emancipation. He did so reluctantly, for he regarded the debate itself as an unnecessary preoccupation with barriers to a process he believed should flow naturally from the interests of an enlightened non-Jewish society and state, as well as from Jewish interests. What, then, did he seek to prove? That the process was completely natural; that religious tolerance follows of necessity from the nature of the liberal secular state and from the values of secular ethics; and that Jewish religion was tolerant, enlightened, and therefore deserving of acceptance. At the same time, he wanted to demonstrate that there was no contradiction between strict observance of the commandments of the Jewish religion within the framework of a voluntary religious community, where religion is not compulsorily enforced, and full integration in the general culture.

Mendelssohn acted as though this was unproblematic from the Jewish point of view even though he knew full well that the rabbis of his time openly opposed his readiness to forgo the coercive authority of halakhah over the Jewish community, or to open the system of Jewish education to general education. The cultural issue Mendelssohn raised is symbolized by the fact that his book, given a Hebrew title, was written and published in German to be read by non-Jews as well as Jews already fluent in German. Thus the emphasis shifted unequivocally in the direction of integration into the German culture to which Mendelssohn continued to contribute the fruits of his mind. He said nothing against the cultivation of Hebrew culture; indeed, he was at the center of a circle of enlightened Hebraists, but in practice he opted for a "Jewish culture" in non-Judaic languages (particularly

German) which relegated Hebrew to the role of an ancient, sacred tongue for ritual religious purposes. In a Germany already engaged in a liberalization process regarding Jews, this seemed the most natural and simplest way.

Raising this issue, in effect, sharpened the distinction between the way the Jewish Enlightenment developed in Germany and the way it unfolded in Poland and Russia. In the former, the direction was toward a Jewish religious culture; in the latter, the orientation was toward the development of a "Hebrew culture."

Though Hebraic culture actually began in Germany and subsequently retained its affinity to the German language and culture as an influential model, all its loyal proponents — even those who functioned in Germany — originated as part of Eastern European Jewry. They all sprang from a Jewish culture acquired through education in a traditional religious system that persisted in eastern Europe for a longer period of time and to a broader extent. Nonetheless, in Russia and Poland there was a continuous process of transformation to a secular, Hebrew national culture. The transition to vernacular Jewish culture came as a third stage.

On the ideological plane, the way of thinking that led to the transition was initially found in the work of one of the important precursors of modern Hebrew poetry. Naphtali Herz Wessely (1725–1805) writer, poet and scholar was Mendelssohn's student and friend, and his partner in writing the *Be'ur*. In fact, without taking into account a short but very influential work by Wessely, *Words of Peace and Truth*, the full meaning of the bifurcation of Jewish culture into its Western (German-language) and Eastern (Hebrew) branches cannot be fully appreciated. This publication was the first to outline a coherent cultural program inclusive of its rationale and values, though these were expressed only in a popular ideological way, not philosophically.

In the first essay of *Words of Peace and Truth*, Wessely proposed a clearcut, simple distinction between two hierarchal domains within religious literature: *Torat ha-Adam* (Human Knowledge/Law) and *Torat ha-Elohim* (Divine Knowledge/Law).* To be sure, the "Law of Man" was included by Wessely among the divine commands, yet each of these "laws" has its own degree of importance and authority, and its own scope of application and content. The "Law of Man" pertains to matters of morals, manners, esthetics and science, to the perfection of the human being in his/her humanity, and

---

* Wessely's use of the term "Torah" for these disciplines echoes the use of "Torah" as traditional Jewish learning. In both its traditional and modern usages, this term embraced both descriptive and normative knowledge; as such, it included both academic curricular subjects and the values — ethics, manners, etc. — guiding the culture and way of life. (LL)

to the achievement of happiness in this world (though understandably as a prerequisite to spiritual felicity in the hereafter). The applicability of the doctrine is clearly understood to be universal — it is aimed at all humankind collectively and at each individual within it. It stands first in rank of importance, and so it is appropriate to be learned first in the primary stages of the educational process. God commands it because human reason requires it for its own temporal considerations. By contrast, the "law of God" is directed in its content to what tradition has defined as beliefs, thoughts and deeds "between the person and God," that are intended for a person's higher spiritual-religious felicity. It applies specifically to the Jews, who were selected as God's chosen people from the whole human race. In rank and authority, it is divine and supra-rational ("by authority" as opposed to "rational" in Saadia's classification of the Torah's laws); therefore it is higher in rank and authority than the "law of man."

In that case, the "law of man" is important, because without first absorbing its teachings and learning its lessons one cannot ascend to the higher level of the "law of God," and the "law of God" is important because it embodies the final destiny and true felicity of mankind.

It is remarkable that Wessely introduced this distinction into the hitherto seamless unity of the Jewish religious sources. All of it — including the "law of man" — is the command of God; ostensibly, therefore, Wessely said nothing new, nothing that was not rooted in the Law. Nonetheless he did sound a revolutionary note when he coined the term, *Torat ha-Adam* — Human Knowledge (actually the Hebrew translation for humanism). He used the term to delineate a universal area of temporal activity, adding the demands inherent in a broad-ranging education without which, apparently, one cannot achieve the human felicity required as a condition for religious perfection. This notion is a departure from conventional religious tradition, if only in respect of the conduct and comportment expected in civil society, not to mention the addition of scientific, professional, and esthetic-artistic education.

Indeed, in Wessely's view the Torah commands us to be accomplished in all these studies and skills that are necessary for our human felicity and perfection. But clearly, learning these fundamentals cannot be acquired by studying only the Torah; other sources and other languages are called for: those of general European culture which Wessely cleverly calls "the law of man" (= humanism), and which is the same for Jews and the enlightened of all peoples.

In other words, Wessely effectively laid out a paradigm that united in one dogmatic theological rubric — and also on the plane of modern didactic Hebrew literature — two cultures, each with its own domain and rank.

The first, "the law of God," was essentially the old traditional religious Jewish culture. The second, "the law of man," was the modern secular-humanistic European culture. The latter required intellectual and linguistic participation in a domain that was defined as universally human, as well as the development of a mediating Hebrew literature that is extra-canonical and secular in character, though written in the language of Torah and deriving its literary resources from the traditional sources.

Wessely was a fully observant Jew. As a Hebrew writer and poet, he felt his main responsibility was to create a mediating Hebrew literature. This is apparent in his Biblically inspired poetry and his essays on the Hebrew language and on religious ethical doctrine. His vision was to create a literary continuity between traditional rabbinic literature and foreign, secular studies. The cultural model he created became a paradigm for modern Jewish schools, those in which the language of instruction was Hebrew and others in which the language of the country was used. The educational curriculum was based on both the general and Jewish spheres, on both languages, and on both sets of values embodied in the components of "modern Jewish culture" according to the rendering of the Enlightenment. It would not be an exaggeration to claim that this is the model used to this day within a wide range of more sophisticated versions.

Chapter Five
THE MEANING OF BEING
A JEWISH-HEBREW MASKIL

The Hebrew essays of Naphtali Herz Wessely, which are marked by outstanding Biblical erudition and a sweep of religious literature, project a sense of sincere and wholehearted piety. Wessely did not regard himself as a revolutionary, neither could he have foreseen the vehement reaction of the rabbinic leadership to *Words of Peace and Truth*. The leadership saw itself as attacked and threatened. Ultimately, the placating words he uttered did indeed couch an emotional plea to the rabbis of his country to promptly and voluntarily obey the 1781 edict of Austrian Kaiser Joseph II to send Jewish children to the new schools that were to be established instead of the traditional *ḥeder*. There, in addition to Torah and Gemara, they would study German and general education in the German language as a preparation for acquiring civil rights.

Wessely seems to have believed in the Kaiser's benign sincerity. He did not fear for Jewish education; on the contrary, he regarded the innovations as a necessary corrective in and of themselves. They would serve to return Jewish education to the ways of the early Jewish sages: after all, the distinctions he proposed between Human Knowledge and the Law of God, and their application in a school curriculum, were in keeping with the spirit of enlightened, authoritative views of such great instructors of learning and halakhah as Saadia Gaon, Judah Halevi, and Maimonides. But his frenzied opponents were apparently less naïve than he in evaluating the magnitude of the revolution required of them and its concealed threat.

Wessely's program was unprecedented. Even Maimonides, who had made far reaching proposals for teaching science and philosophy as the acme of Torah study and a religious way of life (in his construction, the sciences and philosophy were in the realm of *ḥokhmat ha-Torah al ha-emet*, "the wisdom of the Torah on the plane of truth") did not propose that all Jewish pupils be offered advanced study in the sciences and philosophy, in Arabic. Such instruction was to be restricted to those who had exhibited special ability, and then only after they had made satisfactory achievements in the study of both the Oral and the Written Law, and had demonstrated perfect faith and a strict performance of the commandments.

There was a categorical difference between Maimonides and Wessely. It could be said that, paradoxically, Maimonides ascribed a much higher status to the study of the general sciences and philosophy than Wessely did, but he did so precisely from a religious point of view and therein lies the difference. In Maimonides' opinion, prophecy was identified with the most sublime degree of perceiving scientific, philosophical truth, and one ought to strive towards the sublime by orderly stages. Maimonides' halakhic religious position maintained that study and a religious way of life were sufficient in themselves to ensure the first educational stage, the stage that shapes and guides one's personality in all its behavior and aspirations. He incorporated scientific and philosophic studies *within* a Jewish educational framework. This was not Wessely's plan. Wessely granted general studies, which he seemed to rank below traditional Torah studies in importance, the right to form part of the first and most inclusive framework of studies, of which Torah studies would itself be only a part — though central and respected — within the culture defined by the universal and worldly "law of man."

The sequence of studies in the curriculum took on primary decisive importance. Immediately upon beginning one's education, every Jewish child would study the traditional *humash* (Five Books of Moses) with Rashi's commentaries, and go on to *gemara* (Talmud). But along with these topics children would learn German and a variety of subjects that could serve as the preparation for their auspicious integration as citizens and would enable them to find decent employment. They would also be strictly supervised in their civic behavior and appearance in order to be acceptable to their non-Jewish neighbors. In addition to prayers and the routine performance of the commandments, they would be taught good manners, character and precepts of religious ethics, and how to develop literary and artistic taste. It is clear from this that a complete overhaul was unavoidable in the priority of studies and their content, in the relative importance of various subjects, in one's appearance, and in character development; in a word, their whole outlook and way of life. It is obvious that should they remain religious and pious, their religiosity would be only one component in the totality of a *universal* culture. Even if the students regarded religious studies as on a higher plane, these studies would not be the formative value which gave shape to the totality of their education. There was reason to assume that language and the subjects that taught citizenship, helped acquire social position, a good livelihood, etc., would determine the direction of a young person's life in contrast to his forebears who were educated purely towards the worship of God.

As the theory was applied to the educational process, the full significance of the cultural revolution outlined in *Words of Peace and Truth* was laid bare. The important practical question was: How did the new educational program mold the image of the *maskil*?

The answer, found in the curriculum of the new school, is seen in the value emphasis placed on four components of the curriculum; collectively they constitute a realization of the humanist cultural ideal in its Jewish rendering:

1) Language studies: Hebrew and modern languages, and the importance attributed to the ethical, esthetic, and intellectual significance of linguistic knowledge;

2) Education in ethics and manners, and articulating their spiritual significance;

3) Socialization — achieving social status in accord with one's economic, social, and political usefulness to oneself and the society;

4) The aspiration to broaden and deepen one's knowledge for its own sake, realized in the whole of humanistic studies and not just religious studies in the narrow sense.

We begin with the study of languages. The Haskalah movement stressed the pragmatic value of learning languages because this was the most likely argument to convince the masses of the importance of enlightenment. Acquiring proficiency in the language of the country, at more than the vulgar level that was acquired from the everyday encounters in the marketplace with the gentile masses, was now a prerequisite for anyone who wanted to make a decent living. Necessary as it was in traditional Jewish occupations such as commerce and handicrafts, proficiency was all the more a necessity for the liberal professions. As far as the enlightened non-Jewish society with which Jews came into daily contact, there was a cultural advantage in knowing the local language. A Jew who wanted to earn a living had to interact with enlightened non-Jews. Cultured people are precise in their language and do not trust anyone who does not share their culture and whose language is vulgar, corrupt or ridiculous. The precise and grammatical study of Hebrew, too, had a clear advantage for a precise and profound understanding of Torah, prayer, and halakhah.

In any case, the curriculum of the Haskalah school emphasized the value aspect of this approach through its manner of instruction and the grammatical, stylistic norms that it set. Beyond the technical, minimal aspects of conversation as a means of communication for daily needs, language was taught according to the ideological demand that one be meticulous regarding purity, grammatical accuracy and stylistic norms.

(Even the mistakes customary in the vernacular of the masses were to be avoided; words had to be authentic, using words borrowed from other languages or from inappropriate linguistic strata was to be avoided.) The choice of one's words — their richness, phonetic clarity, elegance, and rhetorical flourish — all had to be exact and refined.

We are speaking about a linguistic ethos that regarded speech and writing as superior cultural values which immediately reveal a person's spiritual qualities: language is the national spirit and cultural persona of a people; style is the man. Therefore one should cultivate language as a value in its own right. This lays the foundation for humanism as a scholarly discipline: language embodies sensory, imaginative, affective, and ideational qualities. It embodies the cultural totality that language itself created out of various languages (musical, plastic, etc.) which occur along with it. The differences that exist among the languages of peoples and the stylistic differences of individuals and periods of time are neither external nor contingent; they are qualitative and essential in a way that rules out any full or exact translation of a linguistic expression that deals with the most profound thought and feeling. There are times when translation from language to language changes the deeper dimension of meaning. A person of culture is thus one who knows his language to its very depths, and the scope of his culture is measured by the number of languages that he knows intimately.

The value-laden, humanistic approach to language was especially emphasized in the Jewish Enlightenment movement because it wished to repair the distortions of ghetto culture. This movement's most blatant manifestation was its revulsion against the language of the Jews in the ghettos of central and eastern Europe, namely Yiddish. They defined it not as a language but as a "jargon" — a mish-mash that promiscuously combines and perverts two honorable native languages — Hebrew and German. The differences between these languages in vocabulary, phonetics, rhythm, grammar and syntax could hardly be greater. Consider — if language embodies the essential characteristics of a culture, what kind of culture could a jargon such as Yiddish embody? Or to take another example, what kind of culture could rabbinic Hebrew embody, which is a hodge-podge that includes not only Aramaic words from the Talmud but also words from the Greek, Persian, Latin, and French, and exhibits carelessness and disdain for the principles of grammar and syntax? Consequently, the *maskilim* swore allegiance to their cultural ideal in a war that gave no quarter to Yiddish or rabbinic Hebrew, and was unyielding in the demand to teach grammatical Hebrew of Biblical purity on the one hand, and grammatical German of classic literary purity (particularly Goethe and Schiller) on the other.

The study and mastery of grammar became one of the hallmark traits of the cultured Jewish person of enlightenment. It could be said that in his equal devotion to the two languages, the *maskil* sought atonement and correction for the sins of his Yiddish-speaking fathers. By returning to the unsullied source languages, the *maskil* wanted to reinstate the linguistic authenticity of Jewish culture and open it to the expanse of universal culture. But in discussing the characteristic features of the Jewish cultural ideal, one should emphasize not only the joint study of Hebrew and German, but also the significance for one's values and personal identity that they attributed to accomplished and elegant speech and writing in both these languages.

In the areas of decorum and ethics too, the Jewish Enlightenment was implicitly critical of traditional rabbinic education. *Musar* (moral training) and *derekh eretz* (proper conduct) were always important elements in Jewish education. The abundance of moralistic literature, whose origins are found in the Bible, confirms this. Actually, "education" and "*musar*" were perceived as synonymous for highlighting diverse aspects in the transmission of rabbinic tradition. The *maskilim* took note of this of course. They never tired of mentioning and citing various Jewish ethical classics such as the *Ethics of the Fathers*, Saadia's *Book of Doctrines and Beliefs*, Bahya's *Duties of the Heart*, Maimonides' *Eight Chapters* and *Book of Knowledge*, and more. But their biting criticism of Jewish religious education in their time was made precisely on the basis of their familiarity with the ancient tradition. They claimed that halakhic religious education, undeniably a product of the ghetto, over-emphasized the laws and commands pertaining to an individual's relation to God, but was careless when it came to interpersonal conduct.

This criticism had two aspects. First, it was a protest against esteeming the value of the ethical commands too lightly even from a religious perspective. In the view of the *maskilim*, the rabbis of the generation placed excessive emphasis on ritual commands that had no other reason than worship of God through obedience, because they were unique to Jews, identifying them and keeping them separate from gentiles, while attending less to ethical commands, precisely because the latter were "rational" and a person could arrive at them from his reason in any place or culture. True piety is expressed precisely in observing commands that serve no human utilitarian function. It follows that sins in matters such as kosher food or "family purity"* are regarded by the ultra-Orthodox rabbis as immeasurably more severe than major sins in the interpersonal sphere, especially when one is speaking of issues of economics and livelihood, social respect and the like.

---

* "Family purity": abstaining from marital intercourse during the time of the woman's menstrual flow and aftermath (see Leviticus 15:19–30, 18:19).

Second, it was a protest against applying a double standard to Jews and gentiles, for by a certain prevalent conception one did not have to respond to sins against Jews and sins against gentiles with the same severity. One might even ignore or condone sins against gentiles, as long as they did not come to public knowledge, whether because of their application of the maxim " [when the law specifies] 'a person' — this refers to a Jew"* or because of a view that the full force of ethical injunctions applies only to "your neighbor — i.e. a fellow-Jew," not a gentile who is not "one of the covenant," and especially when the relationship with gentiles was typically marked with hostility.

The practical motivation of the *maskilim's* criticism of the state of ethics in the religious Judaism of their time was obvious: the serious damage, internal and external, suffered by individuals and the Jewish community because of such invidious norms. One must also take into account the excuse that this double standard gave the gentiles for their anti-Jewish resentment, and the obstacle that it posed to emancipation. But it is clear here that in addition to the practical motivation, the criticism also contained a categorical motivation, beyond religion, whose source was in "the law of man," i.e. in humanism. From humanism's point of view, the moral law, precisely because it is autonomous and decreed by human reason, takes priority over ritual law. It is precisely in the moral commandment that one finds the most profound relationship between man and God as enunciated by the prophets; moreover, the moral commandment is binding for man by virtue of his being a man, and not because he is a Jew. Therefore, this precept is more sublime and expresses the Jewish mission among the nations. Only through a universal application of the moral commandments to all human beings can the claim that the Jewish people is a chosen people be sustained.

But the humanist demand to recognize the pragmatic and universal validity of morality is not enough. The cultural, academic ideal of the

---

* In interpreting Biblical law to derive the detailed provisions of rabbinic jurisprudence, the rabbis had to decide which provisions of the law treated Jews and non-Jews alike, and which applied only to Jews. The analogy would be which provisions of a civil or religious code — covering such diverse topics as voting, taxation, welfare benefits, commercial contracts, religious communion, etc. — apply only to citizens or insiders and which apply also to resident aliens or outsiders — not always an obvious determination. Medieval anti-Semites and modern anti-religious writers would take these views out of context and cite them as evidence of Jewish misanthropy and invidious elitism. Against abuse of this tendency, the rabbis promulgated an opposite principle, *mipnei darkhei shalom* — that when in doubt, one should give the gentiles the full benefits that a Jew would receive under the law, "to promote intergroup amity." In fact, the debate between exclusivist and universal values persisted internally within Jewish thought itself in all periods — Biblical, rabbinic, medieval and modern. The debate within the Enlightenment that Schweid discusses here is thus one episode in a continuing Jewish controversy. (LL)

Enlightenment mandated an adaptation of manners as an esthetic, ethical value in its own right and attached great importance to it. Sometimes it even appears to supersede the value of morality. The practical impetus for this preference is not difficult to determine: conformity of external manners shows a willingness to adapt to the environment. In other words, it embodies the social-cultural dimension in the realization of the Emancipation.

There is indeed a basis for the argument that for the enlightened Jew the acquisition of proper manners — including adapting one's dress and conduct to the accepted cultural standard — was comparable to the importance that ritual observance had for the traditional Jew. It was ritual commandments which isolated the Jew from his non-Jewish surroundings and differentiated him through clearly distinguishable signs; hence their heightened importance for the pious. Now, to the consternation of the enlightened Jews, it was the lack of modern European manners that set Jews apart in appearance from their enlightened gentile neighbors, and not for the better. Therefore, in order not to stand out negatively, the Jew must act with propriety. Decorum took on a moral valence. In the modern Enlightenment value scheme, decorum was primarily a matter of esthetics: that is, attractive external appearance in dress and behavior and the cultivation of friendly interpersonal relations. In the context of the Emancipation, however, decorum takes on the moral significance of the desire to integrate and fit in with one's neighbors, to show respect for them, to be like them and be liked by them. Without question, on the Haskalah's scale of cultural values, this humanist value took pride of place. Therefore, the Enlightenment's educational theory called for decorum and morality not only for their own sake but for their special significance as ethical and meta-ethical, decorous and meta-decorous values which would inherently ennoble the Jew.

Education as a socializing process was the most important practical aspect of the Enlightenment because it confronted the question of a person's contribution to society as he made a decent living and acquired status and influence. From this perspective, the *maskilim* — in their critique of traditional Jewish education — wanted to tackle two serious challenges that were bound up with each other. The first was poverty and the culture of poverty that had overtaken Jewish life because of the natural increase in live births in the modern period, as well as industrialization, urbanization, and the development of modern economics that made large sectors of "Jewish" livelihood inefficient and redundant. The second dealt with the criticism that Jews earned their money unjustly through clever exploitation of their surroundings rather than through actual contributions to their society — or that, in socioeconomic terms, they were non-productive, making their money mostly as middlemen. Thus one of the most important challenges of the emancipation in its social aspects was the migration of Jews from the despised middleman role to honorable productive occupations, so that they might achieve economic prosperity, be accepted by their neighbors and so neutralize one of the most potent causes of hatred and prejudice that prevailed against them among the gentiles.

The *maskilic* critique of traditional religious Jewish education on this point was perhaps the sharpest of all. This could very well be the root of all the other evils. Indeed, Jewish religious education, based in the *ḥeder* and the yeshiva, never broached the issue or sought to prepare its pupils for their roles in society, either in the economic or the civic arena.

Who did prepare young people for life in this world? To the extent that this was done by anyone, it was by the parents as they took their children into commercial enterprises that did not require much knowledge, or into apprenticeships as simple craftsmen. Official Jewish education prepared and qualified its students for one goal only: Judaism or "Yiddishkeit," the worship of God through prayer and performance of mitzvot, the study of Torah for its own sake. The only livelihood one could derive from such a religious preparation for life was to become part of the official religious establishment: rabbi, judge, ritual slaughterer, mohel (circumciser), or *batlan* (idler) whose livelihood depended on the charity of the community. But how many religious functionaries could a community support? And what contribution could these persons make to the general society which Jews wanted to enter as citizens and in which they wanted to earn their living?

The *maskilim* believed that an entirely different socio-educational orientation was needed. Jews should enter those productive occupations considered to be most useful and consequently most rewarding. The school should undertake the task of preparation for an adult life at its most general and serious, which is to say, its mundane sense. One could no longer expect parents to fulfill this complicated function by themselves: after all, a transition to new occupations that required greater knowledge was required. Only good elementary and secondary schools could provide pupils with the tools they would need to strive for advanced, productive occupations. Wessely's "human knowledge" focused particularly on training for such occupations.

However, we should emphasize the objective of learning for its own sake. The enlightened primary school that taught reading, writing and speaking in the language of the country, arithmetic, science, and geography laid only a general foundation for choosing a productive, modern occupation, but there was no talk here of specialized professional training, that one could only get at a university or an apprenticeship rotation in the suitable workplaces. In the framework of the school, preparation for life was not therefore a preparation for actually functioning as a professional; it was rather the groundwork for a new kind of cultural orientation which was expressed in the way one lived in the family, the community, with one's friends, and in the society of one's city and country. Integration was the avenue into accepted occupations in an enlightened, progressive society. Obviously, a restricted, religious preparation was insufficient. Civic education was necessary and beyond that the ability to enter into discourse with people of the this-worldly culture on science, philosophy, literature and art. Here, too, an examination of the Enlightenment curriculum shows that internalizing the content of secular topics was not merely a means but an aim in its own right.

At this point we come to the fourth component of the overall educational theme: the humanistic world view of the Enlightenment movement. The message was transmitted primarily in the polemical literature which repeatedly described the ideal figure of a *maskil* as distinct from an assortment of obscuratanists. The *maskil* was first of all "an enlightened person," a fact that set him apart from every kind of darkness: ignorance and illiteracy, meanness and baseness, villainy, impoverishment, backwardness and failure. The metaphor of light dispelling darkness filled a central role in general European enlightenment and was strongly emphasized by the Haskalah.

"Being enlightened" included a wide variety of features. In the first instance, intellectual enlightenment was a type of broadmindedness, an aspiration to become constantly more knowledgeable in many fields. But it should be emphasized that this was restricted to a certain type of knowledge, for the obscurantists have their kinds of knowledge too. In the modern European and Jewish ideal of enlightenment, there is a turning away from religious mysticism and from scholasticism (of which Talmudic *pilpul* is a Jewish variant), and to a large degree against the whole metaphysical preoccupation of philosophy in the Middle Ages. In place of these, there is a turn to the sciences and scientific method, which are rational, objective and based on experience — in other words, worldly knowledge. Second, we are speaking not just of knowledge itself but the ethos of knowledge, a recognition of its value-laden importance to life expressed in an interest that went beyond curiosity to a concern marked by a caring commitment or an acknowledgement of the obligation to know. All this was the impetus for the ever-expanding involvement of a person active in his society. Such an interest called for broadmindedness and openness in relating to the social and natural environment for which the enlightened person felt responsible.

This being the case, it is obvious that enlightenment in its intellectual sense relied on and was completed by enlightenment in the moral sense. Thus enlightenment was a kind of character, a kind of stability and determination constantly directed toward advancing desirable, positive, beneficial goals that could elicit confidence. The enlightened person was a man of integrity, who had no truck with devious ways, who never disguised his aims and did not employ subterfuge; he was objective and unprejudiced in his judgments, and entirely trustworthy. The quality of *faithfulness* is extremely prominent in the moral ethos of the Enlightenment.

It seems that this is the proper place to present the "enlightened man" of the Enlightenment as a religious believer, because it will be seen on close examination that the emphasis on "faithfulness" as a matter of character comes as a moral and existential response of the *maskil* to the criticism that was leveled at him by the "obscurantists" that he denies the faith and throws off the yoke of observance. We should therefore emphasize again that although the Jewish Enlightenment movement was worldly from the outset, it did not originally imply renunciation of religion: not of God, nor of Torah, nor of Jewish law. In the second generation it indeed split and gave rise to several radical tendencies that broke with rabbinic Judaism (especially in Eastern Europe), but there too it remained mostly within a framework of faith. The distinction was drawn between enlightened faith based on knowledge and strong moral convictions, and superstitious faith based on ignorance, deception and delusion, and on uncritical, slavish obedience to the *Shulḥan Arukh*. The enlightened man believes in God, in human beings and in himself. His faith rests on broad worldly knowledge and on a moral orientation that proves its worth through ethically salutary deeds, as well as by fine social achievements: honor, wealth, influence, which are its certain reward. The *maskil's* ethical faithfulness to others is the direct expression and convincing proof of his existential, enlightened faith.

From here we come to the moral significance of the term *maskil* (from *sekhel*, "intelligence"). It combined an intellectual aspect and a moral aspect, which were fused in a flourishing activism. To be a *maskil* meant to be wise, and wisdom was undoubtedly an accumulation of broad and encompassing knowledge, an acquaintance with the totality of things, and an understanding how the details combine to form a unity. Still, the *maskil* was qualitatively different than the Talmudic sage, different than the philosopher in the Platonic and Aristotelian medieval construction (for Jews, Maimonides), and even different than the renaissance humanist who was a polymath, almost the embodiment of a whole university in one person. The perfect *Maskil* — such as Moses Mendelssohn — may stand head and shoulders above the people, but it was assumed and anticipated that many could and should rise to his station, some more and some less. Therefore, wisdom as the totality of knowledge must be a selective principle, focused in the moral will that directs it toward active living. Surely there is value in inclusive knowledge for its own sake, but it must be manifested in the ability of the wise man to carry out the tasks that he undertakes.

The second understanding of *maskil* was the meaning that was directly derived from the context of wisdom literature in the Bible. The wise person, in the Biblical sense, prospers "in all his ways" or "in all his deeds." In everything he says and does, he is a person who knows how to secure a blessing for others and for himself as did Joseph, the son of the patriarch, Jacob. The *maskil* was a sublime embodiment of worldly wisdom. He was a positive person not only from the standpoint of his ethical stance and faithfulness to people and society, but also in the way he saw himself. He was an active person and as such a happy one. Happiness stemmed from worldly social success in ethical ways. Happiness was that great light that shone from him on to his surroundings.

Chapter Six
CROSSROADS:
THE TRANSITION FROM HASKALAH TO
THE SCIENCE OF JUDAISM

Written primarily in Hebrew for the Jews of Eastern Europe, the literature intended for education and school room studies also served to create a Jewish culture for the Jewish people. In central and western Europe, however, most Jews who opted for the worldly ideals of the Emancipation and the Haskalah turned to non-Jewish schools, particularly the gymnasia and university, for secondary and higher education. Their decision to do so was the result of practical considerations and caused fundamental changes: abandoning Hebrew by relegating it to being the language of prayer and Torah-reading in the synagogue (and in some cases, not even this much), and thus abandoning the powerful national elements that were expressed through its language. Educational study was conducted entirely in the vernacular. Inevitably, Jewish knowledge — to the extent that the parents wanted to acquire it themselves and transmit it to their children — had to be imparted mainly in German, and of course at the same standard and with the same tools appropriate to other studies in the gymnasia and the university. In other words, Judaism as a culture had to be developed so that it paralleled general culture at its highest level — the level of scientific, philological-historical inquiry, and universal philosophical study.

The split was unavoidable. Eastern Europe witnessed an impressive, ongoing creation of Hebrew culture, particularly in the character of the new literature: poetry, fiction, essays and scholarly inquiry into Jewish history and literature. This Hebrew culture gave rise to and subsequently cultivated the literature of cultural rebirth and the Hebrew national culture of Zionism. By comparison, in central Europe, a quest for Jewish culture developed whose nature was spiritual-religious rather than national. This ambitious project was undertaken by the movement of *Jüdische Wissenschaft* ("Jewish science," or Science of Judaism), called in Hebrew by the felicitous, broadly significant phrase *ḥokhmat Yisrael* — "the wisdom (or study) of Israel."

Clearly, the dichotomy between these two orientations was not absolute. The Hebrew Enlightenment (Haskalah) in eastern Europe made a respectable contribution to the founding and development of Jewish historical scholarship, while the *Jüdische Wissenschaft* of central Europe exercised a continual perceptible influence on the Haskalah movement and the Hebrew Zionist renaissance in eastern Europe. Still, in general outline the distinction is clear and sharp: the official center of Jewish historical scholarship arose in Germany around the focus of secular-religious Jewish self-definition, in the German language; whereas the new Hebrew literature, whose focus was secular-national, developed and produced most of its notable accomplishments in eastern Europe and later in Israel. Thus two types of "Jewish culture" crystallized, but though there were essentially different, they had a common ground.

Chapter Seven

THE DIALECTIC BETWEEN
NATIONAL HEBREW CULTURE
AND JEWISH IDEALISTIC HUMANISM

The description of the early stages in the ideal of Jewish (Hebrew) Enlightenment tended to emphasize the national-secular character of the European paradigm on which it was modeled. This may have overstated the intention of the Haskalah's founding personalities. One finds a decidedly religious component in the uniquely Jewish aspect of the education that Wessely and those who followed him in the Hebrew enlightenment literature proposed. Still, there were allusions to a national element as well. The religious component is represented in the plan Wessely defined as *Torat ha-Elohim*, the Law of God, meaning, of course, studies necessary for transmitting belief, a religious way of life, and commandments; that is, the Bible with its traditional interpretations, the Talmud and its commentaries, the laws, prayers, and benedictions. The national component in Wessely's plan is found in the study of Hebrew grammar and the fostering of an affinity to Hebrew literature that experienced a renaissance, largely in consequence of Wessely's example, on secular European models.

The disciples of the Enlightenment educational program were recruited partly from the special schools, but more commonly from students of traditional yeshivas who taught themselves modern culture from the auxiliary Haskalah literature in Hebrew and the vernacular (such as Mendelssohn's Bible translation and commentary). These formed the Jewish public who were destined to be the next generation of writers and readers of the new Hebrew literature.

It was indeed this literature that created the feedback-loop of ideas, experiences, and social movement between reader and writer. The basis for a popular, Jewish secular culture with a national linguistic character emerged against the background of eastern European Jewish life in the 19th century. In that period, the dense Jewish population which was concentrated in regions and small towns where they were the majority had no practical ability to struggle for socio-political emancipation. With this population as a base, Haskalah literature was used to develop a popular, secular Jewish culture that had national and linguistic characteristics. Initially, this was done through the Hebrew language. Subsequently similar efforts were made in Yiddish.

To fully understand this, it should be emphasized that Hebrew literature proliferated rapidly after Wessely and Mendelssohn's generation: fiction, poetry, essays, literary and historical studies, translations from European literature. An entire cycle of cultural activity was created. Literature mirrored the reality of Jewish life. It shaped the self-perception and world view of the *maskilim*; it was an outlet for national feelings; it revived the national historic memory by drawing on Biblical sources, on secular literature from the Golden Age in Spain and the Renaissance period in Italy, and by means of scientific and literary descriptions of the Jewish past. Literature nourished an experiential and educational socio-cultural endeavor, gave rise to stormy polemics, and set behavioral standards for the leadership of organized movements in the Jewish milieu. This was a vital process not restricted to the printed page whose breadth of activity made up the vigorous national culture of the Haskalah movement in eastern Europe. Therefore, even the actions of the extreme rebels who were against a Wessely-style "law of God," who mocked, derogated and criticized Hasidism and the rabbinic leadership's code of behavior did not lead to assimilation. Instead, the rebels translated their criticism into the language of a secular-national revolt against the enslavement of Jewish culture to religion. Furthermore, a pre-Zionist national-political trend arose that seized upon the secular political thought of Spinoza as its inspiration for Jewish national renewal in the Diaspora.

As noted, conditions in central Europe were not conducive to the development of a secular national-political rationalism. The effort to advance the Emancipation and to overcome the obstacles to it by internalizing the German national culture through its language and literature, resulted within a single generation in abandoning Hebrew or restricting its study to its use in prayer and reading the Torah, without developing the ability for reading modern Hebrew literature, let alone creating such a literature.

Both as producers and consumers of literature, emancipation-thirsty Jews in the post-Mendelssohn generation embraced German literature, creating a unique Jewish dimension in the literary strata which non-Jews soon became aware of, though that was not the aim. As far as the Jews were concerned, they simply wanted to take part in the national German literature. The slow and gradual development of the Emancipation required that Jews relinquish, even reject, a separate Jewish nationality in the name of total identity with German nationality. This meant that the only way to maintain any Jewish cultural identity was either through a sophisticated cultural transformation of religion, or through the creation of an idealistic, humanistic Jewish religiosity. Mendelssohn had created devices and provided a direction but the atmosphere and the necessary tools for a parallel socio-cultural development in the emancipation-eager Jewish public were created through the rise of idealistic humanism, the spread of the socio-cultural influence of Kantian philosophy, the dissemination and influence of Hegel and Schelling's philosophies, and the consolidation of philological-historic study in German universities. These served as entry routes into German culture for Jews as active participants.

The turn to an idealistic-cultural direction was expressed in the development of two parallel and complementary disciplines in which the Science of Judaism prided itself and by means of which it formulated its Jewish cultural ideal: modern scientific historiography and modern philosophic idealism united in formulating a philosophy of history, or historiosophy, as the self-awareness of a developing cultural creativity. How was the role of scientific historiography understood? What was the historical concept on which it was based? History is the common memory of a human society regarding the events and deeds that shaped it as a collectivity in the past and impacted on its present institutions, on its self-awareness in the present, and its expectation and vision of the future. Historiography in its modern scientific sense is an objective, critical study of the totality of documentation which embodies the collective memory within itself. The aim was to reconstitute from documented memory the flow of significant social and cultural events *as they actually occurred,* to uncover the causality that operated in them so as to achieve a profound, well-founded understanding of present social reality, and to design an orientation for future expectations and goals of society. The subject of history therefore is the presence of the collective in its broadest scope. In general, a particular people is unified through its generational continuity, its language, and the territorial boundaries of its country, or better still, a people is a national entity whose unity as a group shares a common memory that is institutionalized in an inclusive framework which is consolidated and easily distinguished from any co-existing group that relates to it as a *state.*

The notion that flows from this is that the unifying political framework, its leaders and those who shape it, the course of its development, how it changes, and its events are all elements of memory and historic research. In effect this is how history has always been written. It has always been a function of statehood or institutionalized religion.

But since modern scientific historiography is predicated on exhaustive research of a subject — an understanding of its causes, components, and laws — historiography only attached an importance to the political institutional framework in so far as it served as a unifying framework. In this way historians endeavored to gather focused, well-defined information about the resources, institutions and enterprises on which the framework was established, existed, and to which it gave collective expression. In other words, historiography places the emphasis on culture as the content of the collective life of a society both in how it functions as a civilization and in what it produces as a culture. By means of the political framework, scientific historiography focuses its attention on the collective cultural memory of a society: the nation and the people.

Furthermore, when one defines history in this way, one discovers that the principle role of history goes beyond a study of political or political-religious functions of the past. The cultural function becomes primary to historical study, and historical study itself becomes a part of cultural creativity. Through history, culture preserves the content of collective memory, transmits it as the content engaged in an unbroken process which nonetheless is developing, changing and renewing. Through the historian's activity, he means to project the efforts of a culture to study itself in order to assure the continuity which it transmits from generation to generation. Historiography was considered an instrument by which culture could potentially shape the past, the present, and set expectations and future desires. In other words, history was defined as culture's creative process; historiography as its process of becoming known and transmitted.

Thus was formed a meeting-ground between historiography and philosophy. The task of philosophy according to its classic definition was: man's critical self-knowledge and self-understanding in his relation to the environment in which he lives, namely man's knowledge of himself in the world and his knowledge of the world around him. In order to fulfill this ambitious role systematically and critically, it is necessary to examine instruments of knowledge and the way in which knowledge is verified. Subsequently, the wealth of knowledge that has been amassed by humanity in all fields is evaluated and summarized: knowledge of nature, of human nature (man's spirit and psyche), of human society and all its institutions, knowledge of the metaphysical and the transcendental; all these, of course, to the extent that such knowledge is available to man.

This is the way western philosophy defined its role from its beginnings in ancient Greece. It is clear that culture, both in its material and its spiritual aspects, was one of its central topics. It is also clear that it recognized itself as a human spiritual product — i.e., as a cultural product — and judged itself accordingly. Despite all this, because of the essential changes that occurred in the status of philosophy within culture, and because of the essential changes that took place within philosophy itself, there was a dramatic development in modern philosophy particularly vis à vis religion on one hand and the natural sciences on the other. Due to such changes, in both methodology and the substance of truth, philosophers had to take the phenomena of constant change in philosophic thought into account. This was despite the fact that ostensibly there ought to be but one eternal, permanent and immutable philosophical truth.

Philosophy was thus required to give a philosophical account of its own history and its affinity to the changing subjects that it explored and which had caused the changes within it: perhaps understanding these transformations in terms of their causes and underlying laws might lead philosophy from relative, changing truths to the one absolute truth for which it always strove! Without considering the developments which had occurred in thought, linked to the developments that had taken place in all objects of philosophic inquiry: the sciences, including psychology, cognition, social and political institutions, religious faith, and so forth — in other words, in all levels of cultural creativity — without such a reckoning philosophy cannot fulfill the role it undertook. Philosophy had to summarize the historic development of culture in order to achieve an examination of its own underlying truth.

The conclusion was simple: philosophy in its all-embracing scope, and not just in some of its parts, is the general knowledge of human culture as the totality of knowledge, and since culture develops in response to causes and in accordance with laws (that one must of course investigate and uncover), philosophy also develops. It is historical both in content and method. In this way it constitutes a culture's historic consciousness. The function of summarizing, interpreting, transmitting and guiding culture is not therefore the role of the historian who amasses and arranges documented memory but is the role of the philosopher who examines history as the formative process of culture in order to uncover its laws, sources, and goals.

On the strength of this insight, idealistic philosophy created a new philosophic discipline: historiosophy. It could be said that, in effect, this philosophic subject displaced the metaphysics of classic philosophy and of theology in institutionalized religious thought. It could also be claimed that this subject expressed the humanization, or the secularization, of the metaphysical and theological functions in order to provide an overall orientation for the creation of a secular culture whose sources are of a worldly, changing nature rather than in an absolute divine truth.

If that was the case with the highly-developed cultures of Europe which arrived at self-consciousness in the modern age, then it was certainly the case with the culture of the Jewish people that had just now arrived at the threshold of emancipation. This meant that one had to see emancipation not just as political liberation but also as cultural advancement, and one must establish the totality of the Jewish people's cultural legacy as a historical legacy equivalent to that of the historical-cultural heritage of the peoples among whom they lived. In this way, the Jewish people fully develops its cultural uniqueness at the highest plane of creativity within the overall cultural creativity of its surroundings, perfecting and realizing its own goals.

What must be done to this end? First and foremost, simultaneously develop the two cultural disciplines — scientific historiography and the philosophy of history — which, because of historical exigencies, had hitherto hardly developed in Jewish culture. It was these disciplines that were meant to be the instruments of Judaism as a humanistic culture.

Chapter Eight
THE PHILOSOPHIC HISTORIC FORMATION OF JEWISH HUMANISM: A MODERN GUIDE TO THE PERPLEXED

The earliest stirrings of humanist-idealism were felt by German Jewry, indeed, they were the first to perceive the need for and create such a Jewish culture, but it is instructive that the first formative work that combined historiography and philosophy and proposed a complete model of humanistic-idealist Jewish culture was actually written in Hebrew and in eastern Europe (Galicia). One can see in it the direct influence of German idealism (Kant and Hegel) but the specific context of the east-European Enlightenment movement is recognizable in the Jewish-nationalist tendency of the work. We are referring to the book that had an influence throughout the second half of the 19th century and the first half of the 20th century on most of the modern Jewish movements both in Germany and in eastern Europe: *The Guide of the Perplexed of the Time,* by Rabbi Nachman Krochmal (1783–1840).

The appearance of the work against the backdrop of Galician Jewry was not accidental. The Jewish Enlightenment movement of Galicia provided a bridge between those of Germany on the one hand and Poland and Russia on the other hand. Traditional Jewish scholarship and critical historic research, German idealistic philosophy and Jewish medieval philosophy, and the spontaneous Jewish national sensibility (that had still not been dampened by the Emancipation) met at this juncture and were mutually enriched. This is evident in the multi-layered cultural texture — linguistic, literary, historical, legendary, halakhic, theological, and philosophical — in *A Guide of the Perplexed of the Time.* The educational processes of traditional Jewish culture had greater difficulty with the historical and cultural themes of German idealism (which had developed against a burgeoning German nationalism) than with its universal, religious message. As a Jewish philosopher, Krochmal, however, appears to have found it natural and unproblematic to accept the universal religious message (which seemed consonant with Jewish sources) as well as to accept and fully integrate the national message without apologetics or reservation. Krochmal saw external influence as an occasion for adaptation and accommodation, not assimilation.

A Guide of the Perplexed of the Time is a highly unusual work. Rabbi Krochmal was primarily a historiographer, a critical scientific researcher of Jewish history; he was a philologist and a student of literary sources of Jewish culture; and he was an original philosopher of the idealistic school. The book is a blend of his achievements in all three fields. On the most basic level it is a survey of Jewish history from its beginning in the Biblical period to the Bar Kokhba rebellion. On the next level one finds a discourse on the history of the literature of the Oral Torah from the period of the Sages onward, including trends of Jewish thought (particularly Kabbalah and religious philosophy).

And on the third and unifying level, Krochmal lays out foundations of idealistic historiosophy and how its assumptions can be applied in interpreting the political, cultural, and religious history of the Jewish people: the structure of its periods, its governing laws and goals, and its relation to the history of other nations.

The result is a book that is not only a scientific discourse on the political and cultural history of the Jewish people, but a kind of quintessential summary of Jewish tradition as it is represented in the Jewish sources: Bible, Mishnah, Talmud, Midrash, Kabbalah, literature and philosophy — particularly Maimonides' *Guide To The Perplexed* and his *Mishneh Torah*. Jewish culture presents a familiar structure of a continuous series of literary sources — in each period in its history, a new source was created that recombined the content of the previous sources through interpretation, recapitulation, and re-application so as to be responsive to the needs and challenges of a given period. In every period, Judaism as a whole — its past, its present, and its future hopes — was represented in the classic literary product of that generation, and the task of continuity was met by learning the continuous series of previous sources through the vantage point of the last one. The book *Guide of the Perplexed of the Time* was written within this historical-cultural progression with the objective of fulfilling this same educational-cultural need. Its closest and most influential literary model was of course Maimonides' *Guide of the Perplexed*. Krochmal's book was intended to prepare the reader who had already acquired a suitable preparation in Jewish sources and general humanist studies to enter into the full gamut of the developing thought-world of Judaism. He would be able to participate in the process of receiving it, creating it, and passing it on.

One could say that just as the Bible in its day, the Mishnah and Talmudim in their day, and the Maimonidean *Guide* and *Mishneh Torah* in their day provided the all-encompassing "Torah" appropriate for each age, so the *Guide of the Perplexed of the Time* was intended to be the "Torah" in the traditional sense for Krochmal's era: it was intended as an emerging, all encompassing work for students preparing to become teachers. But there was a highly significant difference in both methodology and content — Krochmal's book makes no pretense at being the transmission of divine revelation in the traditional sense for, in the author's opinion, from its inception the Tradition was an unusual cultural historic work by human beings who regarded their national, spiritual creativity as the product of divine inspiration or direct divine revelation. This being the case, the particular cultural, educational role of the book was to confront the problems inherent in a transition from religious to cultural idealistic consciousness. It is obvious that Krochmal regarded such a transition as inevitable for Judaism's survival in the modern period, but he recognized that a severe spiritual crisis was intrinsic in such a transition.

This explains the name of the book and its declared primary, educational purpose: a modern guide to the perplexed. Intent is unambiguously declared in the title, and with necessary adaptations to the needs of the period, in the methodological structure as well.

The derivation from Maimonides is direct and straight-forward. Maimonides' *Guide to the Perplexed* was meant to be the guide its title implied. It was composed as a systematic pedagogical curriculum for certain types of students. At the outset, Maimonides states for whom the book is intended: students who demonstrate certain intellectual achievements in several distinct areas of knowledge. He then goes on to present the studies, both theoretical and applied, in such a way that the students who merited them — and they alone — could pursue them, in stages, as they mastered a scholarly and theoretical competence. Upon completion of their studies, they move from being pupils to students capable of independent, creative progress, who could, in turn, qualify as teachers.

Krochmal's paradigm had a traditional core. Maimonides did not create outside the context of source literature: both the Mishnah and the Talmud were written as study texts for the academies and were applied in the learning process itself. But Maimonides applied this traditional model as a transition from instruction at the halakhic religious level to instruction at the philosophic religious level. It was for this reason that Krochmal chose Maimonides as the model for his work, even replicating it. Like Maimonides, Krochmal's vital challenge was to confront the same kind of philosophic spiritual crisis which both termed "perplexed."

But to the classic title coined by Maimonides, *Guide to the Perplexed*, it is significant that Krochmal added the words "of the time." What was the meaning of the addition? His first intention was simple and obvious. Krochmal informed his readers that in writing his work he wanted to do for his contemporaries — modern Jews — what Maimonides had done for the

Jews of his time. He wanted his readers to know (in an ostensibly simple and clearly understood message) that the profound solutions of Maimonides which had responded convincingly to the questions and spiritual perplexities of medieval Jews were no longer convincing to the perplexities of modern Jews. There were new questions and new perplexities. New responses were required.

To veterans of our post-modern era this sounds almost banal, but against the background of traditional religious culture, even in terms of Maimonides' philosophic construction of Judaism, this is not a statement that can be taken for granted. Does it really imply that the conception of religious truth that is based on revelation can change between one *period* and another? As did all his predecessors, Maimonides too recognized that halakhic decrees must constantly be renewed if they are to be consonant with the needs of each period, and that interpretations of the Torah and its methods of instructions also need renewal in every period. But it never occurred to him that the perception of religious truth that was transmitted in divine revelation would change over time. On the contrary, in Maimonides' opinion, his conception of truth was the very same as that taught by Moses and the prophets, and by the Sages. Furthermore, he believed that the method of teaching that truth, if not always identical, was always similar in its principles.

As a scientific historian, Nachman Krochmal recognized this fact. But based on his research as a scientific historian (a discipline which neither Maimonides nor his predecessors required or knew about in their time) Krochmal came to the conclusion that the conception of religious truth did indeed change over time. Because Maimonides' perception of truth subsumed a considerable measure of Aristotelian medieval science and philosophy, it was not identical with that of the prophets or the Sages.

The far-reaching conclusion that followed from this was the key to the final meaning of the addition of the word "time" in the book's title: since the conception of religious truth, given through divine revelation, was indeed liable to change from one time to another, therefore time itself — i.e., temporality and the process of change that it measured — was the greatest cause of perplexity, and it was the primary and most profound cause of the special perplexity of our own time. Why? Because ours is the time that is marked by the awareness of time.

The awareness of time forces us to recognize the phenomenon of historical change that Maimonides, like his predecessors, embodied in their creative work without being forced to pay attention to it. It is a profound and basic difference in the cognition of truth which now had to be acknowledged.

Not surprisingly, this gave rise to great confusion raising questions such as: Given the far reaching changes that have occurred, are we still inheriting and transmitting the same Judaism handed down to us by Moses, the Prophets, the Sages, the medieval thinkers, and Maimonides himself? Isn't modern interpretation nothing short of heresy and a break in what has been bequeathed over the generations? Such questions emerged with great gravity. It would appear that only if one attends to the phenomenon of "time" in its fullest, historic sense can the greatest perplexity of all be overcome, the one caused by time itself. It must be added that an answer which is contingent on an understanding of the consciousness of historic time turns divine revelation itself into a historic process; that is, a cultural creation.

In any case, the perplexing issues of Krochmal's period were an outgrowth of scientific historiography. When any period in a people's history is examined as a totality of the events and processes that occur in cultural institutions, and periods are compared to another, one discovers that the outstanding differences (which people in every generation are somewhat aware of) are not exclusively of a type that can be defined as circumstantial or accidental. Examples of this would be the succession of kings and dynasties, outbreaks of internal conflicts or wars between kingdoms, changes in geographic and climatic factors or the discovery of resources, techniques, and receptivity to the cultures of other peoples each of whom possesses a spiritual and material civilization peculiar to itself in language, style, and religious values. Initially, the scientific critical historiographer discovers in the period he is examining there are substantive conceptual and value differences between how the people of the period perceived and evaluated the importance of the institutions they created and the events that befell them, and between how — on the background of his overall historic experience — the scholar understands and evaluates them. Thus he recognizes that there are qualitative, conceptual and value differences between his period and previous ones — as there are differences between the periods themselves — and that as a result of these conceptual differences there are not only changes in leadership but in the form and function of leadership. This change in form and function finds its parallel in almost every area of human cultural activity, even when it occurs in the same country, with the same language and with identical natural resources; it is true even when the changes result from new forms of economic, political, ethical-social, scientific, artistic, and religious functions.

On the one hand, there is continuity. The people is the same people, the language is the same language, the literary tradition is the same tradition, the culture is the same culture. But from another aspect, everything is different. Language itself changes greatly in vocabulary, concepts and expressions as well as the principles of speech. For instance, when we observe the difference between the First and Second Commonwealth periods of the Jewish people, qualitative differences are immediately apparent in every area. It would be sufficient to note the disappearance of prophecy as an institution and the appearance of "wisdom" as the institution that supplanted prophecy, or simply to observe differences in form, language, concepts, and essential values between the Mishnah and the Bible. But if scientific philological inquiry shows that there is no foundation to the midrashic claim of the Sages that the words of the Mishnah and the words of the Talmud were uttered in the exact same form by Moses at Sinai, and transmitted by him to his followers among the priests and prophets as the Oral Law (rather than acknowledging that this is what the Sages articulated in their own unique language, according to their concepts and in response to circumstances that could not have existed during the prophetic period), it must be admitted that both continuity and substantive differences exist. The continuity is expressed in the consciousness of the Sages that their words derive from a tradition given at Sinai; the differences stem from a distinct thought process which is generally more critical, more complex, and more sophisticated.

This then is the challenge raised by historiographic research. Who will find the solution and where can it be found? Of course if one seeks a scientific solution to a scientific question, one ought to restrict the inquiry specifically to events and historical processes. In other words, the solution ought to be found in the causal relationship and in the context between events and processes within each period, and between periods. And the role of discovering the solution, after the facts have been gathered by a historiographer, belongs to a philosopher of history. He creates the necessary sophisticated instruments with which to discover that which transcends the external appearance of events, processes and institutions. It is the distinction noted above — the qualitative substantive differences between cultural function and modes of thought in the various periods — that points up a progressively greater degree of critical retrospection, sophistication, and complexity which is how the *theory of historical development* originated.

It is, of course, understood that the notion of "development" is not a novel concept discovered by modernity. The fact that each plant and living creature, not to mention man, are the result of development was always obvious and the basic assumption of any educational theory, even in antiquity. The fact that cultural institutions also reach a high point and then deteriorate did not originate with modernity; it is a trait of every culture because culture is an outcome of the process of development. Thus, reading through the books of Joshua, Judges, Samuel and Kings offers a clear, conscious description of the development and decline of institutions such as the monarchy, priesthood, and prophecy. And yet the theory of *historical* development is a new modern insight, an insight that may be correctly offered as a substantive advance on the theory of development that was current in ancient and medieval times. The difference was accomplished by adding the following three assertions:

1. Development applies to the totality of social-cultural processes that take place in a given society, operating in parallel fashion in all areas, not only on particular individuals in their private life-cycles, or on particular institutions that strive to achieve completion and perfection in their functioning.

2. Development does not reach its outer limit with the maximal creative achievement of individuals and institutions, only to repeat this cycle on the same level, in the way that plants and animals are born, develop and decline in the natural cycle. Rather, it continually progresses from stage to stage, so that every generation is more developed than the previous, and each new cultural institution is more developed than its predecessor. In other words, development is not relative and cyclical, but linear and absolute.

3. Development follows a certain regular pattern that is susceptible to scientific analysis and subsequently enables certain prediction of the future.

By applying these three insights of the theory of historical development, which Krochmal adopted from Hegelian idealism, to the interpretation of the political and cultural history of the Jewish people, Krochmal was singularly equipped to deal with the challenge of modern historical consciousness. His intention was to demonstrate that the continuity and unity of Jewish culture persevere not only despite its increasingly great transformations, but precisely by means of them: the changes which have their origin in the continuity are those developments that preserve it and bring it closer to its goal. This means that Jewish culture can continue to be transmitted over the generations precisely through knowledge of the transformations which are consonant with its purposeful regularity.

Krochmal intended to implement his theoretical research in three avenues of cultural creativity and thereby make his own contribution to the process of transmission: 1) the historical memory of the Jewish people among the nations; 2) the study of the literary sources (particularly the Oral Law) which shaped the Jewish peoples's religious way of life; 3) the development of religious thought which expresses Judaism as a world outlook in tandem with world philosophical thought. All three will be assessed below in order to understand the form and content of the culture he wanted to transmit to future generations, even as he reshaped it.

The historiographic presentation of the history of the Jewish people in *A Guide of the Perplexed of Our Time* is intertwined with a historiosophic context. Section Seven opens with a succinct preface that is intended to explain the structural principles of historic processes in general. It is a straightforward, lucid presentation of the approach which says that history is a developmental process in the culture of nations, and it describes a general, structural paradigm of culture. Krochmal posited that this historical-cultural viewpoint is true of the Jewish people as well. We shall see below that the history of the Jewish people is markedly unique and that it is rooted in a singular culture but, from the qualitative standpoint of culture and the way it develops in history, there is no difference between Israel and other peoples. Judaism, too, is the culture of a specific people; it too develops as every other culture, and the laws that are found in the process of Judaism's historic development are the self-same socio-cultural laws that appear in the history of other peoples.

Krochmal opened this section with assumptions of classic Aristotelian anthropology which he enunciated in a style similar to that of Maimonides: by his nature, man is a social creature. Two empirical facts are set out: as distinguished from all other living creatures, man develops the intellectual, creative potential that is peculiar to him only in a society; and he cannot survive — certainly not develop as a human being — outside society. But a careful reading of Krochmal's work immediately shows that his outlook differs significantly from both the original Aristotelian approach and from its Maimonidean version.

The difficult question that arises after the empirical determination that man develops and survives as man only in society is: how do individuals, ostensibly born as solitary beings, join society even before their humanity is manifest, so that it can become manifest? Granted, within the historical process individual humans are born into an existing society and develop in it. But how did it begin? How is a beginning possible? Clearly the question relates to understanding the essence of sociality as a human phenomenon in general, not simply to understanding the processes of beginning. An answer to this question is actually an answer to the questions: What is culture? What are the special powers revealed in it? What is their source?

The simplest answer which the empiricists tend to give is that society is the consequence of a common nature which human beings share with other creatures: instincts, drives, hereditary and emotional attraction. It is these impulses which unite individuals into societies. After the fact, one can substantiate such a theory by means of observations in nature: there are certain other creatures that also exist in societies — herds or swarms; and there are some among them that, like human beings, cannot survive outside the herd or swarm. From these observations one learns that these creatures are impelled to join a herd or swarm in response to a natural genetic instinct. It is this instinct that directs their functioning in concert, not unlike the instinctive mutual functioning of the parts of a living organism. But does this apply to human beings? Does human society embody common instincts only, or does it exhibit an *a priori* quality which must be attributed to the uniqueness of the human sphere — that is, *will* based on a consideration of values?

Both Maimonides (who was Aristotelian) and Krochmal (who was Hegelian) rejected the assertion that the particularly human quality of sociality could stem from natural instincts. At least in their initial claims, they both based themselves on empirical observation. But it appears that each of them relied on a different aspect of human sociality. Maimonides noted that, paradoxically, man is innately social, yet he is also asocial. That is, although man's nature is not seen (nor does it exist) outside a social framework, it is also true that from the standpoint of man's nature as a creature he cannot be compared to other creatures who themselves band in a herd, certainly not to bees who are programmed to function in permanent and marvelous harmony. Just the opposite! Man is by his nature an amazingly anti-social creature. Precisely because he is more developed and complex than other animals, he displays a marked individuality. Human beings as individuals differ markedly in their motivating urges and their feelings. They are also extremely selfish. Therefore only a willed decision can bring them together to act in accord. Such volitional decision can be explained only as a response to external constraints.

In other words, no human society can persist in the absence of an authority capable of enacting laws and enforcing them. Human beings may be in need of society to survive as human, but one must force this on them. If so, how does an organized human society (as opposed to a herd of animals) arise? How did it begin? Maimonides' answer is essentially religious. In his view, it is not possible to attribute the establishment of society to natural human motivation alone. "Providence" — i.e., supernatural and supra-human divine intervention — is necessary at least as a founding event. It seems that Maimonides even considered this assertion empirical: all the political institutions that Maimonides knew were religious institutions that relied on a certain kind of revelation of supra-human spiritual powers to give force to their authority. The founding individuals — legislators and rulers — were always exceptional leaders, possessed of special spiritual powers that they exercised over their human subjects, a power that operated by charismatic attraction and the power of dominance. Such individuals exert their will in the name of a superhuman authority that was revealed to them, indeed that emanates from them. Subsequently, they institutionalize the authority in a hierarchical religious-political system.

It follows from this that the differences between political institutions of different peoples are rooted in their different religions. To better understand Krochmal's parallel but different argument, we may add: Maimonides believed, on the basis of the Bible's testimony, that all the various religions developed from one true foundational religious revelation, through a process of idolatrous corruption and degeneration. Only the Jewish religion bears the original authentic authority in its basic law. Still, the general assertion remains valid: human society is not rooted in law, but in supernatural divine initiative. It is a matter of providence.

Krochmal rejected the claim that human society is rooted in natural instincts because of his recognition of another kind of empiricism. He did not repudiate the notion that human beings too have a herding instinct. Such an instinct is reflected in family and tribe, and it cannot be denied that initial sociality stems from it. But it is also true that such instincts can hardly account for the rich framework of human relations even on the elementary levels of the family and the tribe. In its human sense, a family is not limited to the coupling of a male and female, and the birth of offspring. A tribe is not merely a herd. The human family possesses an additional element, which is discernible in the unique, voluntary quality of relations between individuals. How so? Perhaps first of all in the fact that human beings establish *communication* among each other through speech, and then they *institutionalize* it.

Admittedly, other living creatures have forms of communication, but there is an essential difference between instinctual communication and verbal communication. Speech is a special property — cognitive, volitional, and transcending nature; it is this uniqueness that differentiates humans from animals who act only instinctually, without benefit of institutional structures. Following on Hegel, Krochmal calls this special quality the spirit,* or the spiritual. Human sociality is *a priori* spiritual. It is founded on volitional consent. If this is so, where does the spirit dwell? Where does it come from? It is difficult to give an empirical answer because while the spiritual manifests itself in the speech and overall creativity of individuals, it is utterly impossible to limit it to the individual, as such, if only because the spiritual is, in its essence, communicative. It is not found in the activity or creations, tangible or perceived, of a solitary individual; rather it exists

---

* "Spirit": *Ruah* (Hebrew), corresponding to the German *Geist*. For its rich and broad meaning (embracing the intellectual, the cultural, and the religious), there is no better explanation than the current passage! (LL)

in the relations between human beings. Or, to be more exact, the spiritual sometimes manifests itself in an individual as an interior monologue (thought); yet even then it appears to him to be a circuit of communication that transcends individuality in its objective meaning because, as an internal monologue, it has the same objective meaning for every other thinker. Therein lies its claim to truth. The manifestation of spirit thus assumes that speakers possess language as an active capacity to understand each other, to function together, to intend the same meaning, to derive an objective claim out of subjective experience, and (on the basis of all these) to amass knowledge.

Krochmal thus concludes that the spiritual is not found in each individual in isolation but is present in him only to the extent that each individual is part of a society in which he is related to all other individuals. If this is so, it means that society is actually composed of the individuals who constitute it but the spiritual reality that unites them is a universal objective reality that precedes them as individuals. Spirit is universal, not individual-particular, and society is based on it. It is manifested in the creative works of human individual that have universal meaning — in other words, culture. This is the historical order of how these things came to be. In learning, however, one becomes aware of culture as a collection of tangible creations. In this progression, culture is the empirical, objective embodiment of the sociality unique to human beings. Culture originates in the *spirit* which it carries in itself, and the spirit is a sphere of reality which transcends nature and the individual. When an individual partakes of it through his society and culture, he actualizes his own spiritual potential in deed, in speech, in relationship, and in creativity, and thus actualizes his own humanity. But (and one must emphasize this "but" to draw the line between Maimonides' outlook and Krochmal's) — spirit is not a divine dimension of existence *beyond* man. On the contrary, it is that sphere of reality that is unique to man and in which he exists: the socio-cultural spiritual dimension is identical with the "human," it is the essence that transcends the individual physical organism. The dwelling place of the spiritual is not in the heavens but in worldly cultural creativity.

In the sequel we shall show that Krochmal also explained religious phenomena this way. Religion is one of the highest creations of the human spirit. If so, then it would seem according to his view that society must have been religious from the outset. Every national culture is identified through its highest symbols, which are its religious symbols. Still, there is an essential difference between Krochmal and Maimonides: according to Maimonides, what Krochmal defined as "spiritual" can only be a primal prophetic emanation coming from a divine, supernatural (and hence supra-human) sphere.

It is not a human creation. According to Krochmal, the "spiritual" is supra-natural but not supra-human. On the contrary. The spiritual is completely identified with the process of man's coming into being, as he transcends his biological being.

The formation process of human society as it rises from one cultural stage to the next is gradual and manifests itself in history through the ascent of human society from one cultural stage to the next. Krochmal describes this process as a parallel development along three adjacent and complementary tracks. The first is the establishment of a social framework — family, tribe, and urban centers — to a point where a complete and comprehensive political framework comes into being: the state which unites a people. The beginnings of social life seem to be natural and spontaneous, but it quickly emerges that a human social system requires, and therefore creates from within itself, the first kind of spiritual creativity: set customs that constitute norms of social conduct conferring meaning and value. Subsequently, the customs are improved upon, crystallized, and institutionalized in law. It is this development which enables a transition to socio-political forms of organization that are more comprehensive and efficient. Once having arrived at the perfected forms, the autonomous goal of that society emerges: justice, the moral good as the supreme value embodied in law. This being the case, what motivates the development from one stage to the next?

If an explanation is sought in the first stage of a culture's creation, a second plane of activity becomes evident — that of providing for those needs which are, ostensibly, the sole reason individuals have for intensifying and increasingly institutionalizing cooperation between themselves. In order to provide for the multiplying material needs of family and tribe (whose numbers are also multiplying) not only must the social framework be developed but also, and primarily, instruments must be created and improved, skills, trades, arts and commerce cultivated. To this end, it is necessary to enhance the level of social cooperation in a continuous cycle. As a result, occupations and economic activity become increasingly sophisticated to the extent that, out of the process of improvement itself, a new quality emerges and becomes an art form. This articulation of innate beauty parallels the aspiration for innate good and justice found at the legislative level: *ideas* are derived from a plane of spiritual aptitude rather than from the level of pressing concerns that man originally faced. At this stage, spiritual aptitude and talent are no longer means but an end, an inborn expression of that which is human.

Still, the creative strata of man are not yet fully covered. A fuller examination will show how societal and legislative processes became institutionalized, and how those processes which created tools, perfected trades, arts and commerce as processes of spiritual creativity came into being. It will also show what makes them what they are: constantly growing accumulations of knowledge that are increasingly refined, exhibiting a more detailed, precise and sophisticated organization. This, too, originated in the earliest stage of cultural development since the evolution of customs, rules, tools, skills, trades, instruments and implements all require knowledge. Impelled by their self-interest, human beings collect and employ various of types of information which is continually and creatively processed: first as science, subsequently as philosophy, in a desire to know the inherent all-inclusive truth. It is not surprising that philosophers see philosophy as the grasp of man's knowledge in its totality; in so far as knowledge is knowledge of the *truth*, it is a revelation of the all-embracing human spirit, for its own sake. This is the most sublime stage achieved by the human spirit as it becomes known to itself as a universal spiritual reality.

To conclude: It would appear that at the start of the historic process of cultural development, achievements are material: economy, power, and authority are the goals for which political and societal arrangements are constituted, just laws are enacted, instruments forged, arts and occupations developed, and knowledge acquired, but gradually this materialist assessment is overturned. Once a culture arrives at its peak, the manifestations of man's spirit are discernible in his most sublime creations: the sciences, art, higher religion and philosophy. These are the actual aims that motivated man, initially without his even being aware of them, but they became clear by dint of observing the essence and properties of the creative process. Nations arise, acquire independence, create a material and spiritual civilization, degenerate, and die. Yet the highest values of a culture are eternal. They are taken over by younger nations who turn the achievements of their predecessors into their own civilizational infrastructure continuing, at an even higher level, the creative discovery of that which is *spiritual*. It emerges with certainty therefore that, ultimately, it is through these eternal values, and for their sake, that culture exists.

If spiritual-cultural developments that went on, stage by stage, over historical periods are re-examined from the standpoint of the philosopher, one discovers three contingent strata of activity that propel each other onward. A pattern surfaces which has a certain structural logic. 1) There is a natural and spontaneous beginning in which there is neither self-awareness nor understanding of the purpose of society; 2) As it continues, there is an avid desire for material achievements which, at this stage, already exhibits an awareness of society's specific talent for attaining the goal it has identified as an interest; 3) A stage of refinement is reached in which spiritual aptitude and its implementation as spiritual expression acquire an inherent value along with material interests; and in Krochmal's view, ultimately 4) Spirit becomes aware of itself by virtue of its "gifts" and "legacies" — every cultural product is a gift or legacy to be transmitted (the ethical-social and organizational-political arrangements, the variety of occupations and trades, the basic sciences, and the primitive religions) — as the underlying reality which is the source and unifying purpose of the entire endeavor (systematic science, the higher religions and philosophy).

We have reviewed four stages of development; in each, several sub-stages with the same developmental pattern can be distinguished. It is possible to analyze such a structure with quasi-scientific exactitude as follows: Every human being is born, educated, and develops in a society and culture of which he is part; in his behavioral development, he personally passes through the civic, moral, social, and scientific stages which his society has reached. An important cultural conclusion can be drawn from this: every stage in the development of a culture, including the most rudimentary, retains a value. It is neither forgotten, lost, nor without present relevance, because the educational process of each generation (admittedly in abbreviated form) passes through all the stages from childhood to maturity. Moreover, the most consummate achievements encompass previous attainments, not only as rungs in a ladder but as components. Which is to say, the highest achievement is a *synthesis* of all the components that went into its creation. In order to reach this stage, the entire road must be traversed and each of the stages recalled.

Most people do not surpass the "horizon" at which their civilization has arrived. Still, creativity goes on. The question is, How? It is accomplished through individuals who are especially gifted spiritually, in whom the genius of the universal spirit is manifest as an exceptional creative force. It is these individuals who develop the culture in preparation for the next stage in which the entire society will be the beneficiaries of their creativity. If this is the case, we can discover the structure of this development by examining the educational and socialization processes in the progression to adulthood. Based on the achievements of contemporary geniuses, one can surmise what the next stage will be. It is clear that these structural stages present in each individual's education are the original stages in the historical development of a people's culture. Each stage is a period in the history of a given society, constituting an independent unit in the annals of a particular people. A people is founded, creates a culture, and at a certain point reaches its spiritual acme. Subsequently, as with every organism, it degenerates, is destroyed, is dispersed and disappears. But have no fear, it leaves its cultural heritage. Krochmal claims that every important people undergoes a cycle of three stages that parallel the developmental and deterioration stages in the lives of individuals: childhood and youth ("the period of growth and development"); independent, mature creativity ("the period of vigor and enterprise"); old age and death ("the period of decline and annihilation"). Just as the legacy of individuals is inherited by their offspring who take it to the next stage (and this is their immortality), it is true as well for the outstanding cultures of peoples. They are eternal.

In fashioning a developmental, historic model of culture which could be employed to assess the uniqueness of Jewish culture and its place among the cultures of other nations, the questions that exercised Krochmal were: If we have but a single model for the development of a structure that exhibits the spiritual presence, how did cultures become different from one another? What is the relationship between them? Is there a universal culture and does it have a general history? If the answer is yes, how did it manifest itself and what is its structure?

Empirical historical observation is the prerequisite for the study of such questions. In retrospect, one sees development from the standpoint of the relationships between peoples. The cultures of prehistoric peoples developed independently, each in its own locale, in total or relative isolation. At that stage there were marked differences between them caused by the direct impact made on each people by its own unique material conditions: geography, climate, resources and the flora and fauna peculiar to a specific region. Undoubtedly in the initial stages of civilization when it is an outgrowth of primary material forces, these elements leave a particular imprint on language, customs and laws, tools and implements, economic arrangements, and political organization.

Subsequently there is contact between civilizations: commerce, wars, conquests and the transmission and purposeful absorption of mutual influences. The cultures of peoples grow closer to one another, and their fate is determined through their relationships to one another. At the same time, one can discern the conscious reinforcement of a particular national, cultural selfhood, a component of internal national unification and solidarity in the face of external physical and spiritual challenges. At this stage every nation tends to develop a certain kind of spiritual creation (its *portion or birthright*) which has a relative advantage over competing cultures. The nation defines its advantage and focuses on it. Indeed, it identifies itself through it.

The three strata enumerated above — morality, legislation and political organization; instruments and tools, occupations, skills, and arts; sciences and religious symbols — are found in the culture of a society, and a type of deliberation or *wisdom*. Each culture selects the special values that orient its morality and its expertise in occupations and economic pursuits, a particular stylistic quality of beauty in art, and a specific area on which its sciences are focused. Moreover, should a comparative study between the preferences in these various areas be undertaken, similarities will be discovered: there is a connection between the orienting moral quality (for instance, generosity or bravery or honor) and the type of economic activity engaged in, and between it and the qualities of beauty and areas of knowledge which the nation elects to develop for their own sake. Further study reveals that this specialness is expressed in identifying symbols that unite and guide the people in its historic development. This is expressed in the properties of the gods of the religion unique to each people, and in the characteristics of wisdom that each nation prides itself on as the totality of its highest achievements.

The conclusion is evident. Through the union of natural conditions and resources, and particular spiritual talent, each people develops its own characteristic spiritual quality. In the religion unique to it, a people elevates its distinctive cultural quality to the level of an ideal, or a deity. This is the relative truth which Krochmal found in all pagan religions: their truth is the express aspect of the *spiritual* that came to the fore in the people's culture. Nonetheless the truth of pagan religions is relative, because it is the incomplete truth of an incomplete culture. When the nation that subscribes to a partial truth opposes or deprecates the religions of other nations which, like itself are adherents of a partial truth, it misleads itself and others. It also misrepresents when it puts its own partial truth forward as the only, universal and superior truth. At this point, one could add that it is only monotheism, because it aspires to a universal culture *that unites the achievements of all partial cultures,* that may claim to possess the one, absolute truth.

Religions that seek to defend the autonomous selfhood of competing nations cannot dismiss the reality of mutual influences. Every nation wants to acquire the cultural advantages of competing peoples that endanger it. Therefore, when nations exhaust their enterprise and disappear as the result of external or internal wars, the new nations which supplant them not only commence at a higher level of cultural development but are also the result of a more complex cultural synthesis. Genuine development requires a higher level of comprehensiveness and fullness. In any case, the process of historical development of nations is also a process of cultures drawing closer. It is necessary to be precise in this definition: convergence to the point of integration cannot be achieved by a mutual destruction, or by a destructive defeat of one culture by another, or by negating the uniqueness of cultures which have reached their acme; rather it is achieved through integration into a more complete and complex unity. It stands to reason that as cultures rise from the stage of material self-interest to that of recognizing their spiritual goals, a more complex integration develops which is achieved through cooperation. Instead of internal, societal struggles and external wars between nations, positive cooperation increases to the point where the history of peoples meld their cultures at the highest level of spiritual awareness which, of course, is expressed in pure monotheism on one hand, and rational philosophy on the other. These become the standard bearers of a common denominator. Based on this common denominator, each nation continues to make its contribution which is a recapitulation of its unique historic path.

Such was the sweep of Krochmal's theory of historical development. What is the place of Jewish culture within such a process? What sets it apart?

An empirical observation of Jewish history shows two strikingly obvious external facts that differentiate the history of the Jews from that of all other peoples. 1) This is a people that has undergone overwhelming destructions, expulsions from its land, and persecutions in exile. 2) In the face of these trials, the Jews persisted as a people.

Does this mean that the Jewish people is immune to the laws of history which apply to other peoples? Religious thinkers of the past and the present claim that this is indeed the case and attribute the uniqueness in the historic fate of the Jews to divine providence conferred on them as the "chosen people." Obviously, as a philosopher of the idealistic school, Krochmal could not substantiate such a claim. While he could accept the notion of divine providence, he equated it with the purposeful laws that operate *within* history, and saw providence as a law that determines history. How could he exempt the Jewish people from the orderly function of general laws that operate in history, laws which he had observed in his scientific work? Indeed, in his comparative empirical observations, he himself came to the conclusion that the laws which operate in the history of all peoples apply to the Jewish people as well. Like all peoples, the Jews progressed through the three standard evolutionary periods — growth and development, vigor and enterprise, decline and annihilation, as they developed their culture. They experienced decline and annihilation not once but three times as they passed through *the entire cycle* of youth, maturity and old age three times. (The ending-points of the three cycles are marked by the destruction of the First Commonwealth and the demise of the House of David; the destruction of the Second Commonwealth and the end of Bar Kokhba's reign; the expulsion from Spain, the Cossack pogroms of 1648-49, and the debacle of the false messiah, Shabbetai Zevi.) In effect, this is what accounts for the entire difference between the Jewish people and other peoples. Other peoples went through the cycle only once, and then left the stage of history; whereas the Jewish people is repeatedly reborn following each destruction, each calamity more sweeping than that which preceded it, adding another distinctive flowering to its culture.

What is the explanation for this unusual historical phenomenon, seemingly outside the natural order, a kind of miracle of resurrection? Not outside the natural order, in Rabbi Krochmal's opinion. Far from being a miracle or beyond natural law, it validates his earlier statement that history is a process in which the spiritual is made manifest in the cultural creation of each people. We have seen that peoples persist until such time as they fulfill their spiritual mission. Having done so, they become redundant, disintegrate, and disappear. Apparently all peoples — with the exception of the Jews — fulfill their mission in one historical-cultural cycle. Because the Jewish people did not complete its task in the first, the second, or even the third cycle, it is destined to be reborn after each destruction, and is currently in a stage of renewal for the fourth time.

At this point, an interpretation of the special content of the Jewish people's mission is called for. This "mystery" too is amenable to empirical analysis: monotheism originated with the people of Israel. It is their spiritual uniqueness, and it came to the fore in their earliest days. The people of Israel became a nation by virtue of their monotheistic Torah; they were repeatedly renewed through the Torah, and for its sake. To be precise, true to his concept, Rabbi Nachman Krochmal believed that monotheism as a *living Torah* — which is to say, as an encompassing culture — is the historical, this-worldly explanation of *netzaḥ Yisrael* (the eternity of Israel) as opposed to the religious explanation in which all things are contingent on divine supernatural providence. It was not a supernatural deity that engendered the miracle, but the monotheistic ideal — which is the ideal of the Absolute Spirit evident in the nation from its inception — to whose realization the nation devoted itself through its integrated living culture. This ideal was the constant that maintained the Jewish people in its unbroken history. In Krochmal's thought, monotheism, of all the national religions of the world, is the sublime embodiment of the universal human spirit expressed in the historical-cultural product of one people. Such a statement calls for clarification.

What is monotheism according to Krochmal? In the dogmatic definition of Maimonides, there is but a single spiritual God, Creator of the universe and its Master, as opposed to polytheistic paganism which believes that there are a multiplicity of gods, and as opposed to pantheistic paganism which is a belief that the universe itself is replete with gods. Initially, Krochmal adopted Maimonides' definition but, as we have already seen, Krochmal's philosophic rendering of polytheism and even pantheism, was more complex. Krochmal did not reject such religions out of hand but detected partial and relative truths in them: the truth of judicial, ethical, scientific, and artistic creations. What necessarily follows is that his grasp of monotheism was also different from Maimonides' in an affirmative, content-laden sense: in Krochmal's opinion, monotheism integrates all the partial, relative truths of pagan religions *within* itself, elevating them as a totality to the level of the Absolute Truth. In doing this, one also postulates a different understanding of the notion of divinity from the standpoint of the relationship between God and the Cosmos; and particularly from the standpoint of God's relationship to humanity which expresses itself in man's cultural, spiritual creation.

Krochmal unequivocally rejected pantheism, even in Spinoza's philosophic formulation; for Krochmal, God is external to the material world and transcends it. Krochmal also conceived of God as the Creator of material nature; nonetheless, God initially manifests Himself through nature as the Source of the unswerving orderliness with which nature operates. This regularity is the constant activity of the Spirit. Whereas spirituality is a characteristic of man, God is Spirit itself — the Absolute Spirit which one finds immediately in all spiritual products, in everything true, everything good, and everything beautiful which has so far been discovered and is yet to be discovered in cultural creativity. We could rephrase this in the following way: everything true, good, and beautiful which has been discovered and is yet to be found in cultural creation is the manifestation of the Absolute Spirit by means of relative, partial creations that constantly strive towards an integrated absolute perfection. Consequently, when in the process of cultural creativity, all peoples arrive at a fully comprehensive expression of every aspect of truth, goodness and beauty — actually integrating them at their most sublime as a totality of knowledge and deed — humanity will reach the ultimate discovery of the Absolute Spirit. It will be found in the full compass of cultural creation.

What then is the meaning of *belief,* whether in a multiplicity of gods or in the One God? From what has been said above it is clear that the recognition that there *are* gods or that there *is* a God is merely the first stage: an awareness that is still almost entirely devoid of content. It is merely consciousness of a cognitive, emotional and pragmatic role which has to be filled with content. That content does not *transcend* a this-worldly reality in which people live and create spiritual products; rather it is identical to the *totality* of spiritual creativity itself. From the standpoint of content, monotheism is identical to the cognitive, spiritual creativity which appears in all possible avenues of human expression. It is an on-going process which seeks to unify multiplicity by integrating and elevating it to the highest degree of truth and desire for good. Or, alternately, to believe in God means to live cultural life to the full — in all spheres, through a steadfast aspiration that life ought to be elevated to its most sublime level in society, the state, in science, etc.

At first glance, this appears to be a daring and revolutionary innovation, and so it is. Is there a precedent for this in the Tradition? Indeed, monotheism came into the world as the event in which the one God revealed Himself to His people so that the people would know their God. But as early as that formative event, the direct and actual content of the revelation was *the Torah* which God gave to His people: an instruction of the entire truth about the creation of the world and man, a compendium of ordinances about desiring the good and achieving it by establishing a civil order in the world and a culture in keeping with God's design so as to heighten and complete creation. Rather than an imagined or abstract impression of a single divine persona, this was the *a priori* substantive content of monotheism, a fully articulated theory about the universe and man; one must learn the composite parts of its truth through constant, profound inquiry, so that man can apprehend and know in detail: What is this world, and humanity within it? What is man's purpose in the world? How can it be fulfilled? To this end, one must study all the components of the Torah, including its commandments which are to be carried out in detail according to strict norms that pertain to real life.

When one observes the behavior of believers, one arrives at the same insight. It is in learning and scrutinizing the Torah that their belief rises to its highest expression; the intention of this inquiry and research is to understand the scope of truth in the Torah as it is the totality of truth about man and the world. Study is accompanied by a constant effort to perform and maintain the ordinances of the Torah — the most sublime goal expected of man. In effect, the Oral Law was a constantly expanding cultural enterprise that based itself on the written Torah. It did so by means of the aggadah and halakhah, the literatures of Midrash, *musar*, philosophy and kabbalah, and the practice and observation of mitzvot. Monotheism is the constantly expanding totality that seeks to find all truth and to practice all good as it was understood by the prophets, the authors of the Mishnah and the Talmud, the Geonim, rabbis, philosophers and kabbalists.

What, then, was Rabbi Krochmal's innovation? How did he advance beyond the views of his predecessors or raise their insights to a higher plane? Apparently, in his consistent application of the religious principle that the Divine must be wrested from an authoritarian extra-worldly sphere from which the Torah was handed down as a teaching of the truth dealing primarily with divine-human relations, and relocated in the totality of man's spiritual activity. Krochmal saw the Divine in all the manifestations of man's spirit whether focused in nature or in the human sphere. He went so far as to formulate the radical idea that the totality of man's cultural creation is in essence not merely the study of what God taught and commanded in the Torah, in the narrow understanding of that formulation, nor merely the observance of God's commands in that same narrow sense. Rather, human cultural creative activity is *itself* the act of divine revelation, and is itself the divine commandment, especially when drawn from every source of knowledge and information, from all empiric experience and thought available to man.

To sum up: according to Krochmal, the Torah is revealed and exists in everything one learns, in all the tools available to man, in all the sources from which man derives knowledge, in all the emotions he expresses, and in all their avenues of expression, in all man's ethical qualities and moral insights, in every field of human endeavor, in all laws that humanity legislates, and in all enterprises by which man advances. Thus Krochmal extended the traditional identity of God and Torah to a radical modern notion which equated Torah with the cultural process itself as it progresses to greater comprehensiveness, integration and perfection.

With this significant departure in the understanding of monotheism, Rabbi Krochmal was able to interpret the special mission of the Jewish people among the nations and its unique historic fate. As we saw earlier, in its own cultural creativity every nation discovers a part, or a single component, of the totality of cultural creation meant for humanity as a whole, and it is here that the notion of the multiplicity of gods originated. In contrast, the Jewish people's faith in monotheism was emblematic of the conviction that all the parts combine into a supreme unity, that the aspiration to realize that unity in practice could be achieved through a gradual integration of all the parts and their elevation to the highest level of spiritual life. What this means is that the Jewish people was not devoted to any fragmentary cultural creation. Such conceptions can be found in its culture, but they originate in external sources that are clearly identifiable in the cultures which the people encountered in its history. The unique and original contribution of the Jewish people is the notion that everything is one, and that achieving such a unity is the cultural task which the people itself must undertake. To do this, the Jewish people must absorb and amalgamate into their own culture all the creative products found in the cultures of major nations, and develop them through all the unfolding stages of culture which other peoples have undergone. Thus the Jewish people would create a totality, integrating and unifying it as a cultural model for all nations.

To authenticate his statements on the singular task of the Jewish people and the uniqueness of its monotheistic culture, Rabbi Krochmal, as a scholar of history and culture, examined the significance of historic facts which attest to the people's fate among the nations and analyzed the development of its literary religious creativity: the pick of its cultural heritage.

On the historiographic plane, Krochmal noted that the Jewish people repeatedly began its own course against the background of important cultural developments in the history of nations. As early as the emergence of the Israelite tribes in the Patriarchal period, Mesopotamia had reached its flowering and was at the beginning of its decline. The patriarchs, products of the country situated between the Tigris and the Euphrates, rebelled against the pagan degeneracy of that culture. Again, against the background of the deterioration of the great pagan culture in Egypt, the tribes coalesced into a nation in a revolt against the despotic regime that had already sealed the fate of the Pharaonic monarchy. In the Land of Israel, the Israelites contended with the cultural heritage of a deteriorating Canaan, succeeded by the Philistines, the Phoenicians, and the Assyrians, all of whom had passed their prime and begun their descent into despotic paganism. What followed is well known: in its second life cycle, the Jewish people had a similar encounter with the great cultures of Persia, Greece and Rome, and in its third life cycle it confronted the cultures of Islam and the Christian countries of Europe.

The modern era saw the beginning of the fourth cycle when the early stages of national renewal were took place under circumstances of a burgeoning humanistic culture. Humanism synthesized all the creativity of dominant Western cultures in the areas of politics, society, ethics, the sciences and arts, the philosophy of religion and the philosophy of history. At every encounter with these cultures, the Jewish people was exposed to identifiable, definable influences. Early on, in the absence of historical research and the insights of modern historical consciousness, these influences were made to appear — through a feat of creative reinterpretation — to derive from the traditional religious sources themselves. (A striking example of this is Maimonides' claim that Aristotelian philosophy is found in the writings of the prophets.) Modern research clearly shows that such influences were not part of the heritage as it was transmitted at Sinai, nor did they result from interpretations enabled by tools revealed at Sinai; they are rather the outcome of selective use of multifaceted sources from which the culture was created, including non-Jewish sources. In the process, a creative blend of the newly learned strata and the ancient heritage evolved.

This has always been the pattern, and it will continue to be so in the future; admittedly, in new ways that are straight-forward and acknowledged, as with Krochmal. At the same time, clearly the Jewish people did not embrace everything that the surrounding cultures had to offer. They selected those positive elements which were compatible with their unique heritage, they expanded the heritage with the new content that was absorbed, but they rejected everything that stood for the negative, partial, relative and degenerate aspects of paganism.

In light of this, Krochmal had no difficulty explaining the institution of an independent monarchy by the people of Israel in their land during the First Commonwealth; the subsequent break-up of the monarchy into two kingdoms, exile and dispersion and the weakening of political independence in the period of the Second Commonwealth. With the fall of the Second Commonwealth there was a complete loss of political independence. In the Middle Ages, a communal framework was substituted for political independence under the heavy yoke of Moslem and Christian states. In the face of suffering and political repression, remarkable spiritual-religious developments took place, developments that were the outcome of confrontations with cultures highly developed from the scientific, spiritual, religious, and philosophic standpoints. It almost looks as though the loss of political might was a necessary condition for impressive achievements in philosophy and religion in the Jewish sphere, and that the spiritual confrontation contributed to the broadening and deepening of Judaism.

Literary achievements are evidence of this. The Jewish people did not assimilate nor did they lose their national, spiritual identity because of dispersion and exile. The opposite is true. Their identity was strengthened. The Jews moved toward the fulfillment of their historic goal along three complementary vectors: 1) Broadening the scope of their spiritual endeavors from the standpoint of their higher spiritual content. 2) Elevating the plane of their achievements to a philosophic, theoretical level. 3) Disseminating the monotheistic ideal among all the peoples with whom they dwelt as an aspiration to unify human culture at the highest level. Thus dispersion and exile enabled the realization of the national goal.

To summarize: Krochmal saw the historical narrative of the people of Israel as having universal significance: the history of an eternal people whose annals were the unifying strand in the history of the culturally most important nations. This, according to Krochmal, is the history of a nation that grew out of the pre-eminent and most developed cultures in humanity, linking and elevating them in a continually ascending synthesis. Indeed, Krochmal asserted, Jewish religious literature is a synthesis of the best spiritual achievements in the cultures of nations. Of course, this is an assessment of the past for the sake of pointing to what can be expected in the future, and a preparation and orientation for the cultural tasks that will yet face the Jewish people in the modern era. It applies to the political and social status of the Jews among the nations, as well as for the content that will determine their spiritual, cultural and religious identity.

What was Krochmal's vision of the future? Ostensibly it is difficult to project a detailed or exact answer to the question because he did not have the opportunity to complete his book. His descriptions were limited to the first two historical cycles. The third cycle was referred to in a highly abbreviated chapter; and the fourth, the one in which the history of humanity was to arrive at its goal and finale (according to Hegel's theory), had no historical description at all. On the other hand, the entire work was written from the perspective of the fourth cycle, and Krochmal saw himself at its beginning. In itself, the book is therefore a paradigm that actualizes a vision of what is yet to be.

The greatest difficulty is found in attempting to gauge what Krochmal envisioned for his people politically. In the staged progression of the Jewish people from one cycle to the next — a fully independent political entity during the First Commonwealth, political status in the Second Commonwealth that was limited by a foreign power, and a condition devoid of all political independence following on the failure of the Bar Kokhba rebellion — Krochmal regarded the Emancipation as *progress and redemption*. The Jews would achieve civic freedom in the lands of their dispersion, existing among enlightened nations, perhaps with their own communal structure. Yet the opposite assumption could be deduced from Krochmal's writings. In this alternate view, Krochmal retained the hope of a traditional redemption in the Land of Israel.

First, Krochmal's perception of Judaism was undoubtedly a national one. In his book, the Jewish people are described as having a distinctive national spirit in the present, not only in the past. And from the perspective of national existence, the Jews are no different, in Krochmal's opinion, than other nations. A clear indication of his national outlook is evident in his devotion to Hebrew, the language in which he wrote his book, unlike the founders of the Science of Judaism and the modern Jewish philosophers in Germany. Unquestionably, therefore, he did not believe that the Jews would assimilate, but that they would maintain their separate national culture.

Secondly, as a Hegelian philosopher, he regarded the constitutional, national state as both an ideal and a necessary framework for the achievement of perfection in all human cultures. It is not unreasonable then to assume that, just as Hegel evolved a concept of German national culture which would be fully realized in a liberal German state, Krochmal envisioned an ideal, national state which would be in keeping with the spirit of the original vision of the prophets of Israel, in keeping with his own messianic hopes, and consonant with Maimonides in whose footsteps he was following.

Thirdly, although Krochmal had reservations about Spinoza's ideas, he thought highly of him and gained an appreciation of the Torah as an eminently national, political constitution from him. Spinoza believed that it was reasonable to expect that the Jewish people would return to its land and reconstitute its state there because this is the national goal toward which

Jews strive so long as they adhere to the Torah. This conception had a great impact on numerous Hebrew *maskilim,* and there are grounds to assume that Krochmal too would have been influenced by it.

Finally, while the model which Krochmal proposed points to a gradual loosening of the Jewish national framework, in all four cycles the historical progression was not from isolated selfhood toward assimilation into the cultures of other peoples; on the contrary, the influence of external cultures only enhanced and strengthened separate national selfhood. Every historic cycle, according to Krochmal, is centripetal — a movement inward from the perimeter and not in the opposite direction. Abram the Hebrew came to the Land of Israel from the Akkadian culture; led by Moses, the children of Israel quit the Egyptian culture for a singularly independent existence; the same was true in the period of Ezra and Nehemiah, and the Hasmoneans. Consequently, at least in the two initial historical cycles that Krochmal describes in great detail, we find there is a movement from enslavement in exile toward political independence in the Land of Israel. This is the redemptive vector that the people of Israel strive for: the Exodus from Egypt and the conquest of the Land of Israel in the first cycle; the return to Zion from Babylonian exile, and the Hasmonean revolt against Hellenic enslavement in the second. This being the case, there is room for hope that in the fourth cycle, too, the same model will reappear against the background of the movements of national rebirth whose rise is one of the hallmarks of the progressive thrust of modernity.

In the short preface to his book, using Psalm 137, Krochmal illustrated the difference between his own philological-historic method and the interpretive-midrashic method of the Sages. They believed that "By the rivers of Babylon, / There we sat, / Yea we wept when we remembered Zion" was written by King David who foresaw the distant exile in Babylonia, while Rabbi Krochmal stressed the pedagogical advantage of modern research which found that the psalm was written by a Levite who was witness to the historic events. The moral that Krochmal drew for his contemporaries about the psalm is conveyed by his words:

> "…there was a poet in a distant exile whose heart and spirit were melancholy for what had been lost, who vowed not to forget the beloved homeland, not to abandon the desire for vengeance against evil neighbors who themselves had never been forced to leave their land. The entire Psalm bespeaks a burning flame and God's blazing anger for events which the exiles saw with their own eyes; it is a devoted testimony to their unbounded love of their land, their nation, and their God. Such an interpretation can have a beneficial and sacred influence on the minds and hearts of the present generation, enabling all their talent, wisdom and justice to emerge so as to meet the needs of the time…"
> (Rabbi Krochmal's Preface to *Shaarei Emunah Tzrufah*)

This is an unambiguous, enthusiastic declaration of Jewish national patriotism. Admittedly, it holds no explicit hope for a quick return to Zion, nor is it an attempt by Rabbi Krochmal to predict specific historic events in the distant future, a possibility he expressly rejected in the preface quoted above. But there is no doubt that the Preface does attest to Krochmal's burning love for the Land of Israel and the vow not to forget Jerusalem. He saw this as a matter of genuine and present concern, particularly for young Jews open to the spirit of the new era.

In any case, it is clear that Nachman Krochmal did not foresee an assimilatory process, either religious or national. Unlike the founders of the Science of Judaism in Germany, he believed that even in dispersion, even outside the ghetto, Jews could maintain a full, national life through communal frameworks, a cultural and religious way of life, research and educational institutions, and an independent language and literature. The following elements which come out of our previous discussion support this and lend it cultural content:

1. The *Guide of the Perplexed of the Time* was written under the influence of German historical research. Though he was fluent in German, Krochmal wrote in a rabbinic style incorporating elements of Biblical Hebrew, the language of the Sages, and of philosophers and kabbalists of the Middle Ages. He wrote the book for readers acquainted with both Hebrew and the traditional sources, and he regarded knowledge of these sources to be a precondition for the proper understanding and use of his work. Apparently he assumed that present and future readers would also know German, or some other modern European language, and considered such knowledge essential for the development of Jewish culture in the contemporary period (just as knowledge of Greek, Latin, or Arabic had been essential in earlier periods). Still, he regarded Hebrew as the language of Jewish national and cultural selfhood, while European languages were the means for participating in the general enlightened cultural environment.

2. Krochmal assumed that Jews would continue studying the entire sweep of religious literature, from the Bible through modern literature, in Jewish educational institutions. He saw the Jewish student's curriculum as a staged progression which would parallel the study of the modern sciences where one would acquire tools for the scientific study of the sources. The systematic sequence would proceed from the Bible to the Mishnah, from the Mishnah to the Babylonian Talmud and the Jerusalem Talmud, followed by the moralistic and philosophical literature of the medieval period. He took for granted that students of the modern period would study the sources through scientific, historical interpretation rather than through the exegetical tools of the Sages or of medieval philosophers and kabbalists.

Study would thus take on a real significance rather than merely an "academic" one — first, because it was assumed that the earlier strata of a culture meets a vital, pedagogic need in the beginning stages of education and second, because of an assumption that the earlier strata are prerequisite for later progress, as they comprise substantive elements that enter into the synthesis arrived at by later philosophical, historical interpretation. In other words, henceforth the *Science of Judaism* would be more than academic research, it would be a curriculum and a methodology for instruction in Jewish schools, and the new rational philosophy would be an instrument through which a modern Jewish literature that draws on the sources would be created.

3. As the consequence of this sequential study of the sources, a new, rich, scholarly and theoretical Hebrew literature would emerge which would forge a synthesis of Jewish culture with the culture of other peoples along the lines that Krochmal outlined in his book. It would be an amalgamation of the finest achievements of European humanism (at the most advanced levels of the physical and social sciences, and humanities — particularly history and philosophy) with the Jewish heritage. It would emulate the method used by Jewish scholars in the past (such as Maimonides and Ibn Ezra who were models for Krochmal) but with the addition of scholarly, literary, and philosophic tools appropriate to modernity. Receptivity to the finest achievements of the ambient culture would not, therefore, bring about feelings of inferiority or self-deprecation; on the contrary, it would generate pride in the great contributions of Jewish culture to monotheism and humanism. A Jewish culture that incorporated the best of other cultures within itself would serve as a model for other peoples.

4. In tandem with the expectation that nations would eventually accept a purified monotheism and a perfected humanism in the modern era, one could also hope that Jewish religious faith would be revived by a spirit of enlightened rationality. It should be added that just as Maimonides did not intend to displace the primary position of religious faith and halakhah with his philosophy, but rather to bring about an intellectual refinement of faith and a systematic consolidation of halakhah while adapting and interpreting its meaning for his era, so too Krochmal's philosophy was not intended to dislodge religious faith and halakhah from their pride of place in Jewish culture. Rational philosophy would be the estate of the spiritual elite whereas the culture of the people would be unified by religion. Of course, philosophy would refine religion, adjusting it as an educational means for progress and rationality.

5. In the chapters of his book devoted to halakhah and aggadah, Krochmal demonstrated how they were developed in response to the conditions and the needs of each historic period; how the method of instruction, study,

interpretation and application of the halakhah developed in keeping with the level of thought, and the interpretive and critical tools that were prevalent in the culture of the period. Consequently, it seemed obvious to him that this would also be the case in the fourth cycle. Halakhah would be updated to meet the reality of living at peace and tranquility among the nations enabling the Jews to be spiritually compatible with the religions of their environment. This would be effected through instrumentalities suitable to the time: historical-scientific research tools, and the scholarly tools of ethical, political, and religious philosophy. And the rationale for mitzvot would also be interpreted by these tools.

One could summarize by saying that the cultural model which Krochmal posited was made up of an autonomous national framework, a national language, a study of the people's history and culture — the unbroken continuity of the sources — through a contemporary interpretation based on a modern, philosophic, and scientific education. The model was also predicated on an unalloyed national religiosity imbued with a spirit of universal rationalism, and a national religious halakhah brought into line with the social and political conditions as well as the spiritual-cultural plane of the modern age.

It is an integrated model, essentially different from the one proposed by Wessely, and later by Samson Raphael Hirsch; it also differed from the model put forward by the founders of the Science of Judaism in Germany. Wessely and Hirsch proposed a religiously orthodox model that joined two separate cultures without blending them: one innately Jewish, and the other originating externally. Wessely expressed this in his work using the terms "Law of God" and "Law of Man," while Hirsch called this notion *Torah Im Derekh Eretz* (the study of Torah with secular education). Both proposed a model of humanistic assimilation through a synthetic construction of Judaism within the general European culture. As opposed to this, Krochmal advanced the idea of a national, humanistic cultural model which was a synthetic blend of the general culture within the autonomous self-contained culture of the Jewish people.

Indeed, it was this aspiration to forge a modern, integral Jewish national culture that made Krochmal a great teacher of the Hebrew Haskalah movement of eastern Europe, and of the "spiritual Zionism" and religious Zionism that developed from the Haskalah.

Chapter Nine
THE SCIENCE OF JUDAISM —
RESEARCH IN JUDAISM AS A CULTURE

The most important philosophic representation of spiritual objectives of the Hebrew Enlightenment is Rabbi Nachman Krochmal's work, *A Guide to the Perplexed of the Time*. It may also be the most profound philosophic and scientific manifesto of the *Wissenchaft des Judentums* (the Science of Judaism). The movement, which developed mainly in Germany, used scientific research and pedagogic activity at modern Europe's highest cultural level, namely that of scientific research, to implement the ideas of the Enlightenment and the Emancipation.

Krochmal died before his book was finished. The incomplete manuscript, entrusted for editing and publishing to Dr. Leopold Zunz (1794–1886) one of the earliest and most outstanding scholars of the Science of Judaism movement, was first published in 1851. But the Science of Judaism started much earlier with the foundation of an Association for Jewish Studies (*Verein für Kultur und Wissenschaft des Judentums*) and of the journal, *Zeitschrift für die Wissenschaft des Judentums*. This was the beginning of the formal movement. Thus by the time Krochmal's book was published, the first generation of researchers was already well on its way, and the contribution to historical research of some of its leading scholars was greater than that of Krochmal's. This was also true in the field of the Philosophy of Jewish History where a number of important essays, including those by Solomon Formstecher (1841) and Samuel Hirsch (1842), were published in German before Rabbi Krochmal's work. Despite all this, a unique blend of original scientific research and philosophic thought — both at a high level — gave Krochmal's book a symbolic importance, and its influence has surpassed his time and place.

A group of young German Jews, the second generation of those struggling for emancipation (figures such as Edward Ganz, Leopold Zunz, Heinrich Heine, Moses Moser, and Immanuel Wolf) established The Association for Culture and Science of the Jews; the movement that grew out of these efforts came to be known as the Science of Judaism. In 1819, three programmatic tracts were published on the scientific and philosophical approach of the Association whose rallying cry was a concern for science as the central element of "Jewish culture." It would appear that none of these programs had any real influence since not one of them was actually implemented, not even by way of a partial attempt to establish a model of Jewish culture in which science would enrich the Jewish content, and philosophic study would provide topical significance. Nachman Krochmal alone was successful in achieving this.

Apart from the importance this gives his work, it also reflects the development of a movement in which the struggle for emancipation became a more powerful component than the desire to shape a new and innovative national Jewish culture. The name of the association is worth noting. The name refers to culture, and to science as the main vehicle for this culture, but the target is not defined as the culture and science *of the Jewish people*, rather as the culture and science *of the Jews*. In other words, through their research or philosophical papers, the founders of the movement (most of whom assimilated and soon converted to Christianity) sought to become part of *the German nation, as individuals*.

Nonetheless, they genuinely sought to save what they saw as the finest elements of the Jewish people's cultural heritage from neglect and oblivion. As individuals who sought to become part of the German nation, they wanted to be accepted as respected partners with equal rights and responsibilities, integrated in its spiritual and cultural life. Thus it was important to them to prove that they were not, so to speak, knocking at the door empty-handed. They had a valuable contribution to make to modern European culture, particularly in terms of its consummate universalist dimension. This was the motivation for the historiographic and philological research into the repositories of the past, and it was the motivation for the philosophic study of the universal meaning of Jewish heritage through which it could be accepted as part of the historic memory of European humanist culture. The advocates of emancipation believed the ideal would be to blend and enhance the best contributions of the peoples of Europe into a universal human culture. The time was right, they believed, to begin striving for the realization of the universalist ideal which Judaism had expounded from its inception.

From the outset, the movement stated clearly that such a process would not result in a completely *contemporary* Jewish culture. Despite this, the intensive creative processes that continued into the early 20th century (when a major change occurred) proved that the spiritual and cultural motivation of the Science of Judaism was strong enough to establish and develop an impressive, albeit partial, cultural endeavor of lasting value. The Science of

Judaism managed to elevate the curriculum of the Enlightenment move-ment from the school level to the university level. In doing so, it offered a modern cultural alternative to the traditional devotional scholarship of the Beit Midrash and the Yeshiva, both in terms of teaching methods and in terms of the literary and research projects required to enable further research and study. It is an achievement not to be taken lightly. The tra-ditional scholarship of the Beit Midrash and the Yeshiva, and the rich Torah literature which this scholarship renewed from one generation to the next, had always been synonymous with the inculcation of Jewish religious heritage. It was this scholarship that selected, classified and arranged the material, interpreting it and converting it into norms for individual and societal life. Without such scholarship, no cohesion, no continuity or future was possible.

Therefore, the provision of a modern, humanistic cultural alternative (one that was developed through the tools of critical scientific research) to traditional religious scholarship as embodied in the Beit Midrash, was an achievement of the utmost importance for the future of humanistic Jewish culture. The entire attempt to impart this culture, while at the same time re-placing the values of faith and religious tradition with a humanistic world view and culture, depended on it. To this day, the sharpest, most well defin-ed and institutionalized dividing line between those Jews who advocate Judaism as a religion in its orthodox construction, and those who advocate Judaism as a culture in its humanistic construction, lies in the methods of research, teaching and literary creativity adopted by each camp. While the orthodox approach maintains the accepted methods of the Yeshiva, the humanistic approach is based on methods embraced by the university.

Our purpose here is to assess the contribution of the Science of Judaism to the emergence of concepts and programs of Jewish culture as an alter-native to religion. To this end, it is worth describing the institutional achievements of the movement, and the scope, themes, and aspects of the literature it produced. By "institutional achievements" we refer to scientific journals, publishers, libraries, and institutions of advanced research and teaching. The introduction of Jewish studies into established universities was a slow process, possibly one of the most painfully slow processes of the Emancipation. Its beginnings lay in the publication of Jewish journals and books in German and Hebrew. Later, quasi-academic Jewish institutions (rabbinical colleges) were established. In effect, the breakthrough in uni-versities occurred only in the 20th century with the establishment of the Institute of Jewish Studies at the Hebrew University in Jerusalem (though this had been preceded by the establishment of an "academy" of Judaism in Germany). At this point, there was a sufficient cadre of researchers and teachers, and an adequate infrastructure of teaching methods, libraries, research tools and literature; moreover, there was a Jewish population of sufficient size to require such facilities.

The programs for research development that were prepared when the Association was established described Judaism as a complete culture; accordingly, they sought to develop systematic and critical research in all fields.

Two typical examples can be given. In the first essay of its kind, published in 1819 and entitled "Some Thoughts on Rabbinic Literature," Leopold Zunz proposed a full research program. After undertaking a methodological examination, the scientific critique of Jewish culture (in every area but particularly the literary sources) would branch out in three directions: thematic criticism, which would discuss the conceptual content of the sources; grammatical (or philological) criticism, which would relate to the language of the sources (Hebrew and Aramaic), to an examination of literary forms and linguistic structures unique to Hebrew, and a study of documents (particularly the types and history of manuscripts); historical criticism, which would discuss the content of this material in terms of the historical progression in each field. What conceptual content would be dealt with in the first critique? Zunz proposed three spheres which combined to form a totality of the culture:

1) The inner world of the Jew, including religion (theology, mythology, dogma, and ritual) and politics (laws, the theory of law, and morality);

2) The approach of the Jew to the external, mundane environment, including the sciences (astronomy, geography, and mathematics), and the practical professions (medicine, technology, industry, commerce, and the arts);

3) "The universal life of the nation" which related to the overall history of the national culture. Comprehensive historical treatises of this kind would form the basis for a historiosophical examination of the eternal spiritual significance of Judaism. Of course, this was an area that lay beyond the confines of scientific research.

The second proposal, drafted at much the same time as that of Zunz, was put forward by Immanuel Wolf. Wolf argued that the role of Jewish science was to provide a comprehensive perception of Judaism. As such, it would encompass two spheres: Judaism as reflected in literature, and Judaism as expressed in contemporary life. The former sphere would include a philological examination of the sources, laying the foundation for their historical analysis according to three themes — religion, politics, and literature. This process would continue so that comprehensive philosophical observations could be made. The latter sphere would include "statistical" research in order to provide a comprehensive and scientific description of the current socio-cultural state of the Jews.

A comparison of the two proposals reveals a broad similarity despite differences in the schematic division of themes and fields of research. The similarities lie in the distinction between — and the perceived inter-relationship of — historiographic and philological research on one hand, and historiosophy on the other; and in the call to investigate the entire corpus of Jewish literature that was available, in any language and from any source, based on the assumption that this corpus described the reality of a complete Jewish culture in its material, artistic, scientific, political, social, moral, and religious aspects.

Moreover, in terms of overall planning, a similarity can also be seen between both these programs and the one proposed by Rabbi Krochmal. The only difference appears to be that while Krochmal almost completed his program, Immanuel Wolf did not begin to implement his; and even Zunz, who actually began work on his plan, devoted himself mainly to one field (that of synagogue sermons) — a field which he failed to cover thoroughly. It is evident, however, that the difference reflects not only the output of the individuals concerned, but also their research approach and the definition of their goals.

Krochmal's approach was based on the knowledge of religious sources he had gained as a traditional scholar. With this knowledge as a foundation, he applied the philosophical tools he acquired from the German idealist tradition to forge a comprehensive historiosophic view of the nature and history of Jewish culture. Using philological and historical tools, Krochmal then re-examined the sources within the general context of his historio-sophic approach; at the same time he examined and confirmed the overall historiosophic approach on the basis of detailed findings in his critical work. Thus a dialectical exchange was created between a comprehensive philosophy and detailed research. Zunz took an opposite tack: although his program placed "conceptual criticism" before "grammatical criticism," in actual practice he followed the path proposed by Wolf, placing "grammatical criticism" before thematic definition and historical sequencing. From the wide range of options open to him, Zunz chose to begin with the literary and cultural field — whether because of the availability of literary material or because of his personal leanings. He was unwilling to offer a description of the overall historical process until he finished the philological and historical study of the literary documents he had chosen; and he was unwilling to construct a historiosophical framework for his approach until he could describe the overall historical process.

Unlike Krochmal, Zunz rejected the *a priori* approach of German idea-lism; he was committed to the empirical findings of literary documentation. One can well appreciate that in order to achieve the overall historiographic perspective required as a foundation for comprehensive philosophic inquiry, an enormous amount of research would be required, calling for the joint efforts of an entire community of researchers who, moreover, would be unlikely ever to reach agreement on their conclusions. It seems, however, that this did not concern Zunz, just as it did not concern most of the researchers of the Science of Judaism who followed in his footsteps. Detailed critical research into literary documents — an endless corpus offering fascinating surprises that revealed themselves to researchers in libraries and archives — seemed to be, in itself, a worthy act of participation in the spiritual creativity of cultural life. Their research defined them as Jewish in terms of the subject of their studies; it defined them as Western humanists in terms of the methods and context of their work, and as German nationals in terms of the language in which they wrote their articles and books. They had, it would appear, no need for any further dimension.

Along with those exponents of the Science of Judaism who devoted themselves to philological and historical research, there were Jewish philosophers and theologians who offered innovative interpretations of the meaning of Judaism for modern Jews who favored humanistic culture and emancipation. However, the connection between research and interpretative philosophy was loosened at one end, and broken at the other. Those who loosened the connection were the philosophers who used their own standards to distinguish between what they saw as "authentic Judaism" and what they considered foreign influences or distortion; accordingly, they needed only those findings that matched their interpretations. The rest were rejected. However, those who broke the connection completely were researchers who, at best, saw philosophical generalizations as interesting, yet suspect. Even when they saw philosophical interpretations as interesting, they never *knowingly* drew on them to guide their research.

Both of these approaches are reflected in the body of research created by the Science of Judaism in the 19th century. Some studies offer a systematic review of the bibliographical material available in manuscripts and books (the impressive work of Moritz Steinschneider is a case in point). There were also critical editions of manuscripts and books, as well as detailed research works particularly in such fields as Midrash, synagogue sermons, devotional poetry and prayer, Talmudic and rabbinic halakhic literature, the Musar literature and the theological works of the Middle Ages. The application of critical research methods to the Bible in general, and to the Pentateuch in particular, was an extremely sensitive matter; as a result, the amount of research in this field was limited, though modern Jewish movements sought to rely more on the Bible than on rabbinic literature. Despite the strongly critical approach taken by exponents of the Enlightenment to rabbinic literature, its relative accessibility for philological research, and the wealth of historical documentation it offered, made this literature the main object of modern Jewish studies.

The most comprehensive works, those that encapsulated an entire specific field, were written according to the historiographical discipline; it follows that in the 19th century the best known and most influential works of the Science of Judaism were an array of history books. The most renowned of these is undoubtedly Graetz's great historiographic work, *The History of the Jews from Ancient Times to the Present*. Characteristically, Graetz initially sought to present a comprehensive historiosophical perspective of the history of the Jews, and began by establishing a general framework to guide his research. Nonetheless, he strove to describe and document the sequence of events and Jewish religious movements "as they actually were." His basic argument was that Judaism is not a predetermined world-view, but an *a posteriori* product of the history of the Jewish people, particularly the history of the numerous and conflicting spiritual-religious movements that have competed for the souls of this people.

Thus it would appear that the institutionalization of research and teaching of philological criticism, and the historiography based on it, reflects a particular approach to the very nature of modern humanistic culture in general, and to the unique nature of Jewish humanistic culture in particular, and how one identifies and affiliates with these cultures as a contemporary humanist. Such a perspective can be better understood if we take a more profound look at scientific research and its motivation *as a form of spiritual activity* distinct from traditional scholarship.

The word that requires critical examination in this context is "criticism." Both in Zunz' program and that of Wolf, the word criticism embodies the methodological innovation of Scientific Judaism as compared to traditional scholarship. The point both men declared so forcefully, almost as a new "principle of faith," was that criticism was the great innovation they brought to the ancient Jewish culture from modern general culture. Through systematic criticism of every kind — linguistic, thematic, historical — a wealth of hidden content would be revealed in the Jewish sources, and the totality would appear differently than it did according to traditional study, teaching, and interpretation. This would lead to a profound change, both in scope and essence, in the perception of the culture being studied. To be precise, the application of systematic criticism would, at last, enable the culture to be studied as it really was, i.e. as a whole culture.

What does "criticism" mean in the context of research and study? An analytical examination of criticism shows that in its most basic sense it defines any act of study as such — an individual seeing, hearing, or reading anything. The individual who does not confine himself to gaining a passing impression but seeks to study the object, asks himself questions. What exactly did I see or hear? What did I read? In order to gain an objective answer to these questions, he must first examine what was received by his senses, his imagination, or his conceptual thought. Second, he must ask himself whether what was perceived in this way is totally consonant with what he saw, heard, or read, as it actually appears in the context of reality. If such an exact consonance is found between what he read and then re-read, it will have been confirmed, and he will attempt to remember it. If not, he will correct and re-examine himself repeatedly until complete consonance is achieved. This is the process of learning, and the value that drives this process is truth as a value, whether the knowledge gained is seen as a means to some purpose, or as a purpose in its own right.

This applies to learning of any kind. In this sense, and in its own way, traditional scholarship was also critical. Indeed, since it was required to *know* what the sacred Torah literature signified — matters of faith, a truth to be believed and a commandment to be performed — in its own way, traditional scholarship had to be no less critical than modern science, perhaps even more so. Based, as it was, on the belief that the Torah was given by a supreme and absolute Authority, tools of critical study were certainly required. These are the familiar tools of Midrash (etymologically, Midrash [< *darash*, to seek out] means "research"), particularly of halakhah; it is the rationale of halakhic interpretative discourse on the sources designed to confirm its own reliability and accuracy. What, then, was new about scientific criticism as opposed to traditional scholarship, and what was there about it that constituted a reversal of the past?

The exponents of scientific research would sometimes answer this question by pointing to traditional scholarship's lack of systematic, critical professionalism, particularly with regard to those historical and literary areas in which modern science was most interested. Traditional scholarship, they felt, consciously permitted an excess of liberty and poetic license. Even in matters that related to a religious world view, there was an excessive measure of permissiveness, a sanction which enabled elementary rules for understanding the literal meaning of sources to be overlooked. One might almost argue that the literature of Aggadah examines and instructs more by recourse to *invention*, ignoring the basic rules of interpreting literal meaning, than it does by adopting the principles of criticism. Clearly, however, these claims fail to reach the roots of the disagreement. A critical analysis of the argument finds that even the most excessive kind of aggadic interpretation, that which relates to all the paths of "Pardes" (the four traditional methods of detecting esoteric textual meanings) is nevertheless guided by rules of Torah criticism, the purpose of which is to ensure that truths derived from the scriptures do not deviate even slightly from what is acceptable to the religious establishment, or what has been defined in the past as religious truth.

If so, then we return once again to the original question. What is the argument about? What was the innovative quality of scientific criticism that distinguished it as a critical method? One might quip that the exponents of modern scientific criticism believed that traditional scholarship was not critical because it refrained from criticizing its own critical tools. The critical tools it used were not subject to criticism.

According to this outlook, two basic assumptions in the traditional religious system were used which were not, in themselves, subject to criticism. The first was the assumption that Torah sources are the embodiment of divinely revealed absolute authority; and that the interpretative and critical tools used to study and interpret the Torah are also the products of revelation. The second was the assumption that the tradition that passed from one generation to the next concerning the authenticity of the texts (the belief that these texts, and no others, are the original and binding version), and the context in which they were written or transmitted should be understood as completely reliable. Exponents of the scientific approach argued that neither of these assumptions was subject to criticism before being laid down; nor were they subsequently exposed to criticism. They were accepted as authoritative fact on the foundation of a total and fundamental act of faith. The entire process of traditional study and criticism follows this act of faith, on which it is founded.

Based on this unswerving faith, traditional scholarship was able to completely ignore three requirements of systematic criticism — requirements which, incidentally, religious scholars would readily accept with regard to any text not included in the canon of sacred writings: 1) To examine carefully whether the literary work before the student appears as it was originally written; if not — in what ways and for what reasons has it been changed? 2) To determine when and in what historical circumstances the work was written; 3) To consider whether the work is understood now as when it was written; if not, what changes have occurred in linguistic understanding since that time? In the pre-critical period, however, religious scholars or interpreters, including those who confined themselves to literal interpretations of the text, worked by addressing the text in the linguistic and cultural contexts of *their own time*. Innocently, yet sometimes knowingly, the original meaning was ignored and the text imbued with meanings completely foreign to it. In this respect, the approach can indeed be described as non-critical criticism, as opposed to the critical criticism of the scientists.

It should, perhaps, be stressed that such an argument reflects a basically secular, humanistic viewpoint whose origins are found in Spinoza's secular, critical assault on the traditional interpretation of the Bible, particularly the philosophical interpretations of Maimonides. The same critique was the basis of Spinoza's Biblical criticism in his *Theological Political Treatise*. Despite this, however, a critical approach does not, in itself, necessarily imply an anti-religious perspective which automatically rejects the revelatory or prophetic content of Torah sources or their authority. The Science of Judaism and Biblical criticism came to include outstanding researchers who used scientific criticism systematically, without putting revelation and its authority into question. All that was required in accepting the scientific discipline of philology and history was to apply also the discipline of historical philology to literary sources that convey a revelational religious message, based on the assumption that the linguistic and literary transmission of this message was undertaken by human beings — prophets, priests, and sages.

Here, too, scientific criticism introduced a far-reaching transformation which placed revelational truth in a context of secular culture, demanding that the very acceptance of revelation, and of particular texts as the product of revelation, be subject to the critical tools of historical research; and that the Tradition which presents literature relating to revelation and its contents also be subject to the same critical tools used in examining those literary works and conventions transmitted by human begins. A final demand required that content transmitted as divine revelation must be understood and interpreted within the historical context of the period in which it was revealed or transmitted before examining what meaning it might have for the interpreter in his own cultural or historical context. Needless to say, such a process would require a precise definition and a profound understanding of the differences between one period and another, as well as the use of philosophical tools capable of making fine distinctions between the scientific interpretation of the content of the sources at the time of their creation, and their reapplication in the context of another historical reality.

Thus we come to the question of the relationship between the critical philological method and historic research. As a broad generalization, one might argue that all scientific criticism, including the natural sciences, takes place on a historical foundation. What is science as a discipline? As an academic discipline, science is first and foremost the systematic, classified, and categorized accumulation of *all* the information that can be found on a particular subject, with the aim of using this information to formulate definitions which coalesce or distinguish particular elements within the whole. This, in turn, enables the discovery of circumstantial contexts and relationships among all the elements of the whole, and between this whole and other related wholes. According to its Greek etymology, the word "history" means "research." As defined by Aristotle, the making of history is the preliminary act of accumulation and ordering of relevant information on any subject. In seeking to examine social, political, or cultural processes scientifically, it is obvious that the most appropriate manner of discovering the progression of causal relationships is according to temporal sequence — event after event, stage after stage.

In seeking to understand any event, including religious revelation considered binding on future generations, social and political institutions, spiritual movements, literary works, or any such concepts, we must place them within the widest possible framework of relevant information that relates to and forms the context of these notions. This explains the burgeoning interest in historical topics which traditional scholarship never considered. Thus, for example, the Biblical scholar attempts to discover (with the aid of relevant literatures and sources) all historical contexts: geographic, ethnic, economic, sociological, and political, in their entirety. He does so because the broader his knowledge in these fields, the greater his chance of approaching a complete and precise understanding of the religious and moral messages articulated by the Bible in its own time.

We return to an examination of the motivation for this dramatic change. Based on philological and historical research, what was the significance of Jewish affiliation and cultural identity?

The relationship between the Science of Judaism and the desire to complete the process of emancipation by achieving complete integration into the surrounding nation, society, and culture has been referred to several times. At this point, however, a number of distinct strata may be discerned in this relationship. On the overt level, what might be termed the *political* level, the relationship between objective research on Judaism and the Emancipation was of an apologetic nature: the desire to effectively fight prejudice — both early Christian prejudices and new anti-Semitic ones — that blocked the acceptance of Jews at even the highest, best-educated echelons of gentile society. Objective research could refute these prejudices. Moreover, it would prove that the Jews deserved to be accepted, with respect, as equal citizens since they represented an ancient culture with universal value, and could bring this culture to the finest level of the surrounding culture. The second stratum, the social and cultural level, was based on the first. The educated Jew, longing for emancipation, discovered that even if he was rejected in a vain attempt to achieve emancipation in the political and formal social spheres, he could accomplish this at the cultural level where one's success depended mainly on the individual himself. By acquiring a thorough knowledge of the language of the country, by adapting his external appearance in dress and in the customs of the social elite, and by acquiring an appropriate education, he could internalize its culture. The hope was that adopting the culture of the social elite would lead to acceptance by them.

One of the principal results of this process was an internalization of the social elite's critical attitude toward Jews. The enlightened Jew incorporated within himself a criticism of Judaism in keeping with the external values of the social elite, a process which could lead to what is defined as "Jewish self-hate." Indeed, there were many instances of this. However, those who did not lose their personal and collective self-respect (and despite what is often implied, the vast majority were not inclined to abandon either self-respect or the dignity of the group into which they had been born) responded with a counter-critique that enabled individuals to identify as Jews and to find Jewish cultural values worthy of the respect of the critical environment. This necessitated a precise and impartial interpretation of Jewish heritage in terms of the objective criteria of the host culture. Indeed, the need to uncover the full scope of Jewish culture and prove its original contribution to the surrounding culture originated here.

Again, some would argue that the motivation for this was no more than an apologetic gambit — adopting a supposedly objective stance toward the culture one wished to jettison as well as the culture one wished to join — in order to claim that there was no loss of self-identity, rather an affirmation of identity through acceptance. In response, it must be noted that an unbiased approach to the history of the Jewish people among the cultured peoples of the West gave this claim objective legitimation. There was no pretence here, simply a well founded claim. On the basis of the humanistic values in whose name he demanded emancipation, the Jew had every right to criticize Christian attitudes toward Jews. There was a solid basis for proving that Jewish heritage had played no small part in the victory of humanistic values in European culture.

Not only did this process provide Jews with the opportunity to be integrated into the liberal state as individuals, or as a religious group, but it also enabled them to interpret and internalize their own Jewish religious heritage as an important component of secular European culture. Those who reached this position therefore reasoned that their duty to themselves and to their cultural surroundings was not to mask or hide or abandon their heritage, but to bring the best of this heritage with them as a lasting contribution. This was the earnest task undertaken by the Science of Judaism in Germany. It was on this basis that the research goal was defined: to depict Judaism as a complete, national culture, analogous to the national cultures of other peoples, and to investigate it thoroughly as a complete entity. Needless to say, this was not done to facilitate the continuity of Judaism as a national culture; on the contrary, the goal was its continuation as a brilliant thread in the fabric of the national culture of Europe.

Today, the position appears both ironic and paradoxical — a movement that advocated complete cultural and national assimilation nonetheless represented the Jewish heritage as a full national culture. The Jews are a people; they existed as one people, linked together over the generations despite their dispersal among the nations. And it was Judaism as an integral culture, not merely as a religion, that held them together in exile. So the offspring of this people — the inheritors of this national culture — should be accepted and integrated in the full national life of their surroundings. In reality, there is nothing contradictory about such a position; it represents an objective assessment of a historical process fraught with dialectical tension. To break through the barriers and restrictions imposed by Jewish religion and Jewish nationhood, and to enable Jews to integrate into their host countries as individuals, the founders of the Science of Judaism believed it was vital to establish beyond doubt the claim that Jewish culture had begun and developed up to a certain point, as a full national culture. On the basis of their scientific research, some of the most important philosophers of Reform Judaism such as Samuel Hirsch, Abraham Geiger, and Solomon Formstecher, also emphasized that the development of Judaism as a national religion gave it a clear advantage over Christianity, which had developed as a church. This path had saved Judaism from the fetters of dogma, enabling it to develop as a culture and, when the time came, to be smoothly integrated into the humanistic culture that was gradually freeing itself from the yoke of the Christian church and the chains of its dictates.

So much for the second, cultural stratum in the relationship between the Science of Judaism as objective scientific research and the emancipation. The third stratum, philosophy, also stems from its predecessor. The transformation of a religious heritage into a cultural heritage as it is integrated into the surrounding culture brings with it the dialectics of release from the heritage even as it brings identification with the heritage. The problem was how could one identify with the surrounding culture rather than becoming encapsulated within the walls of religion, as orthodox Judaism had done. Alternatively, how could one leave the ghetto without breaking off from a heritage that was still close to the heart? Only an autonomous approach to both cultures — the culture from which one came and that toward which one was headed, only a position that transformed this process into a free moral decision open to choice and synthesis — could enable the problem to be addressed. In breaking free of the binding authority of religious belief and Torah, it was necessary to place the decision to do so on a moral foundation; that is, not an arbitrary decision but one justifiable in terms of moral obligation, truth, and justice. Longing for autonomy as the condition for the moral decision becomes an objective critical stance vis à vis one's own culture; it becomes the embodiment of a supreme moral and cultural value through which one may make an informed and complex decision: to identify and yet to move out; to belong, and yet to expand the circle of affiliation beyond the crumbling walls of the ghetto.

It comes as no surprise, therefore, that the researchers of the Science of Judaism actually saw in the very implementation of the objective scientific method, in their devotion to clarifying every tiny detail, in their exhaustive research, a consummate expression of complete adherence to the value of truth as the supreme spiritual and cultural ethos. It is only one step further to a Jewish philosophical stance bordering on religiosity. For the most outstanding researchers, faithfulness to the value of scientific truth in the history of their people was equal in weight to the orthodox religiosity they had abandoned on their path toward emancipation. What, in brief, is the essence of Judaism (or indeed monotheism) if not complete faithfulness to values of truth and justice? Thus, there could be no more faithful observance of Judaism than to study it as a culture of the generations, employing objective study in order to know historical truth as it was. Often quoted was the aphorism of the great German humanist historian, Ranke, that "God is in the details." If so, then the God of Israel surely dwells in the details of His people's history and culture. The scholar who spends his life searching for the truth of the history of the Jews among the nations is identifying as a Jew; he lives a Jewish spiritual life and transmits a message of Jewish truth to the generations to come.

Chapter Ten
THE SCIENCE OF JUDAISM, REFORM JUDAISM, AND HISTORICAL POSITIVISM

Most of those who devoted themselves to the Science of Judaism were unable to earn their livelihood either as scholars or in university teaching. They earned their livelihood as rabbis or worked in commerce. Nonetheless, to the extent that they could commit themselves to research, they regarded that as their main activity and goal. They found the meaning of their lives in scholarship, and it was through scholarship that they identified as Jews, even as the mode of their religious life found its primary expression in science. However, when the Science of Judaism is seen as a model of Jewish culture for an entire group, the question must be asked, For whom were they writing? What public held their publications in high regard, made material resources available to them, read the publications and provided the writers with feedback, respect, and criticism?

True, these researchers regarded their scholarship as a vocation which needed no audience beyond the small and dispersed community of colleagues whom they reached through journals — at times, only by means of personal correspondence. It is also true that those who wrote in German wrote for the broad community of scholars in Germany and Europe who had an interest in "oriental studies" or the histories of Christianity and Islam; these were a non-sectarian group of scholars (including, of course, many Jews who were writers, teachers, artists, doctors or lawyers). Nonetheless, the existence of the Science of Judaism as an institution clearly relied on the organized and identified Jewish public that supported it and regarded its work as an important contribution.

It stands to reason that the audience which held the Science of Judaism in high esteem was not composed entirely of scholars, or intellectuals and learned persons. Therefore, identifying with the groups was not dependent on scholarship alone, which is after all a matter for experts. The public required a spiritual dimension of a different kind to which it could relate personally and directly, one which would impact — if only partially — on community activity and a way of life. Where was there a Jewish public ready to support and provide feedback to a critical, objective Jewish scholarship, written mostly in German? It was to be found in those communities that identified with Judaism through modern religious movements which emerged at the same time as the Science of Judaism: the Reform Movement; the Positive-Historical (or Conservative) Movement that split from Reform because of its radicalism; and to some extent, even Modern Orthodoxy. The modern religious dimension became an important component in the cultural model of the Science of Judaism. It is a component that bears examining, both in content and in the way it related to scholarly infrastructure.

There is no need to describe at length, or in depth, the theology or the religious philosophy of those 19th century religious streams which had recourse to the scholarship of the Science of Judaism. What does bear emphasis is that as distinct from traditional religious culture, certainly from ultra-orthodoxy, the modern movements turned to theological and religious philosophy as the primary dimensions of their identity as believing Jews; these were the elements that guided the ways in which they expressed that identity in public activity and way of life.

It is certainly no accident that almost all modern Jewish religious philosophers after Mendelssohn and Krochmal belonged to the Reform movement. Nor is it an accident that the founders of the Positive-Historical Movement, as well as the neo-Orthodox, despite their disinclination to have a systematic philosophy, did indeed need philosophic foundations in order to propose a specific ideology for their movements which would serve as a guide to their Jewish world outlook. The greater the tendency to limit the applicability of halakhah to the individual Jew's way of life, or to introduce revisions in the halakhah, the greater was the need for a more theoretical, profound and sophisticated definition of a religious world view. What this means is that to fill the vacuum created by the receding of halakhah, a religious outlook was required which went along with the transformation of Judaism from what had been a religion based on revealed, absolute and total authority to what would be a culture with a religious coloration.

The most far-reaching changes were made by the Reform Movement. Its declared aspiration was to relegate the Jewish religion into a component which only partially set the Jews apart from the general, humanist culture into which Reform Jews wanted to integrate fully. The Reform Movement perceived religion as essentially a human-made cultural creation, humanity's most sublime cultural product embodying man's moral, esthetic, and idealistic rationalism. The Movement sought a full integration of the Jewish religion and its unique rational beliefs into the general culture. Moreover, according to the Reform outlook, by its very nature the Jewish religion's destined historic mission among the nations obliged it to serve as a guiding element in the general culture. Therefore, Jewish religion should not isolate the Jews from the world; and even a partial distancing would be justified only for the sake of a spiritual paradigm for humanity.

To this end, an all encompassing outlook was needed whose spiritual profundity and idealism took the form of intellectual understanding and ethical sensitivity rather than pious observance in the traditional halakhic sense. The Reform Movement defined Judaism as an ethical monotheism based on universal, rational fundamentals of faith and on a historical awareness that interpreted Judaism in a manner similar to Krochmal. However, the Movement detached itself dialectically from the national dimension and from almost all national-cultural components (linguistic, political, literary, scientific, artistic); it focused the practical expression of Jewish identity on exemplary ethical behavior in society at large, and assigned the expression of the fundamentals of Jewish faith to ceremonial, symbolic-esthetic ritual in the synagogue.

In reality, the revised halakhah needed by the Reform Movement had applicability only in synagogue ritual and, to a limited extent, in the family. What need was there for traditional Jewish learning? By implication, what was mostly required was a legitimation of the Reform Movements's outlook and its articles of faith; that is, a justification of the statement that the ideas under discussion were indeed founded in the sources. In addition, the Movement required a certain intellectual weight of historic Jewish literacy on which to base its view of the historic and developmental mission-consciousness of Reform. It has already been stated that this was necessarily an ambivalent dialectic relationship. Defining Judaism as ethical monotheism was propounded initially on the basis of German philosophic idealism, the schools of Kant, Hegel, and Schelling which gave rise to the distinction between what was perceived of as "authentic" (rational) Judaism, and what was perceived of as a "corruption" — the result of pagan influence. Such distinctions were made possible by the increasingly broad variety of cultural resources that the Science of Judaism had begun to examine objectively.

Up to a point, research could be directed to relevant areas of interest by the religious outlook of the scholars, some of whom were Reform rabbis. Yet there was a conflict of interests between the desire for an authentic, critical and objective science, which was the supreme value of the Science of Judaism, and the modern religious outlook of Reform, despite their mutual concerns. The cultural result was a problematic compromise marked by increasingly onerous tensions. Typically, research which was the experts' sphere of activity functioned through a conscious detachment from religious philosophy; religious philosophy allowed itself the liberty of arbitrarily basing its generalizations on a selective approach and on dialectic interpretations that were sometimes as distant from the literal meaning as the traditional homilies had been.

A second unavoidable result of this process was that to a growing extent the Science of Judaism became the domain of leadership and institutional elites, that is, Reform scholars and rabbis, both in terms of scholarship itself and from the standpoint of authority to instruct and to teach. The wider public who identified with Reform congregations sufficed with the homilies they heard in the synagogue; their Jewish education became more and more confined to what they learned from short readings in the Torah and the formal sermons they heard, in German, (or other European languages) in the synagogues on Saturdays and holidays. The Reform Movement needed the teaching and research establishments of the Science of Judaism for the purpose of rabbinical leadership training. But in the Jewish culture which typified the Reform public, the Science of Judaism itself did not become significant either in terms of learning or a Jewish way of life. These were displaced almost completely by a general education and a general social ethos.

In the circles of Conservative (Positive-Historical) Judaism, the situation was quite different. The fact that this movement of modern Judaism grew out of a split with Reform (because of Reform's radicalism) gives some support to the claim that the difference between the two movements was not one of principle, nor was it far-reaching in either theology or philosophy: ostensibly the difference was merely one of mentality, a preference for traditional conservatism as opposed to radicalism. Those in the Reform Movement felt an urgency to achieve complete emancipation. They were prepared to pay the immediate full price of a unilateral adaptation to the political, social and cultural demands of the surrounding culture. In contradistinction to this, those in the Conservative Movement proceeded slowly and deliberately. They expected the non-Jewish environment to also make some concessions — to accept the Jews and their unique characteristics, characteristics that could not be relinquished without religious compromise. In other words, a standard of religion was determined which distinguished between acceptable revisions and those which were unacceptable. According to the Conservative Movement, existing Orthodox halakhah ought to be modified only to the extent that it conflicted with principles of humanist tolerance and ethics, or with the laws of a liberal state that was neither anti-religious nor anti-Semitic, or because of intolerable difficulties caused by the changed circumstances of life in a modern open society. Moreover, revisions should be made only to the extent that the modifications did not create a discontinuity in the life of the Jewish people as a whole: relationships between the various Jewish sectors must be taken into account so that no deep rifts were allowed to occur which would create feelings of alienation between modern Jews and their Orthodox brethren, nor should a severe dichotomy be permitted to come between children and their parents. The continuity of generations must be preserved.

Taken together, these assertions appear to indicate that a basic difference in political views, going beyond a difference in mentality, did indeed exist. The difference will be properly appraised when we turn our attention from the theological-philosophic level (about which most leaders of the Positive-Historical Movement had reservations) to the theological-ideological strata or the anthropological-historical one in which religion is described in the full context of cultural and societal life. The meaning of this is evident from the programmatic ideological principles which caused the Conservative Movement to call itself the Positive-Historical Judaism.

1) Rabbi Zechariah Frankel (1801–1875), the founder of the Movement of the Positive-Historical Judaism, was responsible for the split from Reform. The debate which precipitated the split concerned a "reform" which, from a formal halakhic standpoint, could have been considered unproblematic; namely, that sermons and worship in synagogues be conducted in German rather than in Hebrew. Why was Frankel inflexible on the question? Because he believed that in the special conditions of modernity this could signal a revolutionary change which would result in a complete cultural, religious break. Frankel believed that without the use of Hebrew, minimally at the level of prayer, Bible readings and sermons, the modern Jewish public eagerly seeking integration into general society would find its relationship to its religio-cultural sources totally severed. Knowledge of Hebrew at such a level was not only the key to prayer as ritual (which according to halakhah really is permissible in other languages), it was also the key to authentic Jewish learning, a familiarity with the full gamut of cultural tradition which gave the religious way of life its original significance, as Hebrew did to prayer itself. If the traditional cultural fullness associated with language and literature were to be diminished, its entire meaning would be changed. Jewish religion would dissipate into an insignificant, sentimental religiosity.

2) The position that only necessary modifications should be introduced, out of concern for preserving the general unity of the Jewish people, was based on an internal halakhic principle: from a halakhic standpoint, the criterion of judging which modifications are justifiable must be: Which ones appear necessary to persons who basically desire to preserve mitzvot, not eliminate them? Which is to say, reform is justifiable only by virtue of a positive attitude toward commandments as the normative system which

preserves a full Jewish way of life. Furthermore, the authority to change halakhah, or to apply it in accordance with contemporary needs, resides only in scholars knowledgeable in the Torah, and in the will of those who honor the commandments, whose devotion is apparent in their behavior and in the questions they put to the Sages. Consequently, the only revisions justified are those agreed to by Torah-learned wise men after thorough investigation and after they have arrived at a decision that the people do indeed require such change. Or, from the opposite perspective, the only halakhic decrees valid are those which the majority of the people who wish to live in accordance with Torah have ratified. This is a democratic concept, a clear historical-cultural concept of the halakhic process even at the level of a decree. Note that according to this view, the process of handing down a decree requires that rabbis are not only knowledgeable in the formalities of halakhah but that they have historical, cultural knowledge, including the ability to compare the significance of various halakhic decisions both at the time they were decreed and at the present time, on the background of a profound and objective understanding of the totality of historic circumstances.

3) The name Historical Positivism, given to the movement by its founders, reflects the concept of historical positivism in general. In the opinion of the thinkers of that school, culture is an organic, historic process whose very continuity is necessary for its development. An organic culture grows from its roots, through its trunk, to its branches. Should growth be obstructed at any point, it is cut off from the sources of its nourishment; it pales, withers, and dies. This being the case, tradition is a cultural value that must be preserved for its own sake. It should be observed simply for being traditional unless it appears to be harmful or incapable of being observed in new circumstances. This assertion, too, clearly underscores the independent value of a people's unique culture as the interpreting and orienting infrastructure for a religious way of life and world view.

As a result of the position taken by Historical Positivism, the Science of Judaism achieved a central place in religious life. The equation was simple: in terms of a religious culture, for generations Judaism had been based on study of the Torah and on the fulfillment of commandments that derived from that study. It was almost unthinkable, therefore, that a Jew could be ignorant. Only a religious culture based on the continuous process of accepting the Torah and transmitting it over the generations, through instruction and learning, as an inherent part of a Jew's way of life, each according to his own capacity, would preserve authentic Jewish identity. Consequently, the difference between Orthodox Jewry and modern Jewry ought not be that an Orthodox Jew studies Torah while a modern Jew does not, but only in how the Torah is studied. Modern Jewry needed to be based on modern Torah study, a discipline that would relate to the full scope of general culture; which is to say, the Science of Judaism.

This position was realized in practice with the establishment of the Rabbinical Seminary at Breslau, the most important center of the Science of Judaism in Germany in the second half of the 19th century, and later in the establishment of the Jewish Theological Seminary in New York that achieved similar standing and the same centrality in the first half of the 20th century. It was also apparent in the methods employed in leadership training for rabbis of the Movement, certainly in the conduct of the synagogue and the Seminary of the Conservative community. It is true that Positive-Historical Judaism did not have an articulated theological philosophy to equal that of the Reform Movement. It is also true that to this day the Conservative Movement regards theological philosophy with some suspicion and does not attach importance to its study even as a historical discipline, but it would be inaccurate to say that Conservative Judaism has no theology whatsoever. In effect, its theology is the Science of Judaism as a philologic-historic discipline which transmits knowledge of the Jewish people's religious sources and national, cultural history while serving as the underpinning for halakhic deliberations, and this can be defined as a cultural-historic theology.

The leadership of Historical Positivism redirected the Science of Judaism to the same status and function which Rabbi Krochmal had assigned to it in the context of a religious culture with a national cast. This, by the way, accounts for the closeness between Krochmal and Heinrich Graetz (1817–1891) who was a founder and leader of Positive-Historical Judaism along with Rabbi Zechariah Frankel. The only national dimension which they had to jettison in favor of the Emancipation was the political-societal one though it must be added that a leaning toward *Hibbat Zion* (the Love of Zion) and spiritual Zionism manifested itself at the very beginning of the Movement. (This was particularly true of Graetz.)

For the Orthodox Jew who sought emancipation, modern Orthodoxy (founded at about the same time, the middle of the 19th century) limited the application of halakhah to the sphere of his way of life in such a manner that no revisions were needed in the accepted halakhah. It accomplished this by making a clear delineation between a religious way of life — familial and congregational — and the sphere of society in general. Educationally, in terms of what was done in the classroom, the separation was effected in a way similar to what had been proposed by Wessely in *Words of Peace and Truth*, by differentiating between the "Law of God" and "Law of Man." In the parlance of Rabbi Samson Raphael Hirsch (1808–1888) who was the founder of the movement, it was the distinction between Torah and *derekh eretz* (secular education). The difference lay in fully implementing the claim that Torah calls for total devotion; therefore in importance and in the allotment of time, study of Torah takes priority over secular studies which are merely elective. From the halakhic standpoint, a distinction was made between that sphere which continued to be governed by obligatory commandments, and the spheres of cultural activity that had opened to Jews in the Modern Era. These spheres had no halakhic restrictions, therefore participation in them was optional, permissible in terms of halakhah. There was room to ask: Did the Torah relate positively to the participation of Jews in these new areas? The leaders of modern Orthodoxy answered with an unambiguous yes; in their opinion the Torah affirmed the activity of Jews in the life of the country, its society, the professions, and the natural sciences. They even assigned a religious value significance to these activities because the Torah is actually a doctrine of life intended for the benefit of man, the prosperity of the Jewish people and the betterment of humanity.

Such an understanding turns the Orthodox advocate of emancipation into a full citizen of two cultures on reciprocal, neighborly terms: an Orthodox religious culture which is based on absolute obedience to a divinely revealed Torah with an affinity to humanism, and to a humanistic, worldly general culture that has a positive attitude to the values of faith and ethics. To be more precise: in terms of modern Orthodoxy, the sphere of life guided by Torah is not in the category of a *culture* because it is under the jurisdiction of absolute divine will; whereas the sphere of secularity is within the domain of a culture that affirms the religious way of life as a vital facet.

Inherent in such an Orthodox view is an unequivocal criticism of the Science of Judaism as a scholarly discipline, particularly as it applied its critical methodology in the study of religious sources, primarily the Bible. The Orthodox position affirmed a reliance on traditional yeshiva scholarship in everything related to "sacred studies." But modern Orthodoxy also needed to reconcile the discipline it used in the study of Torah with the discipline it used in the study of secular general topics: literature, art and philosophy, general science and behavioral sciences. As a result, certain notions of the Science of Judaism were adopted; at the same time a hesitant attempt which did not make much headway in the 19th century to develop a specific discipline of critical Torah Science. This approach, which hinged on an axiomatic acceptance of the divine source of the Torah as an absolute historic fact, recognized that the application of divine commandments in the individual's way of life has an aspect of cultural creativity.

The two earliest and best known examples of this type of scholarship are the academic and theoretical works of Rabbi Samuel David Luzzatto

(1800–1865) and Rabbi Zvi Hirsch Chajes (1805–1855). Their tradition continues today, particularly in the universities of modern Orthodoxy — Yeshiva University in New York, and Bar Ilan University in Israel, which are however part of the story of 20th-century Neo-Orthodox Judaism.

From this description, we may conclude that throughout the 19th century there were primarily two religious movements in which the Science of Judaism could find a home and design at least a partial culture for the Jewish community and its educational institutions in the Diaspora. Given its institutions, the educational processes it successfully fostered, and the religious movements that had recourse to it, the question was whether the Science of Judaism could also develop a culture which would minimally ensure the continuation of the enterprise. (This, in light of the fact that its work was initially written in German, and subsequently in English, with the aim of conducting *pure*, objective research intended for a scholarly community.) In other words, could the Science of Judaism become the exclusive source of Jewish learning for the development of Jewish scholars, could it create a readership drawn from the second and third generation of the Emancipation who would seriously regard the Science of Judaism as a profound, spiritual source on which they could draw? Moreover, could the Science of Judaism educate Jewish intellectuals whose Jewish learning would serve as the foundation for literary, artistic and wide ranging philosophic creativity that could be regarded as a distinct Jewish cultural expression?

It is instructive that from the beginning the founders of the Science of Judaism, such esteemed scholars as Zunz and Steinschneider, tended to answer these questions pessimistically. They regarded themselves as entrusted with saving the cultural treasures of Judaism from extinction. In their opinion, they were the last generation to have an adequate linguistic and Talmudic-rabbinic education for a profound, wide-ranging and serious search into ancient Jewish literature. Once they had gone, there would no longer be anyone capable of plumbing the depths of the books and manuscripts that were fated to become dead letters. While their pessimistic forecast did not immediately materialize, one cannot overlook the fact that the second, third, and fourth generation scholars of the Science of Judaism were not the products of its institutions, its methodology or works, nor were the pupils who made use of the Science of Judaism. These pupils came mostly from the yeshivot of ultra-Orthodoxy, particularly Eastern Europe, admittedly as an act of rebellion and rejection. Indeed, most of the foremost writers of Hebrew and Yiddish contemporary literature also came from yeshivot, not from the institutions of the Science of Judaism, again generally as an act of rebellion. From the viewpoint of those who saw the "salvation of Judaism" limited to its *dignified* preservation in archives and dusty tomes available to a handful of scholars in university libraries, there was no satisfactory answer to the question of the future of Judaism, either as a culture or a religion. As this became evident, an important question arose. Had the Science of Judaism gone in the right direction? Was its failure in the process of transmission rooted in some basic mistake that was not only in the linguistic instructional orientation of its publications but also in setting its direction and methods of study?

In the early days of the 20th century, with the advent of the fourth generation of the Science of Judaism, a major critical assault was mounted by the Nationalist Movement and the Socialist Movement. The great challenge presented to the supremacy of the Science of Judaism was the new concept of Jewish culture that each movement raised, one in Hebrew and the other in Yiddish.

Chapter Eleven
A CRITIQUE OF THE SCIENCE OF JUDAISM AND THE CULTURAL IDEAL OF THE ENLIGHTENMENT

The critique of the Science of Judaism's cultural ideal, particularly its response to the challenge of emancipation, began as a result of the bitter disappointment with emancipation that occurred during the last two decades of the 19th century. This disillusionment followed on the wave of violent anti-Semitism in eastern and western Europe, the cruel economic strangle-hold which the Czarist regime placed on Jews in the Pale of Settlement, and the "crisis of humanism" and "crisis of liberalism" in western Europe. It was all too clear that under the Czarist regime there was no prospect of achieving emancipation, or even "productivization" — a process in which the Jewish masses would be "productively" integrated into the general economy. At the same time, in western Europe where emancipation had been achieved, a generalized, potent hatred of Jews was unleashed, and there were doubts as to whether it would prove possible to overcome such hatred and survive with dignity. This was the backdrop for the appearance of the principal movements which offered revolutionary alternatives to emancipation in the 20th century: Jewish nationalism, socialism, and the combination of the two, Socialist Zionism. The social-cultural ideals of the Science of Judaism in the West, and of the Hebrew Enlightenment in the East, were portrayed by these movements as shallow, rootless, and even laughable anachronisms.

In eastern Europe first, and later in central and western Europe, the assault on 19th century Science of Judaism was led by the fourth generation of scholars and writers who gained prominence during the last decade of the 19th century. Included were such personalities as Ahad Ha-Am (1856–1927), Micha Josef Berdyczewski (1865–1921), Ḥayyim Naḥman Bialik (1873–1934), Martin Buber (1878–1965), and Gershom Scholem (1897–1982). To a certain extent, this phenomenon could be seen as a delayed counter-attack by the Hebrew Enlightenment on the Science of Judaism which had preferred the German language to Hebrew. Ahad Ha-Am and Ḥayyim Naḥman Bialik, in particular, focused their criticism on "the sin against the language." They saw the decision to use a foreign language when conducting research on Hebrew and Hebrew-Aramaic sources of Jewish culture as a betrayal, a humiliation, and a form of spiritual suicide.

In writing about Judaism in German, one is obviously addressing a Jewish and gentile audience who share an inability (or an unwillingness) to approach the sources themselves, to become familiar with them and — drawing inspiration directly from them — to shape an ongoing creation with an authentic, national, cultural spirit. Reading such studies could provide individuals with some sense of history and the sources, with an abstract notion and generalizations about the essence of Judaism; however, even if the knowledge led to an appreciation of Judaism, it would not produce a single researcher, let alone a halakhic scholar, a Jewish writer or artist.

It is understandable, therefore, why the decision to write in German was interpreted as nothing less than a decision to store Judaism away in a gentile archive, leading to its final demise. Bialik went even further in his angry criticism, arguing that it was foreign-language research itself, ostensibly aimed at translating and interpreting the content of Jewish cultural sources into another language, that contained the germs of suicidal distortion. The treachery was inherent in the research. Bialik claimed that the true content of a culture cannot be authentically transposed into a language other than that in which it was created. A people's authentic language is the living tongue that created the nation; in other words, culture is synonymous with language. Thinking and speaking Judaism in the German language was no less than an attempt to "Germanize" Judaism; surely this could only result in a monstrous misrepresentation. Objective science, which describes the outward appearance of things, could successfully be transferred from one language to another. Philosophy, which deals with conceptual abstractions, could also be translated with exactness. Culture, however, is neither a science which describes things from the outside nor a philosophy that raises them to the level of abstraction. Culture is the direct and complete expression of a subjective and living entity. To put it simply, culture is essentially language itself. In order to live a culture, one must feel, sense, imagine, and conceive of it by means of itself, in accordance with its own rules.

It is worthwhile reading at least part of what Bialik wrote in order to appreciate the force of his rage at the exponents of the Science of Judaism who wrote in German.

They are the ones who brought us this bizarre offering, this strange hybrid, the product of western Jewry called 'the wisdom of Israel in gentile tongues' — something unprecedented in any nation or language. Our physical dispersion is now exacerbated by our spiritual division. The single soul of Israel is rent into ten fragments, and the Torah of Israel is riven into ten Torahs. An iron curtain has plummeted between the nation's spirit and its Providence, and the echo of Providence is heard only through the impenetrable wall of an alien tongue. The spiritual unity of Israel has been annulled and its national creative force no longer rests in a single storehouse...by conjuring up some kind of abstract Judaism, some kind of obscure property without form or image, [the scholars of the Science of Judaism] have seen the language of their people as no more than a vessel inferior to its content, an external garb that can be replaced. They failed to see that language itself is the nation's singular 'spirit', the sole reality of that spirit...beliefs and opinions may change, even the 'commandments will be canceled in the future' — so that if there is any hope for an eternal life and for the soul's persistence, it will only be within language and through language. For what is language if not spirit compacted and concretized?

This is typical of Bialik's prose. A series of echoes is evoked from the sources — the Bible, the Aggadah, the Kabbalah, even medieval philosophy. It is as though a thread has been drawn from the sources, and has itself become a source. The inadequacy of translating these words into another language only underscores what Bialik meant by his furious condemnation.

Ahad Ha-Am addressed not only "the sin of language" but the sin of self-denigration vis à vis the gentiles. In one of his well-known essays, "Imitation and Assimilation," he distinguished between positive imitation, which is a way of learning how to construct an independent creation, and "imitation which is self-denigration." The assimilated Jews of the west, he argued, who wanted to become like gentiles in every respect, had lost not only their dignity but their very selfhood. This could be seen in the proponents of the Science of Judaism who mimicked everything — not simply research methods but the very identification of topics, areas of interest, even the conclusions of gentile researchers. And this was despite the fact that in relating to research materials Jewish scholars enjoyed a clear advantage. Certainly, in terms of ability to read and correctly understand Hebrew sources, particularly rabbinical sources, no gentile scholar could compete with students of a beit midrash. All of which, Ahad Ha-Am believed, proved that the chief concern was to curry favor with the gentiles. Such a process could not result in an authentic Jewish scholarship capable of contributing to the development of a vital Jewish culture.

M. Y. Berdyczewski, who spent most of his creative years in Germany, had himself committed the "sin" of writing studies on Judaism in German, as well as stories in Yiddish. (However, it should be emphasized that most of his literary works were written in Hebrew.) Berdyczewski added another insight: despite the fact that the Science of Judaism's studies lay originally in a secular humanistic discipline, it chose to concentrate on examining religious sources, more specifically — rabbinical sources. Its research, Berdyczewski claimed, almost completely ignored secular aspects of Jewish culture — both in ancient times, when the people lived in its own land, and during the Exile. Particularly overlooked were folk creations, the stories, the songs, and popular art. Hasidism, rich in popular creativity, was not explored at all since the Science of Judaism, as the descendant of the Enlightenment, was engaged in an all-out war against the movement. Berdyczewski believed that the national creative powers which had been stifled during exile could be found in this folk creativity; indeed, even from the little that had survived, one could draw inspiration in the renewal of secular Jewish culture.

Martin Buber, and even more forcefully Gershom Scholem, went still further, noting that the selective and apologetic penchant of the Science of Judaism was totally incompatible with its pretensions to scientific objectivity. In their desire to curry favor with liberal gentiles who based the Emancipation on rational humanism and demanded that Jews do the same, the "Science of Judaism" scholars depicted Judaism from its earliest formulations, and throughout the generations, as a uniform "religion of reason," homogenous, established, and halakhic; they completely censored out, or simply overlooked, the variety of movements and trends that were rife among the Jewish people. Both Buber and Scholem found that the Science of Judaism had arbitrarily ignored the vital phenomena that constituted most of the content of Jewish cultural sources. Buber's criticism related mainly to Hasidism, but Scholem went on to claim that kabbalistic literature formed the most eminent, extensive and important phenomenon in the religious life of the Jewish people, at least since the early days of the Second Commonwealth. Scholem argued that the Science of Judaism had completely ignored the Kabbalah, choosing to see any manifestation of Jewish mysticism as alien and pagan. Why had they done that? The answer could only be in order to present the gentiles with a rational and "respectable" Judaism; they developed a homogenous and uniform model of an abstract Judaism which would enable them to break away from those creative and dynamic forces that offered a potential for renewal. They would embalm Judaism through splendid research before packing it off to the archives. Scholem, of course, was completely opposed to such assumptions and intentions. He believed that Judaism was the total, integrated culture of a nation, and that culture cannot be uniform. There are many facets of Judaism, one of which is rational Judaism — but Judaism is not rationalism. If our interpretation is to be guided by its most original and notable discoveries, it is clear that, for the most part, post-Biblical Judaism actually tended toward mysticism. The philosophical and intellectual stream was a narrow one that had failed to take root among the majority of the people.

The connection between disillusion with emancipation and criticism of the Science of Judaism hardly requires elaboration. In the face of the desire to bring Jewish culture into the lexicon of world culture, such criticism was a clear reflection of the passion to reaffirm with pride a humbled Jewish identity, to reject apologetics, self-denigration and the wish to curry favor with others, and to expose Jewish culture as it had been and as it could be, in all its uniqueness, wholeness, openness, and plurality. The individual Jew could find inspiration in response to his expectations, and those who had absorbed worldly ideals could find sources for developing the secular and worldly Jewish culture they desired.

As noted earlier, at least part of the criticism of the Science of Judaism appears to have been a belated reaction of the national Hebrew Enlightenment to research and philosophy which they saw as having taken a turn toward German nationalism. Ḥibbat Zion, the precursor and progenitor of Zionism in eastern Europe, was born out of the Hebrew Enlightenment movement and continued its thrust. This continuity was particularly evident in the link between the literature of the Hebrew Enlightenment and Hebrew literature which later came out of the movement for national rebirth, eastern European Zionism's most outstanding spiritual and cultural contribution to modern Jewish culture. Nonetheless, a forceful, critical clash emerged between the early ideals of the Hebrew Enlightenment Movement and those of Ḥibbat Zion and Zionism; a clash which was reflected in the works of such leading authors as Peretz Smolenskin, Y. L. Gordon, Mendele Mocher Seforim, and Moses Leib Lilienblum.

The recognition that educational and cultural goals of the Enlightenment had waned along with the fading hopes of emancipation and productivization in the Diaspora led to the conclusion that the values and ideals of Enlightenment culture were insufficient for coping with poverty and the culture of poverty which had spread among the Jewish masses in Russia and Poland. The Jews must follow the path of auto-emancipation; but what was auto-emancipation? At the most basic level, it implied the necessity to address not only temporal cultural forces but, first and foremost, to deal with the elementary material conditions that shape social reality, i.e. the forces of technical civilization and, of course, functional education which would enable individuals to effectively cope with modern civilization. It was necessary to acquire political and economic power; it was necessary for the Jews had to break free of their dependency on the material strength of other nations or classes. Neither spiritual nor cultural adaptation and advancement could provide Jews as individuals, or as a people, with the forces of civilization they required in order to improve their lot. This was a manifestly different approach to culture, and a significant change in the definition of cultural ideals.

Criticism of the Science of Judaism was an expression of new aspirations on the plane of spiritual culture. Basically, however, this "spiritual criticism," whose proponents were actually representative of Spiritual Zionism (the writers of other Zionist streams, as well as the ideologues of Jewish Socialism, were not even sufficiently interested in the Science of Judaism to feel the need to criticize it) was imbued with a recognition of the fact that in order to re-establish an independent Jewish culture dedicated to its own language and historical integrity, not only were this-worldly spiritual ideals required, but also worldliness itself. An actual land was an imperative for an independent civilization that would be founded on a comprehensive national culture, similar in scope to "normal" national cultures, for which the Jewish people would be responsible.

To conclude, Zionism and socialism — along with various combinations of both — proposed the two primary programs designed to effect the course of Jewish civilization thus shaping the fate of the individudal Jew and of the Jewish people within society at large. The path of Zionism led to a renewal of secular national culture in Hebrew; the path taken by socialism led to a cultural renaissance based on a secular social vision, in Yiddish.

Chapter Twelve
ACCELERATED CHANGE
AND REVOLUTION

The multi-faceted and dynamic nature of Jewish cultural life at the turn of the 20th century might be compared to the photographic record of a volcanic eruption. Around the crater, two spiralling movements are seen moving ever more rapidly in opposite directions, while in the center a head-on collision between the centrifugal and centripetal forces bring subterranean and hidden layers to the surface.

The spiraling movements at the perimeter of the vortex represent the urgent and accelerated process of adaptation to the dangers of historical reality, and to the challenges posed by the critique of modern religious movements in central and western Europe and the United States, and the ultra-Orthodox movements in Russia, Lithuania and Poland. The modern religious movements (particularly Reform and Historical Positivism) effectively repeated the process of advocating emancipation (which had been achieved but was in the throes of disillusion) in order to launch an attack once again on the status quo, this time correcting and modifying the earlier extreme approach. Specifically, these movements attempted to halt an assimilation which verged on dissolution by affirming a profound level of authentic Jewish identity.

The process could be termed "the reform of Reform." It must have seemed especially feasible given the prevailing political and social conditions in the United States where the social arena open to Jews looked freer, more democratic and more pluralistic than the nationalist social picture in Europe. There was hope that what had appeared to be on the brink of failure in Europe might prove successful in the New World.

Ultra-Orthodox movements (the large Hasidic movements in Russia and Poland, and the Musar movement in Lithuania) also repeated their earlier stance vis a vis the Emancipation, opting for an increasingly fanatic isolation. Nonetheless, they had no choice but to adapt to the modern economic and political scene through their own national and international political organizations; this required a consolidation of ideological positions concerning the challenges of modernity. The process included first attempts to rekindle religious thought as a response to well-disguised influences of modern philosophy that had crept in, particularly with regard to the Musar movement.

At the center of the confrontation was the revolutionary breaking-out of two protean mass movements: the modern nationalist movement which was subdivided into various shades of Zionism and autonomism, and the socialist movement which was also subdivided along a number of lines. Both movements were indeed of a revolutionary nature. Both quickly absorbed themes from political mass movements on the general European scene and wanted to integrate into these movements, thereby changing the nature of the Jewish people. In the immediate present, however, the underlying objective was for direct involvement on the part of independent Jewish organizations in shaping the societal, economic, and political conditions that would determine the fate of the Jewish people among the nations, or among the classes. Leaders of these movements believed that the time was right for the Jewish people to develop independent political power to promote its own interests, as defined in nationalist terms by one movement, and in national and class-based terms by the other.

In other words, one movement sought to embody European nationalist ideals in an independent political framework of the Jewish people, so that the Jews could be integrated as a "normal" member of the family of nations. The other movement, meanwhile, sought to embody the class-based ideals of the international proletariat in order to direct all of Europe to a new order, an order in which such issues as "the Jewish problem" could no longer arise.

Both movements devoted the best part of their creative energies to establishing material, political and organizational frameworks. Activity in the spiritual, intellectual, ideological and literary spheres was undertaken primarily to achieve these goals. The nationalist movements devoted themselves primarily to issues of organization, politics, finance, settlement, and defense necessary for the creation of a societal infrastructure of modern Jewish nationhood in the Land of Israel (or in other places that appeared open to Jewish settlement). The non-Zionist Socialist movements devoted themselves to proletarianizing the Jewish masses and integrating them into a general economic and social process in which they would be organized on occupational and political party levels. They could then be mobilized for revolutionary action to bring the proletariat to power in the creation of a new economic, social, and political order that transcended nationalism and religion. Here, too, spiritual creativity (intellectual, ideological, and literary) was required to play its part in achieving material goals.

What, then, was the Jewish culture (or cultures) to which these revolutionary movements related? Naturally, all the nationalist movements, and many of the Socialist movements, sought a renewal of Jewish culture with a specific identity. All the movements engaged in practical steps toward the realization of their goals, particularly in the fields of education and ideological literature in Hebrew or Yiddish. It was no coincidence that literature as such, permeated to the core by ideological and revolutionary values, functioned as almost the sole expression of higher spiritual creativity. Only such a literature could speak to the people and create a cycle of dialogue. Only such a literature had the necessary tools to articulate the chaos found at the very core of the Jewish people's soul, spurring them to self-awareness, inspiring faith and hope, and giving the people a direction for the future through the impassioned expression of emotions and thoughts.

While the movements for continuity which were on the periphery of the eruption strove to reaffirm, or develop, existing Jewish cultural themes that formed part of the people's heritage, the revolutionary movements at the center longed for a future that was yet to be built. Even when they were obliged to draw on the heritage — since they had no choice but to base their vision on an existing cultural infrastructure — they did not seek to perpetuate it as it was; they looked for elements within the heritage that were capable of carrying out a revolution, of implementing a future that would be not a continuation of the past but a break with it. The movements recognized that the revolutionary present was, so to speak, an empty space through which a radical transformation could occur between the rejected past which already lay in ruins, and a future still to be created. What use, then, was there to the scholarship of the Science of Judaism? What benefit could there be in a philosophy based on religious canon? Only literature — poetry, prose and drama — might yet be able to absorb the crumbling cultural materials of the Jewish past and, through forceful emotional and symbolic transformation, yield the spiritual strengths from which the new Jewish culture of the future could be forged.

From the standpoint of creating a modern Jewish culture, the various movements within Jewish nationalism and Jewish socialism were distinguished mainly in terms of the sphere of activity in which they chose to specialize (of course, without completely forgoing other fields). In practice, three *pairs* of parallel movements emerged in nationalism and socialism. The most radical movements, in terms of their desire for direct, immediate and sweeping change of the societal infrastructure, chose to concentrate on organization and political struggle. This is true of political Zionism and the Socialist Bund movement, each in keeping with its own goals which were, of course, diametrically opposed. Positioned between these extremes were movements that strove for constructive social materialization, mainly Socialist Zionism which sought to realize Zionism in the Land of Israel by building a new society. In the Diaspora, Jewish Socialism also had aspirations for Jewish autonomy pending the revolution, and possibly even after it (positions reflected mainly among certain moderate Bund circles). At the third level were movements which saw their main role as engaging in cultural creativity based on changes in a societal infrastructure which they espoused and supported. They were well aware of the danger that once expected revolutionary changes were effected, the Jewish people might lose its spiritual and cultural identity and assimilate to the point of dissolution. They saw an urgent need, therefore, to define their cultural vision and to create sources that could already begin nourishing the vision by creating a new societal infrastructure. The proponents of this trend were Spiritual Zionists and Religious Zionists (who competed on the same plane of activity) and cultural Autonomists who believed in the possibility of creating a secular Jewish culture in the Diaspora, chiefly in the United States and Eastern Europe, after the victory of democratic socialism.

Naturally, the major confrontation over the nature and content of future Jewish culture arose particularly with these movements, especially Spiritual Zionism and Religious Zionism.

Chapter Thirteen
THE VISION OF JEWISH CULTURAL RENAISSANCE IN POLITICAL ZIONISM

A movement which seeks revolutionary change in the political, social, and cultural reality of its people, creates its culture through revolutionary activity. In retrospect, it can be seen that the extent and depth of the culture was determined by the scope of the movement and the level of seriousness, devotion and persistence with which it pursued its goal. If the goal is achieved, the members of the movement realize that they have maximized its potential as a life-directing force during the struggle. The leadership of political Zionism focused its activity on the creation of a nationalist organization which was designed to mobilize and demonstrate political power, raise financial resources, engage in political negotiation, create a settlement infrastructure which would enable the absorption of mass immigration, and establish a liberal national state in the Land of Israel (or in another available territory). It could be said that in these nationalist activities, the culture of the movement was realized.

Within the overall context of the activities, it appears that the political and spiritual leadership of political Zionism did not attach great importance or philosophic discussion to the nature of the Jewish culture which would be created in Eretz Israel. This was particularly true in the period when mass immigration was being absorbed and the State established, even more in the dynamic period following its establishment. The assumption was that the Jewish masses would arrive equipped with cultural assets from their countries of origin, from their own social strata and from diverse religious streams and secular movements. Some kind of consensus would have to be forged which would serve their shared goal, at least concerning language and the precepts of societal interaction. Together they would aim to establish an *enlightened* state based on a rationally organized constitutional basis through the progressive, constitutional structure of the World Zionist Organization which was established as a "state on the way." Culture would develop automatically on this foundation.

At the organizational level, the establishment and maintenance of the Zionist Organization required regular, on-going cultural activity. The goal was to recruit people to the idea and to activate them, to inspire, unify, and direct them; in other words, to inculcate the nationalist values and ideals which the movement sought to express through its undertakings. This could be accomplished with the aid of journals (literary, ideological, and political) and by creating an inspiring and unifying national spirit through conferences, ceremonies and celebrations, through national symbols such as the flag and anthem, and such forms of movement folklore as songs, stories, plays, and so forth. In order to provide all these cultural needs, ideological themes borrowed from modern European secular, nationalist movements were superficially adapted to the historic memories, festivals and traditional symbols of the Jewish people. (A notable example of this was the glorification of the Maccabees at Hanukkah, an event which was reshaped and interpreted as a Zionist festival par excellence.)

Despite this, in a general sense, the question of future culture was considered important in terms of language, symbols, social ethics, legal and political constitution, and even "higher culture" as emblematic of the lofty vision the movement sought to realize. The reason was obvious: seeking refuge from anti-Semitism was a negative factor; it was insufficient for achieving the revolutionary objective of Zionism. A positive motivation was necessary, one strong enough to cope with the demands of the struggle, which would reach a level of devotion in which the self-sacrifice of individuals for the good of the nation might be required. Understandably, this was an awesome task, and though it seemed vital in order to save the people from imminent physical annihilation, the limited political power and resources available to the Jewish people at the time must have meant that such a goal was a Utopia verging on illusion. It was only the combination of a negative, material motive and a positive, spiritual ideal rooted in national sentiment and identified with ennobling national memories and destiny that could offer a chance for success. This awareness shaped the characteristics of political Zionism as a nationalist-romantic Jewish sub-culture.

What, then, was the cultural vision offered to their movements by such leaders of political Zionism as Leo Pinsker (1821–1891), Moses Lilien-blum (1843–1910) and even Nathan Birnbaum (1864–1937) during his secular Ḥibbat Zion phase, or by Theodor Herzl (1860–1904), Max Nordau (1849–1923) and Ze'ev Jabotinsky (1880–1940) during the era of the Zionist Organization? The answer lies, paradoxically, in the common biographic denominator shared by most of these personalities: they came from a social stratum of European Jewry which had acculturated to the point of complete assimilation into the national cultures of Germany, Austria or Russia, espousing even the modern, nationalist ideals of those cultures. Anti-Semitism offended their national pride — a pride they had internalized from European national values, and, paradoxically, this led them to engage in a romantic return to Jewish nationalism. It is hardly surprising, therefore, that they saw the future culture as a mirror image of the very European national ideals they themselves had rejected.

Thus Jewish nationalism was imbued with a political and socio-cultural significance analogous to that which was current among the enlightened European nations. The inevitable result was an ambivalent attitude toward traditional and religious Jewish culture. On one hand, the leadership reflected an alienated superiority born of their enlightened secular position, of strangeness, and of superficial or partial Jewish knowledge bordering on ignorance. On the other hand, they showed a positive approach toward clearly nationalist elements of the Tradition, particularly in terms of their attachment to the history of the people during the period when it lived on its own land, the Biblical Land of Israel. These elements were sufficient to enable them to "Judaize" national values they had imported from elsewhere. The assumption was that the Jewish people are a people in the same ethnic and historical sense that makes each people unique and legitimates each nation; therefore, the Jewish people needed a "standard" political expression of its nationality. In cultural terms, however, the people did not have access to a relevant national culture; such a culture, therefore, had to be imported in full from external sources. The reality was that the political framework — independent and autonomous — together with language, and possibly some of the symbols which provided an internal rallying point and allowed for external identification, would characterize the unique nature of the nation.

This cultural vision was not devoid of a certain ironic dimension that reminded one of Reform Judaism's concept of the Jews as the Chosen People, but shifted from the religious to the national plane. The Jewish people, at the starting point of creating its state on foundations free of any previous constructs, could avoid the errors and oppressive distortions of enlightened European cultures. It could cull the best from them and establish a model state and society. The new Jewish culture would be a synthesis of superior and equitable social arrangements in terms of humanistic ethics and the liberal state (in which religion and state are separate, placing individual and rational religiosity as the supreme moral and cultural value.) Scientific education and technological achievements would be drawn from Europe, as well as literature, art, and even the enlightened and humanistic religions of the European peoples. All the nations could then reform in light of this new ideal of civilization and culture — a model authentically based on themselves, yet refined to the point of perfection in the crucible of a nation freeing itself from oppressive rule, passing from slavery to liberty!

This is the essence of the Utopian dream as perfected in Herzl's last and most famous book, *Altneuland*. However, what would the specifically Jewish characteristics of such a culture be? How would such a culture serve as a focus of identification for a nation whose history (the basis of its nationhood and the link with its homeland) was ancient? How would such a culture unite a disparate and dispersed people? It is doubtful whether the leaders of political Zionism really wished to discuss solutions to these confusing questions. Greater urgency was attached to the immediate problem of realizing practical objectives. First and foremost, a state must be established; all the remaining problems could be solved once this political tool was available to the people. Nonetheless, there were practical and immediate questions of culture and education that impinged on current activity, and the demand for decision-making brought about a fierce polemic. There were two main issues.

First, the issue of a national language. For the founding ideologues of political Zionism, this question was even more perplexing than which territory the Jewish people should see as its homeland. From the perspective of modern national theory then current in Europe, a specific homeland and a specific national language were the two key components for defining a proper national entity that demanded international recognition. If the Zionists claimed that the Jews were a nation, and that the "Jewish problem" was a national problem to which a solution must be found within modern international law, the movement had to identify the land that was its homeland, and the language which created the community of discourse that distinguished and identified the Jews as a national group. This being the case, the homeland could be identified (by the very name of the movement — ZION-ism), and the claim supported by the historic memory of the Jewish people, even by the historic memory of the Christian nations of Europe. It was not coincidental that Moses Hess chose to call his book *Rome and Jerusalem*. The Italian people, historic heirs of the Romans who had oppressed Zion and exiled the Jews, had achieved their own independence. In the aftermath of this, Hess asserted, there was a sacred international obligation to return the Jews to their legitimate homeland, which had been usurped. But what about language? If the Jews were a nation despite the fact that they had yet to return to their homeland at the very least they ought to have a unifying national language. Otherwise, how could they prove that they were still really a nation? Did the Jews have such a national language?

The Hibbat Zion movement (which drew both on religious tradition and the national Hebrew Enlightenment Movement) had no doubt as to the answer. Hebrew, preserved as a sacral language throughout the generations, was the national language to which the Jews should return, cultivating it as an integral national, secular tongue. The founders and early leaders of political Zionism, however, had grave doubts on this score. Nationalist and normative considerations favored Hebrew, but practical considerations of communication between Jews who would immigrate to Eretz Israel pointed towards Yiddish as the secular, popular language, and prevailing cultural and political considerations would even have favored one of the European languages. At the time Zionism was established, its founders preferred the language in which they had been educated and in which they continued to identify themselves (even as Zionists) — namely, German. Like the early figures of the Enlightenment, they saw Yiddish as no more than a jargon reflecting the cultural degeneration of the Jews in exile. Hebrew was seen as a "dead" language; while it was respected, it was not seen as a potential vehicle for modern Jewish culture.

The decision on the matter was not made by the political leadership of the movement, but by the spiritual leadership which was rooted in the people, faithfully reflecting its cultural and historic heritage. Hebrew won a resounding victory within the Zionist Movement despite the fact that there were Socialist Zionists who favored Yiddish, at least as a second national language. In the context of what characterized modern Jewish culture as created by political Zionism, three significant factors should be considered:

1) The depth of the ideological debate and the bitterness of the struggle around the language issue. The decision was by no means easy. The process was prolonged, fueling prolonged intellectual and emotional polemics and leading to the creation of a broad body of literature. The struggle may be seen as part and parcel of the cultural experience that shaped Zionism as a Jewish movement.

2) The fact that the decision was made in the Land of Israel and related primarily to Eretz Israel. Accordingly, the Hebrew language came to differentiate the Yishuv — the developing Jewish community in Eretz Israel — from the rest of the Jewish people. Hebrew had not become a national language binding all Jews in the Diaspora — not even within the confines of the Zionist Organization. The international Jewish language continued to be a foreign one — first German and later English.

3) The "revival" of Hebrew as a secular language, and of Hebrew literature as a secular and national literature, were the most important and profound realization of the secular, Zionist version of Jewish culture.

In this respect, a common denominator emerged for all the Zionist streams: the desire to revive Hebrew, transforming it from a sacred language to one capable of functioning in all spheres of civilization and culture; and the passion to inculcate the language — enriched and expanded — in order to achieve the goal. The combination of these two ambitions constituted a key focus in the realization of Zionism, particularly with regard to the renewal of a nationalist, secular Jewish culture. This point will be discussed in greater detail in the context of spiritual Zionism, the movement which led the struggle for the revival of Hebrew and provided the linguistic creation that served the entire Zionist movement.

The attitude of secular, political Zionism to Jewish religion was the second problem to create a grave spiritual and cultural struggle. What began as an on-going cultural struggle between various secular and religious movements that had coalesced around a liberal platform, grew into a head-on collision between two major streams of secular political Zionism. The first of these basic political perceptions posited a separation between religion and state: religion should be respected as a matter of individual choice, shaping personal lifestyle within voluntary social frameworks, but any kind of religious involvement in civil political life, or the granting of political authority to religious bodies, must be rejected. But there was a second perception which recognized that for generations Jewish religion was the only factor that maintained Jewish nationhood, both as an organizational framework and in terms of spiritual content and lifestyle. Moreover, even at the turn of the century the majority of Jews were religious in the Orthodox sense of the word and followed the leadership of the rabbis; at least, this was true of those who seemed to be realistic candidates to immigrate to and establish a State in the Land of Israel.

To appreciate the severity of the clash between these two positions and its ramifications for the cultural reality created by Zionism, it must be emphasized that the liberal perspective reflected international Zionist political interests which required that Zionism be legitimized as an enlightened, modern national movement worthy of the support of the Great Powers. It was not simply an expression of power-based interests in the secular part of the movement from which the leadership came; nor was the liberal perspective simply a source of legitimacy for the secular leadership which had replaced traditional rabbinic leaders. And yet, the practical realization of Zionism required that Orthodox rabbinical leadership enjoy an influential status. In effect, this was the leadership responsible for defining the themes and lifestyle that would constitute *Jewish culture*, alongside its responsibility for Jewish education, since this was the essential condition demanded by the rabbinical leaders in return for their cooperation.

Since Zionism was a democratic political movement, a compromise was essential. The compromise, however, spurred further confrontation between political Zionism and spiritual Zionism. Herzl declared that Zionism, an organization formed to achieve a pragmatic, material national objective, had no interest in intervening in the spiritual argument concerning the nature of Judaism, or in the educational content that would effectively determine it. The definition of Judaism and of its educational system were placed beyond the authority and activity of the Zionist movement. The educational authorities would be distinct and independent. The Zionist movement would continue to relate exclusively to political organization, to representing the political interests of the Jewish people to external bodies, and to negotiating with governments concerning the status of the Jewish people in the Land of Israel (or in Uganda), in fundraising, in preparing settlement in Eretz Israel, and so on. These spheres were defined as the common secular and political interests of the entire people. All the rest — that is, culture — was outside the scope of Zionism. The declaration, which was enthusiastically accepted by the majority of religious Zionist leaders (only Rabbi Kook opposed it) might appear as nothing more than a logical application of a liberal principle, separation of religion and state. In practice, however, its significance was precisely the opposite. Culture was separated from the State, and responsibility for culture was relegated to religious leaders. This, at least, was the interpretation of the religious Zionist leadership as they agreed to the declaration, and the leadership of Spiritual Zionism as they opposed it.

A significant question was raised by both Ahad Ha-Am and Rabbi Kook, each from his own perspective. Could a movement such as Zionism, which sought to achieve a complete revolution in the reality of the Jewish people, avoid direct confrontation over the spiritual and cultural implications of its enterprise, or refrain from drawing on spiritual and cultural messages which served as both motivation and goal? A negative response to the question should have been obvious even to the author of *Altneuland*; its practical ramification was to place the spiritual and cultural message that identified Zionism as a Jewish movement in the hands of the religious faction, thus ensuring (*de facto* if not *de jure*) that the message would reflect their cultural norms. It was for this reason that the rabbinical leadership was so enthusiastic about Herzl's declaration, and it was for this reason that they fought so fervently against the efforts of Ahad Ha-Am and his followers to change the decision. Eventually, following the Tenth World Zionist Congress which did, in fact, change the decision, setting up two parallel departments — one for religious education and the other for free-thinking national education — the dispute was the basis for the withdrawal of part of the religious Zionist movement from the Zionist Organization.

Actually, the second decision did no more than formalize a situation that had emerged following the first one. The most profound, and therefore the most problematic, Jewish characteristics of the culture that was forged by political Zionism, as a global movement, were effectively determined by the *Kulturkampf* that raged within the movement from its beginning to the establishment of the State itself; they continue to characterize the State as the arena for bringing together the contending streams within it.

It was a paradoxical conflict — ideologically uncompromising, yet politically restrained — between four radically different and mutually exclusive concepts of Zionism whose conflicting values, content, and visions for the cultural future could not afford to forgo cooperation in the realization of a tangible infrastructure for the State. There was no alternative but to create an arrangement for dialogue in which each of the parties absorbed influences from the others or was required to accept their impact on the public domain, interpreting what was absorbed from their opponents according to their own standards. Thus, there developed an Orthodox religious interpretation of the political, social and cultural bases of political, social and cultural Zionism; this interpretation addressed matters of democracy, humanism, socialism, scientific and technological education, and artistic creativity from an Orthodox viewpoint. This is particularly evident in the philosophy of Rabbi Kook. At the same time, secular-nationalist or secular-social (liberal or socialist) interpretations of religious motifs emerged, addressing such issues as prophetic morality, the ethical implications of monotheism, the Jewish festivals, the status of the Bible as a source of Jewish education, and so on. (These will be examined in our subsequent discussions of social and spiritual Zionism.)

The major effort invested, however, by all the opposing camps was in the rejection of definitions and interpretations offered by the other side, or their refutation. Even when there was a positive interpretation of a motif taken from others, it was deliberately rephrased in argumentative, vexing terms. The same approach was taken by the faction that described itself as "free-thinking" (with regard to religion), and the faction that defined itself as Orthodox or ultra-Orthodox (with regard to the secular culture of those who sought integration into general European society.) As a result, the conflict led to the emergence of a polarized Jewish identity whose dominant shaping factor was the conflict itself.

While political Zionism continued to provide a broad framework for the preservation and realization of the Jewish people's sense of belonging to a modern nation, it grew to be dominated by a cultural trend toward particularism that sought to equate Jewish national culture with modern secular national cultures. Eventually, the trend led to the desire for a romantic-secular "renaissance": a return to early Jewish history which was seen as natural, vital, and assertive; a return to the homeland and its historical origins; a return to the earliest linguistic and literary sources in order to draw on these in the creation of a modern, *healthy* alternative to the culture of the Diaspora which was seen as defensive, distorted or fossilized.

Behind this form of national and political culture was the myth of national conquest, the myth of renewing the "sovereignty" of the Jews in their old-new homeland. This took on added meaning as it became clear that the Arab majority in Eretz Israel was violently opposed to the Jews "return to Zion" and that the British regime sided increasingly with the Arabs. From the mid–1920s, the return to Zion came to be identified with the struggle against foreign rule. ("Judea fell in blood and fire; in blood and fire shall Judea rise.") It was an appropriate backdrop for the romantic, cultural vision of returning to the ancient sources in order to gain inspiration and valor in battle.

An indication of this trend may already be seen in Herzl's *Altneuland* (though without its bellicose aspect; on the contrary, Herzl argued that Zionism would bring the message of peace to Palestine and to the world). However, the main source of such an approach and its creative application is found in the works of Ze'ev Jabotinsky (1880–1940) who continued in Herzl's path, more thoroughly and profoundly, adopting Hebrew as the national language and Hebrew literature, particularly the Bible and modern Hebrew literature, as the infrastructure on which a new national Jewish culture could develop. The objective was to absorb the best of modern European culture's spiritual, liberal-humanistic themes, and internalize them by their "re-creation" through a process depicted as the renaissance of the ancient sources. This was achieved by means of an interpretative *implant* of European themes into the stylistic and thematic texture of ancient Hebrew sources (freely interpreted) in order to subsequently produce a modern literature, philosophy and ethos which was presented as an organic development based on the particular sources of the Jewish people.

Jabotinsky's literary works, particularly his programmatic Zionist novel *Samson*, illustrated this process across a broad historical and mythological narrative canvas. He proposed the adoption of the Biblical Sabbatical Year and Jubilee Year concepts as a romantic frame for an enlightened social order which he painted in general terms as a vision for the future.

On the level of historical research, one might mention in this context the work of Joseph Klausner (1874–1958); and in the realm of poetry the works of Saul Tchernichowsky (1875–1943) and Yakov Cohen (1881–1960). This was the starting point for the development of a still more extreme national romanticism. Cherished by "the Young Hebrews" (natives of Eretz Israel), it eventually moved toward integration with modern secularism through the renaissance of "Canaanism," in a complete break with a Jewish culture that came to be seen as totally Diasporic.

It must be emphasized, however, that the romantic culture of the Hebrew renaissance (which grew out of a "general" concept of political Zionism) was to be found not only in literature and ceremonial as an ethos, or in the militant struggle of the national educational youth movements (particularly Betar, Irgun, and Lehi), but it was also a contributing component in the curriculum of the educational stream described as "general-national."

Chapter Fourteen

THE PIONEERING (ḤALUTZIC) CULTURE OF THE JEWISH LABOR MOVEMENT IN PALESTINE

Concerned that it would engender controversy, the Zionist political leadership preferred to avoid discussion about the "cultural issue." Their reasoning was practical: the immediate task was establishment of a state. This being the case, a divisive discussion in a period which required unity seemed completely unnecessary. Better to defer the cultural issue to a distant future, and postpone it to a time when it would actually become a question. Indeed, those leaders who subscribed to Herzl's position tended to compromise on such questions, acquiescing to rabbinical leadership. Allowances should be made, in this context, for the assumptions of secularists which legitimized and gave practical validity to their leadership: they had not a shadow of a doubt that religion in its Orthodox form was in a state of rapid retreat. It was necessary to take religion into consideration because at the turn of the century the majority of candidates for "aliyah" (immigration to the Land of Israel) were Orthodox Jews; nonetheless, the secularists felt it would not be long before only an insignificant Orthodox minority would remain; outmoded Orthodoxy would be completely displaced by secular progress. Thus, in keeping with contemporary world circumstances, it was inevitable that when the Jewish state was established it would be as a liberal democracy, or a modern social democracy — a decisive victory of enlightened secularity over benighted Orthodoxy. The cultural issue would disappear; in effect, society would practice an ideal blend of European culture — in the Hebrew language — flourishing in concert with the romantic renaissance described earlier.

A majority of the Jewish labor movement adopted Herzl's political idea: the overarching Zionist goal was the establishment of a Jewish national state in the Land of Israel as the only comprehensive solution to the "Jewish question." Differences arose when it came to the pragmatic steps which had to be taken for the realization of the goal. The Labor Movement believed that to take actual possession of the Land, pioneering settlement was necessary in Palestine. This was to be accomplished through labor (particularly tilling the soil) and by the creation of an egalitarian, cooperative, self-supporting society. Once the foundation was laid for agricultural communities, for an economy, and for a society — all of which would constitute the culture, the infrastructure for the state on-the-way would be in place.

At the same time, in the face of opposition by the Arab population and the reversal of attitude vis-a-vis Zionism by the British Mandatory Government, the Labor Movement recognized that there would be a struggle for national settlement in the Land of Israel. The development of Hashomer, and later the Haganah and the Palmach was a manifestation of romantic militancy which had an affinity to Jabotinsky's outlook (and the members of the NILI group that preceded him), but the emphasis was on collective, agricultural settlements. The Haganah was an adjunct to settlement ("Conquest of the Land and Conquest of Labor" was the slogan characteristic of the Second and Third Aliyot) even as the quasi-military organizational mode of "Gedud ha-Avodah" (the Labor Battalions) was emblematic of a notion that transformed war battalions into labor battalions. All of which called for a re-evaluation of the "cultural issue" since the societal value-conscious attributes of agricultural settlement preceded all other goals. The assertion could be made that societal relationships of the settlements, value-laden as they were, were regarded by the pioneers as the essence of culture. Everything else was commentary.

Yet it is evident that the cultural issue could not be deferred by the pioneering movement to some distant future. On the contrary. The cultural issue was of the moment and urgent for the movement, identified with the very realization of Zionism. The most profound meaning of "pioneering" (*Halutziyut*) was that, in practice as well as in theory, it erased the liberals' distinction between material and spiritual aspects of culture. The material enterprise was regarded as the primary, if not the exclusive, arena in which Zionism and socialism would be realized; the principal, if not the only, province of societal, ethical, and national values. The primacy of the material enterprise was clear, and the pioneers believed it to be even more applicable to the Jewish people as a whole so long as they lacked a material infrastructure. Indeed, the creation of such an infrastructure was the greatest moral challenge the people ought to face, which meant that the "civilizational" enterprise and the "cultural"* enterprise were two sides of the same coin. Furthermore, culture was perceived in the pioneering settlement movement as the very embodiment

---

* See the distinction between "civilization" and "culture" in European usage above, Chapters 1–2. (LL)

of Zionism's great revolution in the life of the people, and in the life of every Jew.

What practical significance could be drawn from all this? It was the realization that Zionism is a life-long task which calls for a total change in the individual's way of life, so much so that he becomes a new person, a new Jew. However, though bitten by the idea of Political Zionism and personally committed to its achievement — even to the extent of making a decision for immediate aliyah — neither the "religious" nor the "free-thinking" individual revised his religious or free-thinking concepts, or his way of life as a person of culture. The most far-reaching cultural implication of aliyah was the question of language: the individual who chose aliyah would have to speak Hebrew. Satisfying his cultural tastes would be restricted to the locally available repertoire of European culture, conceivably not of the standard to which he was accustomed. But from the standpoint of his way of life, values or activity as either a religious or a secular person, absolutely no change was required; the only exception was the interpretation or the intellectual and emotional significance with which he colored his Zionist efforts. By comparison, both in theory and practice, the *Halutzim* whose aliyah was centered on seeking Zionist realization through pioneering, made essential changes in their way of life: language, occupation, daily schedule, societal and family relations, and the gratification of spiritual and physical needs. Everything. There was no area in which far-reaching transformation was not required.

The cultural question was thus how to completely redesign the personal and societal way of life of the pioneer dedicated to Zionist realization. The question of what cultural message their education institutions should transmit arose almost immediately. Kindergartens, schools, and youth movements of the pioneering settlements had special requirements that needed to be addressed; even the university was expected to respond to the special circumstances of the labor settlements. A new national infrastructure was conceived that, in and of itself, was both spiritual transformation and message; that is, it formulated a new, broadly encompassing outlook and way of life. The basic norm was *hagshamah* — self-realization through identification with the collective ideal — the practical meaning of which was *labor*. Consequently, the movement was called the Labor Movement, and the culture it created was called the Culture of Labor.

In fact, labor stands out as the primary characteristic in the basic norm which exemplifies pioneering culture as a way of life. By this, the *Halutzim* literally meant manual labor in trade and industry but particularly in agriculture. They invested labor with a quasi-religious meaning: a secularized equivalent of worshipping God.* Though based on a misinterpretation, in the common parlance of Eretz Israel it was known as the Religion of Labor. (We will return to this issue at some length in a discussion of A. D. Gordon's perception of Jewish culture; Gordon was the Hebrew Labor Movement's greatest thinker.) The theory that guided the Labor Movement in both its cultural efforts and world view must be seen within the overall ideological framework of Socialist Zionism. It was this theory that differentiated the Labor Movement on one hand from Political Zionism, and on the other from Cultural Zionism, giving Labor Zionism its own distinctiveness.

Two complementary yet contrasting versions of Socialist Zionism were advanced by Ber Borochov (1881–1919) and Nachman Syrkin (1868–1924), its founding theoreticians. In turn, there were agreements and disagreements between these socialist-Zionist thinkers and the political-Zionist views of Herzl and Nordau, even of Jabotinsky. Borochov and Syrkin accepted Herzl's analysis which posited a national-political solution to the "Jewish question." But they differed sharply with him about the implications of the social class problem which he totally disregarded. In response to Herzl's *Jewish State*, Syrkin wrote his famous essay, "The Jewish Question and the Jewish Socialist State." The title itself highlights the distinction. Syrkin attempted to show that the Jewish state could emerge only if it was established at the outset as a socialist state, the necessary guiding principle of the process being social justice among individuals and among classes.

To understand the nature of nationalist-socialist Jewish culture as it was formulated by the Hebrew Labor Movement, a brief review of its ideological rationale is in order. The Jewish constituency that identified itself with the Hebrew Labor Movement was committed to the view that Zionism could be realized only if it was socialist; this belief was basic to the motivation that spurred their heroic pioneering efforts.

The claim was simple. While the leaders of Political Zionism correctly saw that the masses of eastern European Jews were, for the most part, still Orthodox, they overlooked the societal and class dynamics which led to an acceleration of radical anti-religious secularization. The economic noose which was tightening around the Jews led the younger generation to undergo a rapid process of proletarization, but the fate of the impoverished worker, who was exploited and discriminated against, held no attraction for them. Consequently the immediate solution to the suffering of the younger

---

* This equivalence was based on a linguistic correspondence: the Hebrew *avodah* (whose root meaning is "service") referred both to the traditional religious service in the Temple and to the common notion of work. (See *Ethics of the Fathers* 1:2: "The world stands on three things: Torah, *avodah* [the Temple worship], and deeds of kindness.") (LL)

generation was to be found in the revolutionary workers' movements. It was the secret of their increasing attraction, and more and more young Jews renounced religion. True, Borochov and Syrkin correctly claimed that the social revolution which had overtaken Russia and other European countries would not straightaway solve the distress of the Jews. On the contrary, it would exacerbate it almost to the point of threatening annihilation: one had to admit after all that the working classes in most European countries were more anti-Semitic than the bourgeoisie of those countries, and that the revolutionary leadership made use of anti-Semitism for its own needs. But if they wanted to convince those masses of young Jews who were undergoing a dual process of proletarization and secularization (as Borochov and Syrkin maintained), the Zionist leadership had to propose a societal-class solution within the context of Zionist nationalism. Because of its strained circumstances, the Jewish working class was the principal social force open to Zionist realization; yet it was only ready to commit itself to Zionism if the movement could present it with a viable social solution to a problem which had become existential and urgent.

The difference between Political Zionism and Socialist Zionism was expressed in programmatic terms. Jabotinsky's slogan, "One Banner," called for a concentration of national effort in a single direction rather than dissipating it in favor of several simultaneous aims: one flag only should be unfurled and it must be the flag of Jewish statism. As distinguished from this, Socialist Zionism coined the slogan, "Two Banners" — a social, political program for the creation of a socialist society on the way to establishing the Jewish state. Clearly this programmatic difference also led to substantive variations in the realization process.

The first problem Zionism was supposed to solve appeared to be more existential and pressing than the social issue, demanding an immediate solution not only in terms of history but also biography. Through their romantic dedication to political activity or to a political-military struggle for the Jewish state, personalities such as Herzl (and the assimilated bourgeoisie Jewish public he stood for) could find a full emotional remedy for the existential anguish they felt in response to the insult of anti-Semitism. Even before the state was established, they could be comforted and gain personal emotional compensation through the organized struggle for a political realization that was imminent in one or two generations. But for a person whose Jewish suffering expressed itself in being poor and in the culture of poverty with all its shocking material, emotional, and spiritual misery, who could not see an alternative in his immediate reality which pointed to an escape route (with the exception of revolution), an activity that would solve his problem in *just* one generation or *at worst* in two, was unacceptable.

Only an immediate practical realization, even one which entailed suffering but was colored by hope, could effect a remedy.

Secondly, the realization of a vision that is not solely political but has a social dimension requires action that goes beyond the political or military. Tangible, direct effort on the part of each individual is demanded, and such action must be an integral part of the individual's way of life. To this end, it is not enough to organize, to collect donations, or to identify symbolically through cultural activity alone. Rather, it is incumbent upon each individual to act out the vision in practice. The workers' class in every country responded to pressures by mobilizing in a daily revolutionary struggle through street demonstrations, strikes, mass meetings and underground activity against the regime. The revolutionary struggle thus became the daily personal life-style of the organized worker. The Jew who was a Zionist needed a similar personal, practical outlet. The only way to bring Zionism to fruition was through immediate aliyah to Eretz Israel and to agricultural settlement, which was the quintessentially direct economic-social action in which both the national and social ideal could be realized. The Zionist worker had to personally settle the Land, to labor and to be economically self-sufficient, to build a society, and to develop a culture by his own efforts. Such realization by the individual was the norm implied by a social revolutionary mentality.

Ultimately, no political negotiation alone, even one that was successful and forward moving, could achieve the social vision. Rather, the dual vision called for a process that put an altogether different set of priorities in place. If one began with a framework of political sovereignty (rather than with social-economic issues) as Herzl, Nordau and later Jabotinsky insisted, the social structure that followed would perforce be the existing social order; the one which, in effect, was representative of the (bourgeois) political leadership. Neither Herzl's nor Jabotinsky's seductive hyperbole about a liberal utopian society would effect social change. As representatives of the existing social-economic order, the prevailing forces in the general Zionist movement would establish an order congenial to themselves. In their hands, the State would be an instrument for the realization of their class interest. By contrast, to achieve the workers' social goal along with the political aim, a different socio-economic base had first to be laid. The desired state would result, a state that would not lord it over society but be its expression.

Another qualitative difference shaped the social-national culture of the Hebrew Workers Movement, both in form and content. Though admittedly secular and leaning toward a more radical anti-religious stance than the leadership of general political Zionism, the constituency represented by the workers' movement was none the less steeped in Jewish folkways. Culturally, it had not undergone a process of assimilation before being caught up by socialism or Zionism. For the most part, it was a constituency that came from religious Jewish communities and from traditional, even ultra-Orthodox families of eastern Europe. These were young people who grew up in an observant milieu, who initiated a radical overturn which was expressed in an overt heretical rebellion against the religious ways they had experienced from birth. However, their decision was not motivated by any preferential attachment to the surrounding non-Jewish culture. On the contrary, that was a culture which they regarded as riddled with gross anti-Semitism, no less objectionable to them than it was to their religious parents. This being the case, elements of religion were equated with an oppressive Jewish existence in Exile and were negated along with the existential situation of the Jewish people in the Diaspora. Both rejections were combined in the radical notion of *Shelilat ha-Golah* ("Negation of the Exile/Diaspora") — which was a core motivating sentiment of the pioneering movement. Yet these self-same religious themes served the pioneers as the basis of their integral Jewish identity, an identity they took for granted. Their personal and national identity required no proof of Jewish validity, neither by its practitioners nor its critics. In truth, the pioneers elected to enact their rebellion within the context of Jewish existence rather than outside it.

This was a crucial juncture. If they opted for revolution in the countries of their birth, the decision would explicitly and implicitly be understood as a decision to jettison future Jewish identity. In opting for Zionism and working for its realization, they decisively confirmed their Jewishness. They regarded assimilation as betrayal and forcefully rejected it. What was the content of their Jewishness? The question itself seemed untenable because their very being was Jewish. Consequently whatever they did for themselves or their people as Jews was destined to be Jewish, even if the norms and values that guided them, and the ideological themes that nourished them, did not originate in a "Jewish source" but derived from modern European national and social revolutionary movements. It was obvious to them that their entire activity was expressive of Jewish feeling and would serve the national interest.

This conviction explains how the pioneers related to the hallmarks of Jewish culture. From the outset, the national and social components of the culture were self-evident: a compelling emotional bond to Eretz Israel as the material (not religious or spiritual) homeland of the Jewish people; a profound emotional bond to Hebrew as the national tongue (not as a sacred language), an intense ongoing bond to the Jewish people's national history (not religious history) and national literature (not religious literature — the Bible itself was perceived as national literature not as holy scripture.) All these commitments would be carried out according to the norms of self-realization in labor. Labor was to be the practical application of the national connection to Eretz Israel; it would also serve as the core assumption on which a new society would be constructed. Built on principles of self-labor, this would be a working society whose social values were embodied in the way one related to one's fellow — laboring for and with one's comrade, working for and in society. This would be a society that practiced equality, co-operation, liberty and moral responsibility for one's fellow man and for the community, not as slogans but as a daily way of life.

From the outset, the principles of such a cultural norm seemed to be so encompassing, so intensive as to obviate the need to add to it, certainly not from the standpoint of articulating the attachment to Jewish culture. But if this seemed to be the picture initially, it changed in time. When the dream of aliyah was fulfilled, a great dilemma arose as a result of the cultural concept itself. The pioneers encountered the bare landscape of Eretz Israel whose soil had to be redeemed, and the Jewish people and the conflicting cultural legacies they brought with them from different parts of the world to Eretz Israel. They encountered the life of physical labor, which was to be the means for redemption. They encountered complex societal relationships against a background of poverty, loneliness, and hardships at work. How would the ethical-spiritual significance of the national-social bond to Eretz Israel be acted out while settling on the Land which was after all only soil? How would the notion of self-realization be achieved through labor which was nothing more than back-breaking toil? How could the significance of labor be maintained while one was engaged in work to which the body refused to adapt and so left the soul in torment? How would the guiding message be transmitted to a second generation that would grow up to a life of work without benefit of the cultural background that had impelled the pioneers, endowing labor with its national and societal significance?

Arising from the realization of Zionism, these questions called for further thought about the relationship between the Jewish spiritual tradition and the Culture of Labor.

Chapter Fifteen
POLAR VIEWS ON SOURCES OF JEWISH CULTURE

The initiators and champions of the Hebrew Labor Movement were deeply, personally rooted in the religious and cultural sources of Judaism: the Hebrew language, the Bible, prayers, Sabbath, holidays, and the religious precepts of daily life. Most of them knew Yiddish well, and the folk culture was close to their hearts. But they regarded it — the Yiddish and Hasidic songs, Hasidic dances, folktales, and Jewish humor — as a secular culture. The scholars among them were well grounded in the literature of the Sages, the aggadah and halakhah, and the rabbinic literature of the Middle Ages. Those who devoted themselves to literary creativity drew on these sources so that their Hebrew was infused with references to them, without which they would not have been able to fully express their thoughts and feelings. Despite all this, it was precisely the literati in the Movement who sounded the existential and philosophic revolt against religion. Sometimes this was effected through satiric exploitation, an indication that they did not want to use the sources for contemporary purposes, at least not insofar as the sources were religious. Had they been able to, they would have skipped over the sources to create a different Jewish culture from which a new generation would spring, but this was impossible because it was precisely through the sources that their identity and motivations were confirmed.

Moreover, what if it transpired that cultural creativity was necessary to give meaning to a life of contemporary Zionist realization, and to that end one needed sources that had been internalized? Since people feel most comfortable with what is already theirs, would it not have been natural to utilize the very sources that had been pushed aside and neglected? Would it not have been natural to institute, both on a personal level and in the life of society and the nation, an understanding of the role the sources played in the revolution which had taken place thus making them relevant to the new Jewish reality in Eretz Israel?

This lacuna was seen as a spiritual vacuum that threatened everyone who took part in the Hebrew Labor Movement's struggle. The perplexities were great, and they became institutionalized in the ideological rigidity of political parties where change is exceptionally difficult. Opinions in the Labor Movement generally differed along political lines which, in principle, can be summarized according to the following three positions:

1) The radical revolutionary position which was adamant about the idea of revolt, demanding total separation from traditional religious sources, substituting for them humanist, socialist, universalistic content. Such content would simply be translated, verbatim, from other languages to Hebrew, and would then be integrated as an authentic element of Eretz Israel.

2) The revolutionary position which insisted on the idea of revolt but sought options within the historic tradition of the Jewish people, on the assumption that a broad, popular, secular tradition existed which was independent of religious and rabbinic content.

3) A position that aspired to continuity within the revolution and sought its options within the traditional religious sources but insisted on a far-reaching freedom of interpretation. Such freedom would subject religious content to a process of secularization. This position, also found in the revolutionary Hebrew Labor Movement, was actually quite similar to the position of Spiritual Zionism. On this point, there was a partial and fruitful junction between the two movements which was parallel to another junction that existed between the Hebrew Labor Movement and political Zionism.

In the following chapters, we will look at each of these positions more closely. Taken together, they represent a focus of turbulent spiritual activity in the Culture of Labor.

Chapter Sixteen
ALIENATION FROM RELIGION AND TRADITION

Yosef Haim Brenner (1881–1921) was regarded by many of his close associates and admirers as a martyr. His works expressed an alienation from religion, belief, tradition and Torah observance in an aggressive, challenging manner that constituted an almost holy war against sanctity. Yet it was Hillel Zeitlin (a religious writer) and Benjamin Radler-Feldman (nicknamed "Rabbi Benjamin") who described Brenner as a prophet devoted to truth — bitter as it might be — who was ready to sacrifice himself for it. Perhaps because his denunciations were redolent of prophecy, they attempted to find an expression of disillusioned belief in his essays which were unambiguous and harsh.

Brenner's words were never phrased as "a cry against heaven" which is really the gesture of a disappointed believer. They were a cry against religion: the establishment, the *Shulḥan Arukh*, the rabbis, and the coteries of pious students whom he considered fools for blindly following rabbis and teachers like lemmings. He had nothing to say about God, or to God, so certain was he in his belief. His negation of religion was experienced with all his being. Nor could he overlook the fact that in his war against religion, he was battling against his own formative training, his childhood experiences, his basic education, his memories, his language, his very way of thinking. He not only fought the rabbis and their followers, he fought against himself. Apparently the secret of his sweeping influence was that, in fact, he was a radical exponent of his generation.

Brenner's anti-religious preaching had a two-fold background:

(1) A personal (but typical) biography which began with a wretched childhood and early youth in a small town in the Pale of Settlement. His impoverished parents had hoped that their genius son would save them from poverty and a lowly social station by virtue of his prominence in Torah study. Repelled by his parents' pressure, he nonetheless did their bidding. He tried to find a surcease for his disbelieving spirit through devotion to the Torah and religious awe when he studied at the yeshiva. Apparently,

however, he found proof of the hypocrisy and dishonesty of belief in the God-fearing piety of his parents which he saw as merely a cloak for their gross material cupidity and their fawning behavior towards the wealthy, forceful members of the community. His spiritual failure in attempting to overcome doubt or to find a positive religious experience in yeshiva studies provided him with a final conformation that although there may be innocent people of faith, they were very rare; for the majority, belief was hypocrisy — conscious or repressed.

(2) The social background of an emerging Eretz Israel was marked by a collision between the pioneers of the Second Aliyah and the Jews of the Old Yishuv. During this period, the Old Yishuv was comprised of a majority that was attempting to assert its authority over a secular minority. This was true even in agricultural colonies where the workers of the Second Aliyah sought employment.

The need to throw off the yoke of tradition appears to have been greater, given this background, than the need to embrace it, especially when the notion that religious tradition could be "interpreted" or "secularized" seemed, to people like Brenner, too much like Talmudic casuistry. He regarded such casuistry as the essence of intellectual dishonesty, hypocrisy, and deviousness, a conscious disregard for the true nature of religion. If Brenner judged anything to be more despicable than religion — which was at least an authentic hypocrisy — it was the quasi-religion of reformers and interpreters of various kinds including Ahad Ha-Am and A. D. Gordon. In his estimation, such attempts were not authentic, even as a form of piety: if you want religion, take it as it is; don't try encasing its initial hypocrisy into yet another one. Here, too, Brenner was a typical representative of the atheist stance dominant in Eretz Israel of that period. The only *authentic* expression of Jewish religiosity — which they loved to hate — was the religion of the ultra-Orthodox. The more ultra-Orthodox, the more authentic; the more authentic, the more they abhorred it. They could not imagine that they might have recourse to its values or symbols.

It is clear that Brenner's critique of religion and tradition was not theoretical or philosophical but rather descriptive and existential. In his journalistic attacks, he had recourse to the descriptive mode. His most trenchant article about the negation of the Diaspora was a sweeping essay called, "Mendele in Three Volumes." In his addenda, he wrote that he had tried to summarize experiential, cultural and religious descriptions of the eastern European Jewish town as he found them in the realistic-sarcastic story-telling of Mendele Mocher Seforim's books, *The Beggar's Book, Vale of Tears, Travels of Benjamin III,* and *My Mare.* It was a painful, derisive portrayal of the culture of poverty that existed in the small towns of the

Pale of Settlement: hunger, whining supplication, begging, an idleness that was spiritually and ethically dissolute, corruption — all the direct result of poverty and cruel repression by the authorities.

Certainly exile. What blame did Jewish religion or rabbinic leadership have in all this? Why did Mendele (and Brenner even more) single them out as the most noxious elements of the Diasporic situation? The answer may be detected in the way religion used its spiritual powers to deal with the material distress of the Jews — their repression by the authorities and the pogroms unleashed by the Russian people; however, it was also implicit in the way in which religion did not even venture to confront these afflictions. In Brenner's view, the spiritual tools of the rabbinate were used to give *spiritual compensation* for material suffering thereby preventing a stark consciousness of the real conditions of Jewish existence. In Brenner's opinion, religion obscured the factual basis of poverty, repression and persecution, blurring the very realization that was a precondition for appropriate response. In doing so, religion created spiritual distortions that resulted in disorientation and a break from reality, convoluted thinking filled with fantasies and delusions.

As a result of religion's position of evading confrontation, the people were handicapped in their ability to incorporate information, skills, and the types of appropriate activity necessary to effectively struggle against the sources of poverty. In Brenner's view, religion itself was a kind of poverty: the knowledge it proclaimed was a kind of ignorance; the truth it taught a kind of sacred lie; and, worst of all, instead of facing poverty and repression so as to vanquish them or escape from them, religion became their collaborator. Religion became a prison in the face of life, a method for suppressing the natural, earthly survival instinct of its believers. In other words, Brenner and Mendele perceived of religion not only as a product of exile, but as one of its causes as well. The claim that the Jewish people's survival for thousands of years was due to religion may have been true, but religion was also the cause for the survival of exile. Significantly then, if the time was ripe for the Jews to redeem themselves from exile, the time had come to first be rid of religion.

Brenner had this position in common with Mendele while he was still in the Diaspora, and Brenner's views were confirmed by the reality he found in Eretz Israel. The question has been asked, was it not religion that maintained the Jewish connection to Eretz Israel and the Hebrew language? Was it not religion that tended the flame of messianic hope and excited an occasional effort to *propel history*, to go to Eretz Israel thereby actually effecting redemption? In effect, was it not religion that laid the foundations for Zionism, including secular Zionism? Brenner's answer was a categorical and forceful, "No." His factual, indisputable proof was the old Yishuv in Eretz Israel: this community of Jews, founded on a fanatic, religious love of Eretz Israel, was a despicable continuation of the Diaspora *shtetl* from which he had fled: the same pan-handling, idleness, degeneration and the same misshapen mind and heart. Before they went into exile, the Jews, as all other peoples, were rooted in their land and language, and acted out of a drive for worldly success. These were the natural circumstances. Eretz Israel was not invented by religion, nor was the Hebrew language, nor the drive for a successful mundane life. True, religion had retained a memory of these elements, but not the elements themselves. Religion achieved this by transforming the temporal homeland into "the Holy Land," by converting the national language into a "sacred tongue," and by altering ordinary sovereignty — the worst of illusions — into a "Messianic" state. This being the case, clearly the realization of Zionism was contingent upon the revolution so opposed by the old Yishuv: to recognize Eretz Israel as the terrestrial homeland which was intended to grow food, to relate to the Hebrew language as a medium for daily usage, to turn the worship of God into unadorned labor and messianism into straightforward political independence. Zionism, therefore, had to insist on Eretz Israel and on Hebrew; it had to redeem these values from the hold of the Orthodox, from the Jews of the old Yishuv who prayed in an Ashkenazi dialect, spoke Yiddish in their daily intercourse, and who opposed the secular settlement of Eretz Israel.

What could replace religion? Or did anything have to come in its stead? If "the naked truth" and "chasm-like despair" which Brenner and many of his comrades spoke of is examined, a religious dimension can, nonetheless, be found in their thoughts; apparently, paradoxically, this is what replaced religion in the stormy spiritual life of those who drank thirstily from Brenner's writings, finding strength there.

Brenner and his comrades were far from a romantic idealization of reality in Eretz Israel. On the contrary, they insisted that there must not be any idealization at all. Literature as well as ideology were expected to describe the truth and document it in all of its cruel nakedness. The encounter with the homeland did not give them a sense of home; the encounter with nature in agricultural labor could not arouse a compensatory sense of romantic experience. Their poverty was a real poverty. The desolation was far greater than anything they had experienced in exile. But in their minds, if a pioneer had made aliyah to Eretz Israel in order to liberate himself and his people from the despairing atmosphere of exile, he should have known this in advance and accepted as the truth. He had to confront reality as it was; under no circumstances could he return to a Diaspora stance. The real difference between Eretz Israel and the Diaspora was that Eretz Israel was the testing ground. In Eretz Israel, one was compelled to face the naked truth, the truth about the state of the nation, the truth about the condition of the Jew. Yes, the truth about what people can do to help themselves and to help others. Even the positive ability of people is limited; they are after all only human. Even the righteous among them cannot be righteous when they are enveloped in poverty and distress.

The courageous person can recognize the bitter truth and still act honestly, work honestly in the face of little hope, and extend decent comradely help. All this as a result of finding within oneself the irrational strength of the will to live. At the threshold of despair, this fragment is all one can hope for. Indeed, Brenner did speak of despair as the only avenue to a hope which, though it may not profit, still has a redeeming value.

Brenner's existential response was reiterated in his rebellion against religious belief and its sweet illusions. Perhaps in this way he lived a spiritual life of inverted faith: if not through religion than against it. An honest man in his generation, Brenner was sufficiently profound to see the paradox that ensnared him. It is inconceivable that he did not know that the elements in his literary creativity flowed from an atmosphere of Jewish religious life, or from those who had been religious so that the texture of their lives was infused with Jewish culture and the vocabulary of Jewish religious literature. He employed these sources and lived them, even as he negated them. He knew that he held these sources in common with the readers of his generation who extracted, precisely from the starkness of the truth he advocated, a kind of spiritual wealth. They found a meaning in the very loss of meaning which he described, a strength greater than hope from the bereavement and failure which he saw everywhere. But if this is the case, it means that Brenner functioned by virtue of the same religious themes that he rejected, that he did not want to transmit; his negative message resulted in affirmation. What could his young followers, born in Eretz Israel without a personal experience of the themes he negated, make of Brenner's writings? What did he transmit to them as the positive content of a life of the spirit?

Brenner's response was straightforward and direct: a modern Hebrew literature existed, and it could serve as the foundation. In addition, the best of the secular cultural heritage of Europe should be translated for the younger generation. Just as science and technology were translated, so literature, thought, theater and art must be translated and integrated into the culture to serve as a basis for the new Hebrew literature, new thought, and new art, reflecting the experience of the people in its homeland and sustaining its spiritual life. Jewish selfhood? Certainly. Whatever was created for independent Jewish life, whatever came from that life would be "Judaism." No norm was needed that would define Judaism in advance because the essential thing was that the Jewish people would discharge the full responsibility for its own life.

Chapter Seventeen

THE JEWISH FOLK CULTURE OF ERETZ ISRAEL

Among the writers of his day, no one better expressed the world-view and experience of immigrants to Palestine, during the second and third waves of aliyah, than Y.H. Brenner; nor did anyone have as great an impact on their ideology. Yet even as the Halutzim lived the ideology he articulated — on the highest spiritual plane — and fully understood his message that Zionist realization was a secular way of life, they felt something meaningful was missing, something of transcendent significance beyond the secular plane; something they would be able to transmit to the generations that followed after them.

There are times when secularity is overshadowed, when even the most hardened, worldly ideologies are put to the test. The pioneers rebelled against religion and threw off the yoke of tradition. Did that imply that as workers or as people with a social vision the Sabbath had lost all meaning for them? Could they go without celebrating their marriages, the birth of their children, or their times of mourning? True, prayers in a synagogue, *kashrut*, blessings and other such rituals *had* lost their meaning, indeed, angered them, and they protested vehemently against them; however, did the rejection extend to such festivals as Passover, Shavuot, Sukkot, Hanukkah, Purim, Tu bi-Shevat — had these also lost all meaning? On the contrary, these holidays assumed a renewed meaning that stemmed from a life of Zionist realization in Eretz Israel. It is true that Rosh Hashanah and Yom Kippur were spurned as days of synagogue worship, but did the memory of a parent's death no longer touch their hearts? Were they no longer impelled to conduct a yearly accounting of the actions between man and his fellow, or between man and his society? And in general, did they have no need to respond to events of great joy or great sorrow, of achievement or of sacrifice that broke the pattern of days?

On the contrary. It would appear that just because the collective life of the community was so central to the culture of realization — a culture that placed socialization as an ideal and not merely a means — that festive occasions were essential as permanent points of reference in the cycle of time, occasions when individuals could renew their contact with the community and express feelings of belonging and sublime comradeship. Whether or not they thought about it on the ideological or political plane that was rooted in socialism, the absence of the Jewish home of their childhood, of family life and community were decidedly felt, and impacted directly on the emotional and personal level. Casting about for an alternative, the early settlers found it in meetings and gatherings. They attempted a partial reconstruction of a core social experience that had been central to the religious culture against which they had rebelled, particularly the experience of the Hasidic *hevruta* (fellowship). Frequently, there were moments when the sensation of loss broke out as a full, living memory, painful as a wound. A new social norm was needed which would enable the celebration of traditional occasions in an existential context that appealed to familial, community, and national emotions, albeit without the direct religious overtones to which they objected.

These were people who came from the ordinary folk, so the spontaneous solution sprang from the popular culture: primarily Hasidic songs and dances, and holiday folklore. Yet the articulated cultural norm (which demanded something beyond spontaneity) had to be relevant to a world view and a scale of national, social values that were the underpinnings of a life of Zionist realization. A theory was called for that could shape the totality of norms into the image of an overall culture.

The creative expressions that evolved in the course of years, by dint of many arguments and uncertainties, are known to this day. Outstanding examples are the Passover *haggadot* and the Shavuot *omer* [sheaf-presentation] festivals of the kibbutzim, tree planting ceremonies at Tu bi-Shevat, parades and dramatic presentations at Hanukkah. Each of these was resplendent with poetic and literary richness, music, drama and dance. At the same time, there was an underlying theory which provided a common denominator for these celebrations as an integral segment of the endeavor for Zionist realization and as part of an overall historic understanding of the development of Jewish culture. The influential thinker who provided the basis for the theory was Micha Josef Berdyczewski (1856–1921).

Reading Berdyczewski's work, it becomes apparent that there is a cultural link between the Hebrew Labor Movement and the Hovevei Zion Movement both of which stemmed from the Eastern European Haskalah. The radical, secular Hebrew movement, which arose out of a bitter critique of rabbinic Judaism, adopted Baruch Spinoza as its modern philosopher-teacher of Judaism. It did this by giving his ideas a national, political proto-Zionist interpretation. Exponents of this approach included such enlightened thinkers as Rabbi Avraham Krochmal (1818–1889), Yehoshua Heschel Schor 1818–1895), Shlomo Rubin (1823–1910), and Fabius Miezes (1824–1894).

131

Orthodox Jewry had responded by ostracizing Baruch Spinoza whom they regarded as a dangerous heretic, calling him "Aḥer" (likening him to Elisha ben Avuyah, a well known heretic of the Mishnaic period.*) Nonetheless, the main thrust of the national wing of the secular Hebrew movement emphasized Spinoza's interpretation of the Law of Moses as a secular, political theory; indeed Spinoza was the first thinker in modern times to promote the notion that the Jewish people could return to political life in its own country.** They related to the ostracized Spinoza as a Jewish philosopher of worth despite the fact that he had broken away from established Judaism. From earliest time there had been an alternative Jewish culture (and an alternative Jewish concept) that went beyond rabbinic Judaism whose focus was almost exclusively on Talmudic halakhah (summarized in the *Shulḥan Arukh*). This parallel culture was essentially political and mundane, close to nature, with an affinity to the natural as opposed to the supernatural. It continued as a subterranean stream in the Jewish people's culture, although after the failure of the Bar Kokhba rebellion it was repressed and severely limited by the rabbinic establishment.

Haskalah thinkers equated the rabbinic establishment with the clerical establishment of the Catholic Church. Just as the time had come for enlightened Christians to rebel against the clericalism of the Church, they believed the time had come to defy their own rabbinic establishment, to throw off the yoke of religion and uncover the secular alternative. But they had no need to go outside historic Judaism nor beyond the precincts of its culture; they could find their paradigm within Judaism itself for from its beginning, the Jewish people had been a temporal people. It had not been established either in Egypt or in Sinai but in its homeland — the Land of Israel — and its original statutes and ordinances were the common law of the people. Its practices were those of a nation which intended to succeed and flourish in the mundane world.

Against the background of its struggle with rabbinic Judaism in the 19th century, the radical secular Haskalah regarded Hasidism (its contemporary) as its bitterest enemy because the latter was a movement for the renewal of religious mysticism. But by the end of the century, it became evident that a remarkable parallel existed between the two movements — both of them were critical of rabbinic Judaism because of its attitude to the common folk. Similarities appeared to be more meaningful than differences. Suddenly, upon deeper observation, Hasidic pantheism which tried to unify

---

* The tragic career of Elisha ben Avuyah is sympathetically recreated in Milton Steinberg's historical novel, *As A Driven Leaf.* (LL)

** See Spinoza, *Theololgical-Political Treatise,* end of Chapter 3.

temporal and spiritual experience through its worship in sensual-corporeal ways (*avodah be-gashmiut*) appeared surprisingly similar to the pantheism of Spinoza. Solomon Maimon, a contemporary of Mendelssohn, noted the startling resemblance, and Moses Hess, who considered himself — both in general terms and in his Jewish-Zionist thought — a disciple of Spinoza, developed the notion into a full theory.

It was at this juncture that Berdyczewski evolved his approach to the development of modern Jewish thought. Influenced by Schopenhauer and Nietzsche, but in sharp distinction to Ahad Ha-Am, he developed his theory of "transvaluation"* which posited a radical continuation of the Haskalah rebellion against rabbinic Judaism, together with a search for alternatives to it within the culture of the Jewish people. Berdyczewski regarded Hasidism as one of the most impressive and realistic expressions of the temporal alternative to rabbinic Judaism.

Brenner regarded Berdyczewski as an elder brother, even as his guide in literary undertakings, criticism and polemical journalism. There are grounds to assume that the sense of closeness to Berdyczewski was rooted in their common, existential rebellion against the religious-rabbinic ambiance of the small Jewish town in eastern Europe and its culture of poverty; against its repressive nature and the restraints it placed on natural life. This was coupled with their grim feeling that outside the Jewish village and the ghetto, no temporal alternative awaited a young yeshiva student who had been bitten by the Enlightenment. There was only a state of being in which he was cut off from Jewish life, in which there was loneliness and alienation in cold, rejecting surroundings. It was out of this despair that Brenner made aliyah to Eretz Israel. Berdyczewski, however, despaired of the hope that as a writer he could find conditions of work in the Land of Israel where everything had to be devoted to physical realization. For the sake of his literary work, he remained in Germany for the rest of his life. Clearly, despite their ideological closeness, there was a profound existential difference between the two men, and this difference found expression in two complementary ways: the vivid consciousness found in Berdyczewski's work, *Ha-Kera she-ba-Lev* (*The Sundering of the Heart*) and its implications, and the sharp awareness of the natural origins of the religious experience.

What was this sundering of the heart? It was a sense that despite the negative attitude that existed towards ultra-Orthodox belief, an observant Torah way of life, or a scholastic Talmudic erudition devoid of universal

---

* Based on Nietzsche's *Umwertung aller Werte* ("transvaluation" or "revaluation" of all values) — proclaimed in so many words in the last line of *Antichrist*, and developed as a theme especially in *Zarathustra, Genealogy of Morals*, and *The Will to Power*, Part III. See Ahad Ha-Am's critique of Berdiczewski's Nietzschean tendencies in his essay, "Transvaluation of Values."

vistas, a former yeshiva student who had been schooled on these sources from infancy had internalized them, so that now they unavoidably shaped his personality, character, feelings, habits, and his accustomed ways of expression. The internalization had been so far reaching, he could never be free of them. He would remain a believer in the depths of his soul even if his speech, attire, and life-style were all characteristic of an atheist who has thrown off the yoke of the commandments. Such a person was bound to make a public display of his apostasy, and his behavior would be the cause of amazement, sorrow, and anger in his religious surroundings. But, in fact, he would be the most grievous victim of his own behavior; his suffering would be immeasurably greater than that of his erstwhile community because despite himself he understood and even identified with the pious world. He repudiates Orthodoxy, and he is frightened by his own denial; he is an apostate alarmed at the destruction he himself has unleashed. There is an unbridgeable gap between the world view which stems from part of his feelings, and the primary religious feeling that preceded them.

There is some evidence in Brenner's work that he, too, experienced such a sundering of the heart. There are many elements in his fiction drawn from resources he had internalized during his early religious education. At a later stage he externalized them by giving them artistic expression. A psychological note seems evident at this point: Brenner was an author of great sensitivity to the sorrow of others, yet he spoke against religion in provocative, irritating terms which were regarded by Orthodox readers as unusually impudent, impious and cruel (and Brenner was well aware of this.) Certainly, then, his intention was to cause aggravation and sorrow rather than to elucidate or persuade. His behavior makes no sense — unless he was attacking himself. Apparently he had a need to convince himself of his position, to act out his rejection so that he could free himself from the negative elements he found in his opponents but which had become ingrained within him as well. It was because he saw the negative aspects of his adversaries reflected in himself that he so abhorred the reflection.

However, the differences between Berdyczewski and Brenner were substantive, not merely stylistic. Berdyczewski constantly reminded his readers of the dichotomy in his soul, bewailing his torment. But also, and more importantly, for Berdyczewski the process of internalizing the religious, rabbinic, and pietistic elements generated a sense of positive identification with them. The differences can be described in the following way. Even as he internalized it, Brenner hated the religious content he had been forced to practice in his youth; consequently a sense of nausea at himself accompanied the internalization. Berdyczewski loved the content from the start and identified with it from his childhood. His criticism arose as he matured and discovered the price one had to pay: what one had to give up for this attachment. Consequently he retained his love for religious content even when he loathed it and did not for one moment think, as Brenner consistently did, that religious belief was rooted in fraudulent experience that was nothing more than hypocrisy and pretense. Berdyczewski could never agree with such a description. He was convinced that Orthodox religiosity, whether in its rabbinic, political projection or in its mystical, Hasidic manifestation, was an authentic psychological phenomenon even when it had negative consequences.

This being the case, Berdyczewski, the secular thinker, had to explain the source of the legitimacy of the religion he fought against, and as a secular thinker he had to offer an alternative of a secular religiosity. This was the second essential difference between him and Brenner. Berdyczewski was consciously a religious secularist; he sought a remedy not only for his secularity but for his religiosity as well.

What did Berdyczewski perceive religion's role to be in cultural creativity? In this context, it is useful to note the essential difference that existed between him and Nietzsche, the great rebel against both Christianity and Judaism. It is a common error to describe Berdyczewski as "the father of Jewish Nietzscheanism," although he did adopt the phrase "transvaluation" as well as some of its terminology from him. However, regarding religious phenomena, in no way did Berdyczewski follow Nietzsche. On the contrary, he was much closer to Emil Durkheim, a French sociologist of religion (of Orthodox Jewish ancestry). Durkheim saw religion as an authentic phenomenon rooted in man's social nature, and as such it was not only the by-product of his actual psychological experience but a necessary component of all cultures.

According to Berdyczewski (and Durkheim) God is a symbolic image of great, absolute emotional-tangible force. In effect, God is created by the inter-human collective. The process takes place in the psyche of the individual as a shared experience which supersedes the boundaries of individuality. Individuals undergo an intensive collective experience as a kind of integration with other individuals into a collective being which they experience as an independent entity. This entity is "greater" than the sum of its parts. The togetherness of the family posits the family as a reality which is greater than themselves; the togetherness of the community, the tribe, and the people are also perceived as realities that are greater than the sums of their parts. Individuals undergo an actual encounter with these spiritual entities in their communal, ritual experiences, and these are presences that are both personal and tangible which transcend them. Physically unseen of course, these encounters are definitely perceived in the unity of the community; they are actualized by means of symbols and take on revelatory aspects in the imagination and the emotions of those who are nurtured by them. At such a time, individuals feel the divine presence as if within themselves, and they subject themselves to its authority and discipline. Berdyczewski demonstrated this by a paradox: human beings are prepared to sacrifice their lives in war for their family, their tribe or their people despite the fact that the survival instinct which, by its very nature is individual rather than collective, continues to operate in them predisposing them to run for their lives and seek only their own welfare. Neither external law nor fear of the state are the reasons for obedience on the part of citizens to commands that cause pain or danger to life, rather it is the fact that they are in the thrall of a sublime authority which they perceive of as being simultaneously directly above them and within themselves.

According to Berdyczewski's doctrine, God is therefore a kind of collective super-ego which encompasses the legislative will of organic societies such as the family, tribe, and people, and which exists above and beyond the individuals who make up these societies. God is the *conscience* of the collective ego repeatedly internalized by each individual as a personal conscience that imposes social obligations on him. The God of Israel, too, the One God, Creator of the Universe and its Master, is nontheless the particular God of the Jewish people; He is the symbolic likeness possessing the absolute might of the Jewish people (*Knesset Israel*) which appears as a collective presence. This was Berdyczewski's understanding of the notion of covenant between God and His people in accordance with the Torah. In the narrative of Sinaitic revelation, the Biblical myth presents the essence of the collective experience as one stage in the establishment of the Jewish people. Clearly the beginning was not a private matter. God appeared at the center of the life of a people that had united after experiencing a wondrous liberation from bondage in Egypt. The people assembled for the ceremony of the covenant, and God was revealed within and transcending the people as its law-giving and directive will. The historic experience by which individuals were elevated into the unity of a people was shaped in the collective memory as a mythic narrative, and was embodied in a concrete symbol: God gave the Torah to His people at Sinai and led them in the desert to His promised land. Subsequently, the memory was transmitted from generation to generation through pragmatic dedication to the study of Torah and observance of its commandments. In every generation, God is revealed anew to each individual who receives the Torah. This ritual, coupled with study of the Torah, united the people, instructing their lives even in their dispersion as they moved from one exile to another.

We will return to Berdyczewski's reflections about the historic significance of the covenant at Sinai and to the connection between it and other covenantal rituals in the history of the Jewish people. What must be emphsized here is that as long as the unity of the people and its way of life was inspired by the Torah and the commandments rigorously observed, the actual experience of the Giving of the Law was transmitted and was periodically renewed. Each individual entered into the covenant and it was repeatedly imposed on him as the fate of an individual within the collective body. Berdyczewski's own experience testified to this. But when the circumstances of historic fate changed and the gates of the ghetto were breached, exposing Jews to the winds of secularism, unity began to break down; the collective experience of increasingly large numbers of individuals changed. They discovered other cultures, other groupings in the surrounding peoples, and began rebelling against the obsessive despotism of the Jewish collective that continued to be portrayed as "the God of Israel." They found that Jewish cohesiveness obstructed them on their road out to freedom, and to mundane experiences. Consequently, Berdyczewski regarded his as a generation in transition. He was forced to undergo the difficult spiritual crisis that stemmed from the destruction of the collective unity of *Knesset Israel* — that is, the destruction of rabbinic religious culture. This was how he defined the problem, and the solution he sought for it.

Before pursuing Berdyczewski's solution, it is necessary to examine his theory of how religion comes into being. If God is the embodiment of the people's collective ego, then organized religion and all its ideological, value-laden, symbolic, and normative manifestations are certainly products of the national culture, so that a religion carries within it characteristic attributes of its culture. The image each people has of God, and the qualitative relation-ship between God and each individual within the people, is directly shaped by the people's historic circumstances, particularly by the pattern of the culture as it develops in all spheres. Thus it is possible to understand the differences that exist between religions, particularly monotheism as it was constituted by the prophets of Israel and the religions-of-nature which, by and large, tended towards various forms of pantheism.

The uniqueness of prophetic-Biblical monotheism does not consist in the idea of a single Godhead (pantheism too seeks unity) but in absolute spiritual transcendentalism. Monotheism oriented its followers in the direction of absolute ethical and ritual sanctity, which overcomes the mundane and transcends nature; halakhic monotheism, which the Sages further developed in the footsteps of the prophets, embodied the absolute spiritual ideal in a total way of life. By comparison, the religions of nature oriented their followers in the opposite direction: the expansion of worldly life, prosperity, diversity, multi-faceted expressions, freedom, and the vistas that these offered. Cultures that maintained a constant and close connection with the particular natural circumstances in their environment developed in this way, and they reflected the natural necessities of their peoples. Religions established states, legislated and imposed their laws, led nations into wars, even insisted on the self-sacrifice of the individual for the good of his people. Invariably, religion's motive was plain — the will to power in all spheres: domination of knowledge, of natural resources, of the sensual pleasures, of esthetics and art. The gods, or the pantheistic gods that were part of nature, were tangible symbols of the complex of goals that a life of nature strove for in order to shape a harmonious order. Not the subjugation of life's goals to a single aim which transcended life, but rather the balanced regulation of all of life's aspirations. In this sense, Israelite Biblical monotheism was the exception to the rule. According to Berdyczewski, it included elements which provoked and irritated but at the same time were remarkable and wondrous: Judaism managed to fashion a supra-natural culture for the entire nation which it governed despite the polar conflict between a supernatural goal and the natural inclinations of down to earth people.

Indeed, the argument that Berdyczewski had with rabbinic Orthodoxy was not a disagreement about the validity of religious phenomena in general; it was rather a profound and bitter argument over the specific kind of monotheistic religion that developed in the halakhic Judaism of the sages, who were the inheritors of the prophets. Furthermore, Berdyczewski's trenchant analysis did not use the tools of theology but employed the tools of phenomenology and cultural critique. What he rejected in rabbinic Judaism were the various aspects of its negation of nature: the halakhic monotheism of the sages distanced the Jewish people from the natural sciences, from the independent creation of a material civilization, and from the plastic arts which aspire to esthetics as an end. The sole aim of rabbinic Judasim was transcendental sanctity, achieved through asceticism; that is, the compartmentalization and repression of physical passions and the spiritual interests they engender. According to Berdyczewski, this was the rationale for the halakhic way of life and the rationale for rabbinic Torah studies: exclusive devotion to a metaphysical aim, and to sanctity; the suppression of physical drives and restrictions of an intellectual interest in nature or the perfection of tools by which to control nature.

Clearly, the prophets ran up against the mundane aspirations of the monarchies in Judea and Israel, as did the sages, subsequently, during the reigns of the Hasmoneans and Herod, which led directly to destruction and exile. Transcendental monotheism emerged against a background of exile and, according to Berdyczewski, exile was also the only form of national existence in which it was possible to realize the ideal of sanctity while avoiding constant collisions with the institution of an independent state, and with secular elements in the people. In exile, the Jewish people was no longer responsible for a civilization which would provide for its modest needs. Such chores were managed by other peoples, as if destined for such service, while the Jews as "the Chosen People" could turn their attention to a concern for the sacred. As long as it was not too severe, suffering, persecution, and repression by the surrounding peoples did not prevent the Jews from practicing their religious devotion. On the contrary, they helped to channel all of life's aspirations toward the spiritual ideal of holiness that compensated for all the deprivation.

Berdyczewski's call for transvaluation must be understood in light of this criticism of the exilic and despotic character of halakhic culture. He called on his people to return to nature, to return to the natural values of life, to return to a natural culture: to the sciences and technology as elements of empowerment, to this-worldly polity, to the ideal of beauty in art, and to the hetrogeneity of temporal life. Of course, all these had an overall religious significance for him: detachment from tyrannical, halakhic monotheism and from the notion of transcendental sanctity so as to return to a pantheistic, natural religion. It must be emphasized again that unlike Brenner, Berdyczewski did not declare war on the religious attitude to life as a totality. His battle was against the ascetic, halakhic monotheistic attitude to natural life.

Did he call upon his people, as individuals, to leave the religion that had maintained the nation throughout its history, to convert to another religion? Did he propose the adoption of some type of modern, secular "paganism" or unleashing a romantic revival of an archaic Canaanism? If truth be told, the pagan or Canaanite orientations are latent in Berdyczweski's theories no less than they are found in the "romantic renaissance" of political Zionism but Berdyczewski as well as his followers skirted around it. He understood the dangers of isolation and excommunication.

Berdyczewski fought a consistent and bitter battle against Ahad Ha-Am whose views were based on rabbinic culture, a culture whose hold he wished to prolong despite his criticism of it. In one key matter, however, he agreed with Ahad Ha-Am completely: the secret of a culture's vitality is its historic continuity. A culture develops organically from its origins, and national self-hood is maintained through the continuity of a national, cultural consciousness from generation to generation. This is especially true when the effort to maintain a national culture comes in the face of the advanced developments of the Modern Era. Clearly, the Jewish people could not begin a new culture by detaching itself from its past. Neither could it return to its primitive beginnings; perforce, it would have to accept the culture of another people; and, even if this was done in its native land and in its own independent political framework, it would assimilate and disappear.

But for Berdyczewski just as it was natural for one to want to continue as an individual, it was as natural to want to sustain the collective, independent ego of the nation, at least as long as it continued to exist in practice. This being the case it is only natural to embrace historical continuity. Such an attachment is the necessary norm for an ongoing national identity.

It is clear then that transvaluation should maintain the historic, cultural identity of the people. Such a solution was contingent upon a positive response to the question of whether or not this exilic people had, within its own culture, a religious-cultural alternative to halakhic monotheism, an alternative linked to its own origins. Could it indeed reconstitute its culture around a continuum of the natural, folk-like state of being that had marked it from the beginning?

For Berdyczewski this question was a drive for research which surely must arrive at a positive conclusion; he knew his search would not go unrewarded. During his early years of Jewish education, he had directly experienced positive aspects of Judaism's folk expression, and he continued to identify with those aspects after his rebellion. He grew up in a Hasidic environment and was acquainted with its pantheistic tendency and adherence to values that were clearly part of a natural folk culture: the joy of life — its openness to song and dance, and its affection for folk tales. Hasidism was an explosive eruption against the notion of a transcendental sanctity and an affirmation of the fullness of temporal life even as it remained with the bounds of halakhah. His first step as a writer, therefore, was in search of a solution to the crisis of disassociation that the heroes in his work faced. Hasidism offered him a vital, creative story-telling tradition possessed of a lyrical quality and a philosophic insight that could serve as a footing for his work. Second, even if he had not directly experienced an alternate culture, he had to assume the existence of a natural life, against which rabbinic Judaism had conducted a stubborn struggle throughout the generations, not only outwardly but within itself. Ultimately, despite exile, the Jews were indeed a natural people. If the Jewish people existed, then by definition, a natural culture persisted within it, even if this culture was suppressed, diminished, and concealed.

Moreover, in Berdyczewski's view, natural culture co-existed with the rabbinic culture that oppressed it because neither could do without the other. He thought it stood to reason that prophetic and rabbinic Judaism could develop only on an infrastructure of a natural culture that historically and ontologically preceded them both because nature precedes spirit. While Judaism fought against natural culture, it also needed it in order to survive in the temporal world. Within certain bounds, therefore, it tolerated natural culture; subsequently, having no choice, it did what it could to obscure what it had accepted and allowed to persist, granting it limited status. Indeed, we can discover signs of its existence in many Jewish sources, some of them unique to the folk culture but most integrated into the sacred sources of rabbinic Judaism itself: in certain strata of the Bible, certain strata of the Mishnah, in Talmudic legends, in mysticism, and in the literature and philosophy of the Middle Ages.

If one approaches these sources with the proper prior expectation, the worldly variant in them is easily discovered. It becomes clear that the Orthodox sources which rabbinic exegesis (as well as the Science of Judaism in the 19th century) presented as a unitary continuity of thought are but an arena for stormy conflicts between adversarial cultural trends; these trends sprang up anew in every generation even as they drew on earlier sources and were influenced by Jewry's encounter with changing temporal cultures in the environment. In effect, the annals of Jewish culture are the history of an ongoing confrontation between two alternative cultures which were in conflict throughout the history of the Jewish people. Generally, rabbinic Judaism held the upper hand and repressed any coupling with folk pantheism under the heavy cloak of esoteric lore. But even under such conditions the dissident version could persist and be transmitted over the generations through its own modes.

Berdyczewski's critique of 19th century Science of Judaism has been noted. Because of its adherence to rational idealism, the Science of Judaism showed a preference for essential ideas of the prophetic-rabbinic school. Berdyczewski, as Buber and Gershom Scholem after him, claimed that the Science of Judaism's modern studies were no less biased or obsessive than rabbinic Judaism. Its scholars completely overlooked and obscured the richest and most vital strata of Jewish culture because of a great passion to assimilate. Research directed at a revitalization of Jewish culture in the interest of temporal, secular renewal rather than assimilation had to look in the opposite direction. Here, too, transvaluation was called for, and Berdyczewski approached his task as a student of the sources of Judaism by declaring that he had two complementary aims. One, to prove that an alternative, natural Jewish culture existed within and beyond rabbinic sources; two, to present the content of that alternate culture in a way that would enable its resources to be utilized for the creation of a natural, modern Jewish culture.

His study resulted in two wide ranging works: the book, *Mi-Mekor Yisrael* (*From Jewish Sources*) which is a compilation of Jewish folk stories, and *Sinai U-Gerizim* (*Mount Sinai and Mount Gerizim*), a comprehensive historical-scientific study. In the second work, Berdyczewski refined his theories and proposed an entire historiosophic design of the twin-layered development of the Jewish people's culture.

According to Berdyczewski, as early as the Biblical writings, one finds two parallel and contradictory historical traditions. Using disingenuous techniques, late rabbinic redactors attempted to disguise the duality but it is easy to detect it and to point out the contradictions and discrepancies. The tradition most emphasized by such rabbinic editorial efforts is the story of the founding of the Jewish people as a result of the Exodus from Egypt and the people's acceptance of the Covenant at Sinai. But, if one examines the meaning of the historic strata in the Bible, particularly the books of Joshua and Judges, one discovers another tradition as well, according to which the Israelite tribes lived in the Land of Israel continuously, even taking into account the descent to Egypt of some of the tribes. The struggle to settle throughout the land, while displacing other people who also tried to occupy it, was accomplished primarily by the tribes who remained in the homeland. From their standpoint the constitutive, unifying national event did not take place at Mount Sinai but at the covenantal ceremony in Shechem opposite Mount Gerizim, a more natural and certainly more ancient rendition. It is the original national narrative, although the account of the Covenant at Sinai also includes a historic nucleus which relates to a small part of the people that went to Egypt and returned to its Land.

The most important implication of this is that the Jewish people was *born*, as all other natural peoples, in its homeland and that the Covenant of Gerizim enacted by Joshua was the undertaking of a military man, a great conqueror and settler, rather than the enterprise of the Prophet Moses who enacted the supernatural covenant at Sinai against the background of an exodus from exile. In other words, we are confronted with one tradition in which the establishment of a people is an act of natural and ordinary temporal statecraft conducted by a military leader, and a second tradition in which the establishment of a "holy people" is brought about by the prophet of the spiritual one-and-unique God whose coming-to-rule can be explained only against a background of exile and enslavement. In the first instance, there is a tradition of prosaic statehood which documents the development of a popular, natural culture. In the second instance, we have a monotheistic-prophetic spiritual tradition which was superimposed ex-post facto on the mundane tradition, overcame it, enacting its own legislation after it had undermined it and returned the people to exile. It is this tradition that was created in the Egyptian exile and prevailed in the Babylonian exile.

The confrontation was repeated during the period of the Second Commonwealth. The tradition of Hebraic statehood was reconstituted by the Hasmonean dynasty. But again a conflict arose between the state on one side and the leadership of the sages, and Ezra the Scribe, who were inheritors of the prophets on the other. Nonetheless, it bears noting that in Berdyczewski's opinion, the sages — just as the prophets — did not intend the destruction of statehood and the resulting exile. They only wanted to impose their spiritual legislation on the secular state and use the state for their sacred ends; however, the unavoidable result was rupture, destruction and exile. Consequently, it becomes apparent that as long as the people lived a natural life on its soil, rabbinic tradition had to reconcile itself to the counter tradition and integrate its narrative, historical and value elements into its own system. The struggle was for control, with the Pharisees fighting the Sadducees for leadership of the people. The unavoidable result was destruction and exile again.

The second exile which began with the failure of the Bar Kokhba revolt re-established a monotheistic-halakhic orientation. But even under the circumstances of the second exile, an exile more repressive and bitter than the previous one, it was impossible to fend off natural tendencies or the growth of a folk tradition, particularly against the background of the mundane-religious cultures of their surroundings. The influence of these cultures was especially obvious in the seed-bed of movements that retained pantheistic, mystic or theurgic elements, and in messianic movements that were inspired to occasional tragic attempts at escape from exile and the establishment of a Jewish state. For the most part, rabbinic Judaism opposed these efforts, transforming the vision of redemption into a passive, spiritual expectation. But it could not uproot its foothold among the people. Indeed, under the circumstances of exile, even natural aspirations to redemption underwent a distorting, supernatural transformation. Ultimately, this is what happened in Hasidism as well. The only movements to effect a genuine historic turnabout in the direction of a temporal, natural existence were the secular rebellions of the Enlightenment and of Zionism.

The implications for the situation at the present time, particularly with regard to the realization of Zionism in Eretz Israel, were clear. There existed an option of a rich, natural folk culture embedded in the traditional sources of Judaism. The task for those who favored transvaluation was to mine that option and develop it through study, research, the creation of a literature, art and modern thought which would be nurtured by all the resources available. The return to Eretz Israel would be a resumption of the temporal naturalness of the homeland, and the temporal naturalness of language and traditional sources. This would be accomplished by reuniting with the natural motifs of Eretz Israel that had been preserved in the sources, particularly those of the First and Second Commonwealths, but also those preserved in the Mishnah and the aggadic rabbinic traditions pertaining to the Land of Israel. The flame of temporal-Jewish Messianism was also kept alive in numerous literary sources of the Exile, and in the rich folklore that sprang up there. Such elements must be taught and transmitted as source material for the creation of literature, art and philosophy and a folk ritual that would express the aspiration for a return to the homeland and the ideational efforts required to take root in it. Such a creation would inspire Jews to live the uniqueness of its landscape, to become acquainted and conversant with all its strata, to penetrate its past, to live the cycle of its seasons, and to develop a philosophic and artistic articulation of all of these experiences.

The extent to which the thrust of all this was absorbed by the Hebrew Labor Movement can be seen in the interpretation that was given to the holidays in the cycle of the Jewish year. Using Biblical and Mishnaic sources, a consistent effort was made to reclaim the image of the holidays as festivals of nature or as holidays of national and political independence: Passover as a spring festival and a holiday of national freedom that emphasized the link to the Land; Shavuot to mark bringing in the first fruits when one rejoices at the bounty of the crop; Sukkot as the harvest holiday of all the crops; Tu bi-Shevat as the tree planting festival; Hanukkah as the festival that celebrates the national victory of a people in its land; and Purim as an outburst of worldly joy.

Hikes and excursions sponsored by the schools and youth movements of Labor Israel filled an important cultural function. They resembled a ritual infused with religiosity whose purpose was to reassert the covenant of the people with its land by means of the personal, romantic, experience of youth. The young hikers walked, Bible in hand, striving to rediscover the unique beauty of the country's landscape and the history of the people when it lived in its homeland, the events that were engraved in remnants of the past and were still visible. As it was with the Bible, a special cultural importance was also attributed to the archeology of Eretz Israel, with an attendant ritual motif. Uncovering the Hebrew past was perceived of as a deed that redeemed the authentic history of Eretz Israel and returned it to the consciousness of the people enabling them to make the transition from an exilic history to the history of the homeland.

The impact of Berdyczewski's message was also evident in the curriculum of the Labor Movement's schools. The subjects in which national consciousness was focused were Hebrew, Bible, Hebrew Literature (particularly the literature of the Modern Period which concentrated on the Land of Israel), history of the Jewish people, nature studies and geography of the homeland. In Bible studies, the prophets were taught as the visionary precursors of social justice which was currently being realized in socialism, while the historical books exemplified the rootedness of the people in its homeland and its temporal political life. In contrast, the Torah, particularly its legal codes, was only briefly touched upon. The Bible was also taught as a classic literary work, the source of the revival of the Hebrew language linked to the homeland.

The preferred texts from the literature of the sages were those elements of the aggadah and the halakhah that were connected to agricultural experience and social ethics. From medieval literature, the secular poetry of Spanish Jewry was culled along with its Eretz Israel motifs and the hopes for redemption found in sacred poetry. With regard to history, the periods of the First and Second Commonwealths were taught. In effect, the exilic period skipped over, however, dismissed as the result of a terrible accident, a tragic digression from what the national history was intended to be. Persecution and suffering were described and, of course, the moral drawn from them was the Zionist lesson that preached negation of exile and negation of the exilic pattern of a culture created and reflecting exilic circumstances. The people must return to its land and to its natural state where its continuing chapters would be written as Zionist history.

This was the model of Hebrew culture that developed and flourished in the Eretz Israel of the Hebrew Labor Movement. From a historic viewpoint, it can be said to have had a firm hold on the reality of Eretz Israel as long as agricultural settlement and cultivation of desert land were at the heart of Zionist realization, and as long as it was possible to regard agricultural labor as the basis for an experiential return to nature and to the cycle of its seasons. After the establishment of the State of Israel and the technological industrialization of agriculture, however, the return to Eretz Israel lost its sense of a romantic return to nature and to naturalness. What did prevail was a connection to the country's landscape and nature through hiking (which retained a ritual character) and a regard for archeology which was seen as a profession with a unique national significance. But it was no longer possible on this basis to design a cultural ideal which could shape the national entity and its way of life.

A number of thinkers and educators in the Hebrew Labor Movement sensed the inadequacy and the transient quality of this solution even as it was being implemented. They were particularly exercised by the unsatisfactory link between the Hebrew Yishuv as it developed a culture for itself and the Jewish people in the Diaspora: could a unified Jewry be sustained in the face of a divisive Hebraic culture? Was it possible to skip over segments of historic Jewish continuity and creativity and still retain national identity with only a truncated link to history? These theorists and educators sought a corrective in the thinking of a third Zionist stream — the stream of Spiritual Zionism.

Chapter Eighteen
JUDAISM AS THE TOTALITY OF A NATIONAL HISTORIC CULTURE

Spiritual Zionism developed as Hovevei Zion's critical reaction to the Practical Zionism advocated by Lilienblum and the Political Zionism of Nordau and Herzl. This intermediate position of Hibbat Zion, as exemplified by Ahad Ha-Am (Asher Ginsberg), was actuated by a sense of national responsibility to what the movement regarded as the dangerous approach of others. After careful examination, Ahad Ha-Am concluded that the political and economic circumstances which existed in Eretz Israel did not hold out any hope for solving the "Jewish problem" there. The answer to the economic distress of the Jewish masses in the Pale of Settlement could not be found in Eretz Israel. The problem could only be solved in America. On the basis of scientific analysis, it seemed obvious to Ahad Ha-Am that the notion of bringing most eastern European Jews to Eretz Israel in order to establish a Jewish state there (with the aid of a world power), in the span of one generation, was a mad delusion comparable to the Messianism of Shabbetai Zevi. If such "tidings" were disseminated among the people, encouraging hopes of imminent redemption, the result would be unavoidable disappointment and a crisis of disastrous proportions that would lead to large-scale desertions from Judaism.

In Ahad Ha-Am's measured view, if the Zionist Movement acted cautiously, in several generations it could establish a Jewish community of spiritual quality, one that was economically, socially, culturally, and perhaps even politically, independent. While such an enterprise would undoubtedly be of great value, it would not solve the pressing *physical* problems of the Jewish people; it would address itself only to resolving the dilemma of Judaism in the modern world — the sense of despair and total indifference to remaining Jewish on the part of young Jews which led to assimilation and extinction. In Ahad Ha-Am's view, this was the principal problem of the Jewish people in the modern era. He considered material problems, including racist anti-Semitism, to be transitory. They would disappear in the face of economic, political, and social progress. In contrast, assimilation stemmed primarily and unavoidably precisely from progress, from modernity itself. It was the outcome of cultural secularization. Religion, which had been the Jews' traditional and national means of identity, was being undermined, ultimately to disappear. Religious culture seemed outmoded to young people, retrograde and confined to narrow horizons; whereas the modern, secularized culture of European nations appeared highly attractive. The only solution would be for the Jews to adapt to the secularization of culture by making it their own form of national-cultural identity as well. They had to develop a modern, national, secular culture like that of the progressive peoples in their environment, a goal that could be attained in the national language, in the national homeland, that is, in Eretz Israel.

Ahad Ha-Am began his career as a national thinker with a negative message, *Lo Zeh ha-Derekh* ("The Wrong Path"). Even his second essay, "The Truth from Eretz Israel" was an honest, unsparing, and pessimistic critique of the situation. His alternative plan came later: a call for a *Cultural Center*. An authentically Jewish, yet modern, national culture would be created in Eretz Israel which the progress-seeking younger generation abroad could be proud of, would imitate, and could identify with. To that end, an elite aliyah had to be educated and encouraged of young, enthusiastic men and women of vision who were prepared to undertake the hardships of the pioneering task on behalf of their people. They would establish a community in Eretz Israel capable of sustaining a comprehensive national culture, including a modern, balanced economy and all the stratification necessary for independent existence, and, of course, institutions from kindergarten through university. Sciences would be taught, arts and trades developed, literature and philosophy cultivated. All would be in Hebrew. Clearly the cultural message that would emerge from this Center had to be a new Torah that went out from Zion to the entire people. In other words, the message had to be sufficiently infectious to elicit pride and identity in the hearts of all those Jews who would find the solution to their Jewish problem in the Diaspora.

Indeed, for Ahad Ha-Am, the solution to the problem of Judaism was as urgent as the solution to the Jews' economic problem. Assimilation raged among the younger generation as a fire in a field of thorns. Something had to be done immediately. Obviously, therefore, he did not propose waiting until the Cultural Center was established in Eretz Israel. On the contrary, the cultural-educational confrontation had to begin at once, and in the Diaspora. Ultimately, the prospect for building Eretz Israel as a Cultural Center was dependent on it: youth had to be educated so that they would undertake a national task that called for sacrifice which meant that Jews in the Diaspora would have to pool their spiritual as well as material resources in order to gradually build the national homeland. The first stage was to be educational: the establishment of a network of national, educational institutions in which aliyah would be held high as the ideal goal for the elite among youth. In Ahad Ha-Am's opinion, any educational process worthy of the name communicated an ideological demand, and the process was complete only when the mission was undertaken in practice. The elite, the best students, would dedicate all their energies to the realization of the national goal, becoming leaders by virtue of personal example; others would contribute according to their ability. Even as it was being built, Eretz Israel would thus fulfill the role of a Cultural Center by a process which would require several generations.

It was clear that the principal and immediate thrust in developing a modern Jewish culture had to be directed at creating a secular, national culture. The urgent need was to define that culture, fill it with content so that it provided spiritual and cultural creativity for the people, and demonstrate the ways in which its ideals could be implemented through detailed programs and educational curricula. Ahad Ha-Am considered this his paramount mission.

From the earlier discussion of Micha Josef Berdyczewski and Yosef Haim Brenner, one learns that personal biography is the key to understanding how the crisis of Jewish identity was confronted. In effect, all the solutions offered by these two were a depiction of their actual experiences and personal encounters with the crisis of identity. Because their attempts at finding solutions were acted out in the way they shaped their lives, their life stories can be seen as models of the search after culture. Ahad Ha-Am, in his early essays, appeared to be a modern intellectual who was at home with rational, scientific, pragmatic criteria for evaluating the goals and achievements of Zionism. He took his Jewish national identity for granted, rejecting manifestations of assimilation with an instinctive moral revulsion; at first he saw no need to offer an explanation for his outlook which he regarded almost as axiomatic. Needless to say, what was axiomatic for Ahad Ha-Am was not so for many of his peers, let alone for the younger generation. Therefore he had to analyze the roots of the phenomenon: why had the sense of national identity, so spontaneous and natural for him, been eroded for others? To properly understand his conclusions, the question must be turned around and asked about him. What brought Ahad Ha-Am to a national identity of such force that he equated it with a biological, Darwinian survival instinct?

Not surprisingly, Ahad Ha-Am's social and class origins impacted on his experience and the ideas he stressed. He was educated in a deeply Orthodox, wealthy Jewish family. As was the case with Berdyczewski and Brenner, his Hasidic religious home did not manage to inculcate its spiritual message within him. At a relatively early age, he became critical of the vulgarity of the Hasidic masses. An outstanding scholar who devoted himself to Torah study, he (unlike Berdyczewski) maintained an aristocratic distance from folkways. His intellectualism led him to Maimonides where he discovered the halakhic legitimation for scientific study that brought him to Haskalah, foreign languages and sciences. He accomplished all this through self-study without leaving his parents' home. In this way he was spared the existential dilemmas usually encountered when an individual abandons a religious world view and a traditional way of life. By personality and intellect he tended toward rationalism with the result that he quickly convinced himself of the justice of the positivist, scientific outlook: in his view, the natural sciences had taken over the sphere of religious truth and replaced it. Moreover, he determined that by means of the sciences, particularly psychology, sociology and anthropology, it was possible to explain religious phenomena, beliefs and commandments, and so retain their vessels and change their content.

In his rebellion against religion, Ahad Ha-Am resembled his two younger critics. Divergence resulted from the fact that his parents came from the upper middle class; their wealth not only ensured his higher education, social status and standard of living but enabled him to devote himself to wide ranging literary activity and public life without leaving home. To put it negatively, the poverty that drove most young Jews in Eastern Europe away from the familiar framework of their parents' religious life and sometimes out of the communal structures of Jewish society as well did not effect him. The opposite was true — affluence kept him within the circle. Like Berdyczewski and Brenner, he did go through a crisis of secularization, but without their existential quandaries; most important, he remained within his family which was ultra-Orthodox. Later, in his Odessa years, he found himself within the compass of enlightened wealthy Jewish society most of whom were nationalist, some of whom observed the mitzvot, none of whom were assimilated. It must be emphasized that he did not regard himself as a "Marrano," that is, someone who professed one faith while surreptitiously practicing another; neither did he see himself as schizoid vis à vis his family and society for they allowed him the liberty of involving himself in his own spiritual concerns. True, he was discreet, keeping some of his thoughts and practices to himself. But he did this with Maimonides serving as a model; that is, with a rationale of responsibility for family, communal and ultimately national concerns, and out of consideration for the feelings of people who were close or dear to him.

The fact that it was possible to explain religion — its beliefs and commandments — by recourse to scientific means made it easier for him.

He was not hypocritical: a scientific explanation of the mitzvot did not necessarily lead to invalidating or ridiculing them. On the contrary. An enlightened individual could understand the importance of religion and its commandments for their own time. Subsequently, one could differentiate between beliefs, practices and observances which required change or replacement because they were outmoded, and commandments that retained some direct or indirect benefit and therefore should be kept at least for a certain period. So it was natural that in his attitude toward religious belief on one hand, and toward secular enlightenment on the other, the changes Ahad Ha-Am underwent did not occasion a crisis of identity. From the standpoint of affiliation — familial, social and cultural — he remained a whole Jew exactly as he had always been. As far as he was concerned, there was no difference in the totality, integrity or Jewish legitimacy between himself as a Jew and his religiously Orthodox parents.

In effect, the basic analysis on which Ahad Ha-Am built his theory of national culture was drawn from the alternatives he had personally encountered. As a result, he was immediately convincing to many young people whose experiences paralleled his; from his own life story he concluded that the most potent factor in shaping Jewish identity was the pervasive impact of the social-cultural atmosphere of family and/or community. After all, religion too operated in such a cultural milieu. Certainly one could not make light of religion as an independent and primary factor in molding the Jewish way of life, but Ahad Ha-Am realized that even when religious faith disappeared there was no attendant break in an individual's bond to family and community; indeed, a separate infrastructure was *uncovered* — a personal-societal one — which seemed to him to be the very fabric of Jewish life. This was the fabric into which religion had, so to speak, insinuated itself, only to engulf it. It was evident that both these factors had always been present, but not until religion was undermined was the personal-societal factor distinguishable as a separate factor because Jewish religion with its all-encompassing nature had simply superimposed itself on the collective spheres, whether familial or societal. Only when religious belief was replaced by a scientific world view did it become clear that the familial-societal infrastructure, with all its cultural hallmarks, had an independent existence. Furthermore, this infrastructure could be equated with an intrinsic personal-societal dimension which could transform views without itself being transformed in the process.

The question now is what kind of cognitive content — feelings, senses, knowledge — makes up the fabric which we perceive of as intrinsic and identity-bearing, whether of an individual or a group? In retrospect, it is evident that this question exercised Ahad Ha-Am as early as his first essays.

Although he did not raise it directly, he did propose an answer in the form of a scientific assumption. Basing himself on Darwinian theory, he stated that the survival instinct was intrinsic not only to individuals but groups as well. There is a national survival instinct just as there is a personal one.

What was the basis for this assumption? Did it have a scientific foundation? The answer is yes. There was a scientific foundation even though one could dispute the methodological legitimacy by which Ahad Ha-Am adapted it to his needs: according to Darwin, too, there is a survival instinct linked to the reproduction and fostering of progeny, not only for maintaining the life of the individual but also, and primarily, for the maintenance of the species. A living organism acts in a way which indicates that it regards its offspring as the direct continuation of its own life, which is why the survival instinct impels individual living things to sacrifice themselves in order to save their offspring when they are endangered. Ahad Ha-Am defined family, tribal, and national groups based on common origins and generational continuity as species, or subspecies, of humanity. Thus he concluded that every individual bears within himself, as a genetic code, the instinct to safeguard the existence of his "species" which is his people.

It is primarily a concern for the future; a concern that the people as a people will not disappear after the death of the individual but will continue to be sustained by his progeny. This is what the individual regards as *immortality*. Ahad Ha-Am claimed that observation of the behavior of healthy, natural peoples proves this, and cited an instructive example from the Bible. It is well known that there is no overt mention of immortality in the Bible. What is said of the dead is that they are "gathered onto their fathers." Where does the individual will to survive express itself? In concern for one's children. For our forefathers, children were the supreme aim of life. While an individual regarded his offspring as the unbroken continuation of his own life, a person who died childless was considered to be cut off from his people. In the Biblical period, the Israelites were a young, healthy, natural people. They had no need for assurances of an afterlife. It was only when the people grew older and its vital forces weakened did individual egoism require a religious promise of individual, personal immortality.

It is unnecessary to stress that in Ahad Ha-Am's view this was a pathological, degenerative process which bespoke biological entropy, not spiritual progress. He needed to relate to this process in order to explain not only why he himself felt a natural and obvious identity with the Jewish people but why so many young Jews of his generation did not share that same natural sense. The implied scientific response was that there was a deterioration in the aging process of the Jewish national organism which was diseased, a process exacerbated by the condition of life in exile. In this quasi-medical diagnosis of a disease rampant within the Jewish people, the condition had to be dealt with by the use of appropriate organizational and educational remedies.

Yet even at this early stage of his analysis, it was clear to Ahad Ha-Am that there was a qualitative difference in the way the survival instinct functions in organisms which are instinctively concerned with the continuation of their species and the way it functions in a human collective. All the biological drives of human beings are *consciously* expressed. This is particularly true for the collective survival instinct. Belonging to a human collective and concern for its continuation is not only instinctual, it is also a type of associative consciousness or a type of spiritual life. Consequently, human beings can alter their thinking and then their behavior sometimes undergoes a polar change. Thus Ahad Ha-Am believed he could deal with the phenomenon of national aging and deterioration of the Jewish people by educational means.

This being the case, what type of associating consciousness is meant? What is its content?

Ahad Ha-Am devoted an entire essay entitled, "Three Stages" to the issue. The main thrust of the essay is the Hebrew translation of a quote from a "Western Rabbi" published in an 1898 German-Jewish publication. The point under discussion was, "Why do we remain Jewish?" The Rabbi, whose imagination had been fired by Zionism, began by rejecting the clichéd answers of assimilated Reform Jewry who explained their gradually weakening affinity to Judaism through the uniqueness of pure monotheism, the loftiness of Jewish morality, or the mission of Jewry to humanity at large. The Rabbi concedes that these are rationalizations which he saw through to find the existential truth that Ahad Ha-Am had maintained in his earliest essays.

"Why are we Jewish? What a strange question! Ask fire why it burns! Ask the sun why it shines! Ask the tree why it grows!…Thus they asked the Jew why he is Jewish. It is beyond our ability to be anything else. It is inherent within us despite ourselves, it is a law imprinted in our nature as a mother's love for her child, as the love of a man for his homeland! It wells up from the depths of our souls, it is part of our heart! It cannot be abolished, defeated, or denied just as it is impossible to abolish, defeat or deny the heart itself…We are incapable — even should we wish it a thousand times — to separate from the roots of our being. The will to live rebels against oblivion…We have been Jews for three thousand years because we could not be anything else; because a power stronger and mightier than ourselves binds us to Judaism and compels our hearts to declare, I want to be a Jew — because this striving to be Jewish is a force of nature within us…"

[The Western Rabbi continues and redoubles his emotional vividness until he reaches the conclusion,] "No! Neither a Jewish outlook, nor the Torah, nor Jewish belief — none of these are the original cause, the first cause! Rather it is the Jewish sensibility, an instinctive feeling that cannot be defined in words. Call it a sense of race, or the spirit of the nation, or more than anything, it should be called the Hebrew heart!"

Ostensibly, the Western Rabbi is simply repeating in emotionally charged words Ahad Ha-Am's assumption made in a dry, scientific style in his first essay, "The Wrong Way." Among other things, Ahad Ha-Am wrote that the will to live rebels against oblivion. However, despite its poetic character, it appears that when the Western Rabbi uses this expression, he is not referring to biology alone, even though he repeatedly alludes to parents' love of their children. In his final paragraph he prefers the phrase "Jewish sensibility" which implies a sense of belonging and a sense of uniqueness about certain characteristic spiritual attributes. When he attempts to define the content of "Jewish sensibility," he proposes two alternatives whose meanings are not congruent: the sense of race, which can be equated with the awareness of an instinct for biological survival; and the sense of peoplehood, which is certainly not biological. Ultimately, he prefers yet a third expression, "the Hebrew heart" perhaps because it is symbolic — the confluence of two meanings for the word heart. In Hebrew as in European languages, the heart is the center of physical life as well as the locus of human feeling.

At any case, when we look at the way in which Ahad Ha-Am himself continues in the later essay, we find that he is not entirely satisfied with the existential statement, We are Jews despite ourselves, therefore we deserve to be respected for being the Jews we are, accepted as equal citizens without demanding that we change. Ultimately this is not acceptable because the principal question being discussed is not whether, when all is said and done, a Jew is anybody who is physically born a Jew. Who could deny this? It is rather a question of how one's Jewishness manifests itself behaviorally and voluntarily. Furthermore, the matter of rights that a Jew is entitled to enjoy as a Jew is not merely the right *to be* Jewish, or even to *feel* Jewish (who could prevent this?) It is rather an issue of the right to act out feelings of Jewishness fully and openly in one's way of life and creativity; indeed, in every area that one could wish to articulate Jewishness. In essence, this is the original Zionist expectation according to Ahad Ha-Am. Because of this he ventured to reject Herzl's political Zionism which in effect was grounded in racial feeling that welled up in the face of hostile anti-Semitism. Ahad Ha-Am's Zionism, it must be kept in mind, was *spiritual,* not *racial.* The aims of Spiritual Zionism were to create the conditions which would enable Jews to articulate their Jewishness in every sphere, expressive of their humanity.

The will to do so was, he felt, rooted in the biological instinct for survival, but it was essentially spiritual. He summarized his thoughts in the essay, "Three Stages." "It is not the complementary relationship between branches in some system that connects human beings in a genuine, internal bond; it is rather the unity of the root itself from which they all branch out. Our ancestors recognized this truth and said, 'It can be said of anyone who rejects idol worship that he accepts the entire Torah.' In the same spirit, today we would say, 'It can be said of anyone who rejects assimilation that he accepts the entire Zionist Torah. If *I, myself* (that is the *ego*) am present, everything is present.'"

If that is so, then what is meant is a *spiritual root* which the biological survival instinct impels us to articulate and act on, and the definitive statement (which we shall yet have to look at more closely) enables us to summarize Ahad Ha-Am's point of view in this essay as follows. *National feeling* is spiritual consciousness and spiritual validation of the national *will to survival* which is instinctive and biological. *National sensibility* shifts the *will to survival* to the plane of spiritual life unique to every people. Granted, this spiritual life is not amenable to a definition according to some system of branches that stem from a *root* (the allusion here is to Rabbi Joseph Albo's *Torat ha-Ikkarim* — *"Theoretical Principles"* in analogy to the Reform view that Judaism is based on dogma) or according to any other defined *teaching*. Despite this, spiritual life does have its own essential uniqueness which is seen in the characteristics of human behavior and human creativity. If we wish to understand why a *Hebrew heart* is the preferred term not only of the emotional Western Rabbi but also of Ahad Ha-Am, we must look at the word he substitutes for this expression in the final line of his essay, which will provide the precise scientific explanation he intended: "I, myself (that is, the *ego*)." The consciousness of self which the *ego* presents is the elevation of the biological *will to survive* to the plane of spiritual existence that is unique to man. Feeling is a distinctive gesture of the ego. It is the content in which the ego exists and which it expresses. In this sense, *national sensibility* displays the *national ego* as an object within the personal ego that parallels the national will to survive which is an object of the personal will to survive and, in and of itself, comprises a specific spiritual content. More precisely, it is the source from which all other contents flow.

Ahad Ha-Am's influential and well known essay, "Past and Future"* develops this notion in a theory which posits the connection and parallel that exist between personal ego and national ego. He deals first with the substance of ego. Ahad Ha-Am proposes that the ego is equal to the

---

* Found in *Selected Essays by Ahad Ha-Am*, Jewish Publication Society, 1936.

consciousness of internal continuity held by a subject conscious that he lives in the time continuum. The key sentence defining the ego in Ahad Ha-Am's system is the statement that the subject has a consciousness of continuity within the constant change in time: I am who I was and will be. In his simpler formulation, ego is the encounter between a memory of the past and an expectation of the future. The intention, of course, is that the ego is a subject that remembers and observes, identifying itself by means of both. Without a memory of events and experiences that occurred in the past, and absent expectations of these memories for the subject's own future, there is no ego because there is no identity. Ego is basically identity. Examination shows that the only way one can answer the question, "Who am I?" (or "Who are you?") is through registering characteristics of acts and events that occurred to the subject in the past. I am the one who was born to…at such a time…and such a place…this is my profession…these are my actions…these are my attributes…and I am the one who expects to be in the future or act in the future…on the basis of the aggregate of all my past achievements. Anyone who does not have a memory of his past is incapable of telling others, or even himself, anything about who he is: he has nothing with which to identify himself in the present. Which is ultimately why amnesia is the ego's loss of consciousness. But anyone deprived of a vision of the future towards which he is proceeding on the basis of a memory of the past, has also lost consciousness of ego. Not having a vision of existing in a future that is based on the past is, from the standpoint of the consciousness of self, tantamount to death, a life that has been cut off in the present.

The implication of this is that in every individual the ego is identified with biographical memory as a scaffold for future aspirations, and to the extent that one can speak of a group ego to which individuals belong through consciousness of themselves or through their identity as individuals who belong to a societal continuity, this too constitutes a consciousness of continuity between memory and expectation. The difference is that one now speaks on the historic plane: the wide-ranging, ancient memory which the group has and its expectations for an expanded and distant future. A group that has lost its historic memory, or a group that no longer holds common expectations based on its memories of the road traveled, has lost its collective ego, has perished and no longer exists.

If national feeling equals the consciousness of individuals who identify with their group, and if one speaks of a group that has existed as such over a number of generations, then in essence national feeling is a kind of historic memory which shapes an orientation of the future. Through this we arrive at an understanding of the concrete and defined contents of the term, *national feeling*. One could say that the terms *historic consciousness*, which in and of itself is linked to the content of certain historic memories, and *national feeling* are interchangeable. Still, in this context, it bears emphasizing that not every historic memory is historic consciousness or the content of national feeling. Objective data, even when related to events that personally occurred to an individual, are still not an identifying personal memory which express the person himself. Only that which is perceived as a personal experience, and is encased in memory as a formative experience, can be classed as an identity-shaping memory.

This applies as well to the identity-shaping historic memory of the collective ego. Clearly individuals cannot remember their people's history as personal events that occurred to them or that will occur to them. The variegated content of their history must be learned as objective data. It is only after this has been internalized as a contemporary, recurring personal recollection that it becomes a component of one's historic consciousness which shapes a specific orientation and specific expectations for the future. To sum up, for both the individual on the level of personal biography, and for a people on the historic plane, only that which can be classed as an actual experience of remembrance, and an aspiration for the future, constitutes an identifying, consciousness-shaping element of the ego. In this sense, Ahad Ha-Am's formulation, which initially may appear simplistic for purposes of popularization, is none the less precise: the ego's consciousness is always situated in the present — the arena in which past and future content meet; it is always recollection which shapes expectation, and expectation that is nourished by recollection.

Culture is, of course, a composite of content (events and deeds of national importance, social processes, spiritual creativity) which fills the formative memory of the national ego. Culture is the cumulative expression of national feeling that is motivated, as will be recalled, by the people's instinct for survival. It was from this concept that Ahad Ha-Am derived the following methodological approach for the next stage in the discussion of Jewish culture, its circumstances and contemporary problems. First: to learn about a people's culture and understand the particular attributes of that culture, the actual accumulation of memories found in its literature (and other means of creative documentation) must be examined in a historically scientific manner. For Ahad Ha-Am, this meant probing the process of accumulation by which the national memory documents the sequence of events as part of an ongoing confrontation of the national feeling with the challenges, problems, and difficulties that flow from changing objective circumstances of national existence on both the material and spiritual planes.

Second: one must distinguish between culture as a repository of the historic memory that every people possesses (in keeping with the extent of its history and its degree of development) and the current *state of its culture*. At any given moment in the present, the cultural state is concerned with the degree of communication possible between the content of national memory that has been accumulated in the past, and the people who live in the present. It is also the extent of communication between the members of a given generation as they confront the challenges of the national reality at a given time because, in actuality, culture is not an archive of memories but a tangible encounter with its content. Which is to say, the question of the *state of the culture* of a people is the question of the applicability of culture as a repository of national memory in the circumstances that exist in the present: is it still capable of functioning in ways that will insure the national ego a historic future that is based on its past?

Third: should it transpire that there is a discontinuity between the contents of national memory and the existential functioning of the nation in the present, one has to ask what changes and adaptation are required in order to overcome the dysfunction and assure continuity. And such changes should be presented as a categorical command of the national will to survive.

"Teḥiyat ha-Ruaḥ" ("Rebirth of the Spirit"*) the most wide-ranging and important essay that Ahad Ha-Am devoted to the question of contemporary Jewish culture, opens with the methodological assumption described earlier and a parallel, paradoxical claim: scientific inquiry into the history and literature of the Jewish people shows the civilization of the Jews to be among the richest, most culturally developed. It is a culture that had met challenges and ensured its continued existence throughout generations overcoming obstacles which other peoples had been unable to do. Through scientific, historical observation, one can demonstrate that Jewish culture adapted itself to new circumstances by displaying the firmness necessary to preserve selfhood; at the same time, it also exhibited the flexibility required to adapt the heritage to contemporary needs. In the modern era, however, an especially severe crisis occurred which found the Jewish people in circumstances of unaccustomed cultural poverty.

The crisis originated in the break that occurred between generations. The old generation, overwhelmingly religious, clung dogmatically to a blind, fanatic memory of the past and zealously refused to adapt to contemporary circumstances and future needs. The young generation clung to cherished needs and aspirations for the future with a similar degree of fanaticism, and were completely alienated from their heritage as the carrier of the national ego. As a result, the two generations which lacked any positive communication with each other were, in effect, bereft of a culture. The old generation held

---

* Translated as "The Spiritual Revival" in *Selected Essays*.

on to a memory that was unusable in its own contemporary life: minimally, the ability to act as transmitters of the heritage to their offspring; whereas the young generation had no historic memory at all. From the standpoint of the national will to survive, this was the greatest danger one could imagine since being cut off from the future, just as being cut off from the past, means national extinction — utter fossilization on one hand, rampant assimilation on the other.

In terms of national feeling, therefore, the following question arises: what must be done to repair the way culture functions as the means of communication between generations so as to make the component of memory applicable to the present and an orientation for the future?

It is important to note the vantage point from which Ahad Ha-Am approached the pragmatic issues of Jewish culture. Naturally, it would be from his own position as representative of the *intermediate generation*, a generation that was able to see the problem from the perspective of parents possessed of cultural memory, as well as from the perspective of young people striving to live the present and aspire to the future. Thus he was able to create the necessary historical perspective for both sides in order to overcome the break between them. Indeed, historical perspective was the advantage he had in successfully confronting problems in which he could feel the pain that emanated equally from each side. To some extent he could be a spokesman for the parental generation (while at the same time counseling them to use a measure of moderation and flexibility in their relations with young people); nonetheless, as a man of the intermediate generation, Ahad Ha-Am's main educational thrust was directed at the younger generation.

The first question he addressed was: What were the practical criteria for defining the Jewish people's culture as an ongoing repository of historic memory? In other words, out of the broad compass of the documented national literature, what could still be considered an available heritage, worthy of being studied, a heritage out of which meaningful useful contents could be gleaned for use in the present?

The answer to the question was not only necessary, it was urgent because the rupture with the young generation had already become so severe that they expressed it as a denial of the very existence of a meaningful Jewish culture even in the past; in effect, a denial of the past. Ahad Ha-Am took aim at two types of denial that were current — ignorance and distortion. Ignorance was the province of the assimilated, even those such as Herzl and Nordau who had returned to Jewishness via Political Zionism. It was a group certain of its judgment that Jewish culture was so outmoded, backward, medieval, rife with superstition and foolishness that it was incapable of competing with enlightened European culture. They neither bothered to learn anything about it nor discover what it might hold for them. Even more serious, more grave was the outlook of such young Jews as Berdyczewski and Brenner who were Jewishly educated and well acquainted with Judaism but, as a consequence of a bitter and painful conflict with their parents, tended to regard Jewish culture as valueless, sick, deformed and inferior. They were prepared to jettison most of it or, at least what appeared to Ahad Ha-Am, those features which shaped its essence.

Discrediting Herzl's and Nordau's views was relatively easy. Their statements were founded on ignorance and nothing further was required of them than that they study the topics on which they had expressed an opinion so that they could discover the truth. They had only to take the trouble to identify specific Jewish spiritual contributions to that European culture of which they were so proud, to be convinced of the folly of their judgment. By comparison, Ahad Ha-Am found the critique of those young people who propounded a theory of radical negation of exile far more serious. Their theory was predicated on a misinterpretation of genuine knowledge, and as such it was perverse, even wicked. In effect, their sole points of reference were Hebrew, Eretz Israel and perhaps the Bible, as the content of positive Jewish national culture. Their outlook totally negated as an exilic deviation anything that had been created in the Diaspora, including most Talmudic literature and the rabbinic creativity of the Middle Ages. Aspiring as it did to a temporal, emancipated and enlightened culture, the younger generation could not relate to this part of the heritage.

Ahad Ha-Am countered the arguments of the younger critics on two basic grounds: first, the pragmatic-pedagogical. Culture does not operate in fits and starts. It is permissible, sometimes even necessary, to winnow out the substance and to jettison that which is less important. But one may not dismember the living continuity that binds the culture, not even to clutch at an earlier chapter in its history. In other words, it is impossible for the culture to be maintained in the present leading toward the immediate tomorrow when there is a break with the immediate yesterday. The vital links between the present and the periods which preceded the immediate yesterday are transmitted through that same yesterday. Should we cut ourselves off from it, we will in effect cut ourselves off from a living connection to the past.

For example, the Bible does not come to us as it was inherently understood at the time of its writing; it is transmitted by means of interpretive observation exercised over the generations. Should we disengage ourselves from that interpretive continuity, we will be left with *archeology*, which may be fascinating scientifically but is not productive as a source of contemporary cultural creation. Consequently, if we divorce ourselves completely from the Mishnah, the Talmud, Midrash, the Siddur [Jewish prayer book], halakhic and *musar* [moralistic] literature, and the religious philosophy of the Middle Ages, as well as from Hasidic, Haskalah, or modern Hebrew literature, what remains will be neither a living Hebrew that is rich and original, nor a continuous historic bond to Eretz Israel, nor even a vital creative link to the Bible.

Secondly, the radical view that invalidates everything our people created in exile, because it was created in exile, is entirely without foundation. There is no basis for a distinction between contents found in the Bible and contents found in Talmudic literature. It is the same emerging heritage which develops not only in its religious content but also in the ethical, societal, judicial, political, philosophic and poetic content. Moreover, Talmudic literature is closer to the modern Jew than the Bible, in point of time as well as criteria of values and the applicability of its content to contemporary life. Furthermore, the historic fact that the Jewish people was able to survive, to maintain its identity and create cultural products even under the most difficult conditions of exile attests to the great vitality of Talmudic and post-Talmudic creativity. Instead of dwarfing the image of exilic heritage as merely illustrative of exilic experience (of course it does contain such an element) we should value the spiritual force it demonstrates, despite exile, because it is that vitality that enabled the Jewish people to persist. Clearly, evaluated in this way, one is convinced that this creativity has a meaning that goes beyond exile, particularly when seeking a content that unites the Jewish people living in its own land, and in the Diaspora.

With this as his basis, Ahad Ha-Am's outlook can be defined as *universally Jewish*. Yet Ahad Ha-Am, too, postulated a certain "negation of the Diaspora." In his opinion, existence in exile had harshly negative implications for the circumstances of the nation and its culture; indeed, from a national and Zionist point of view, he rejected certain habits and behavior that had emerged in exile. This was particularly conspicuous regarding the issue of a national language for the Jewish people. In the acerbic argument that broke out over the question of Hebrew versus Yiddish, Ahad Ha-Am came down strongly and unambiguously: Hebrew and Hebrew alone.

It was a decision colored by universal Jewish considerations: while Yiddish remained the language of many of the Jews of that generation, in effect, it was only partially the national language of a segment of the people in a given period. The aim of a genuinely national language ought to be to unite all the dispersions throughout the generations. Only Hebrew could address this need. There was a second consideration, one which reflected the view of the *maskilim* and the Zionists, in which an element of negation of the exile resonated: Ahad Ha-Am saw Yiddish as a jargon, an irregular language encompassing the aberrations which inhere in partial assimilatory processes. Consequently, he categorically rejected a recognition of two languages, and the two literatures created in them, as the dual languages and literature of the Jewish people. In his opinion, two national languages in one people was a harmful and abnormal phenomenon. No model existed for this in any nation or language. Moreover, it would be a waste of the national creative energy because Yiddish had no future; Hebrew alone would be the language spoken in Eretz Israel. In the emancipated countries of the dispersion, most Jews would prefer to speak the language of their countries for purposes of communicating with the cultural environment in which they were integrated. Hebrew would serve them for purposes of identification with their historic culture because it alone was capable of serving that function, and it was unlikely that they would either desire or be capable of being loyal to yet one more national language.

Ahad Ha-Am believed that the historically continuous culture of the Jewish people was replete with a wealth of content yet, despite this, there was already a profound break between that culture and the younger generation that had turned to modern secularity. The historic reasons for this, and Ahad Ha-Am's proposed program of a Cultural Center in Eretz Israel to overcome the predicament have been noted. But, in reality, could the serious question of principle that had sprung up in the strained, alienated relationships between the pre-Zionist Old Yishuv in Eretz Israel and the new community growing up there be resolved? How could the obvious contradiction between the halakhic religious nature of a historic Jewish culture and the temporal values of a secular modern culture be bridged? Or, put differently, was it possible to mine a rich secular culture from a culture that was essentially religious?

The answers to these questions were to be found in the most striking element of Ahad Ha-Am's theory of a Jewish culture.

To describe this, we return to his own point of departure: his recognition that despite the fact that his religiosity had been replaced by a scientific world-view, he remained a Jew in his way of life, his world outlook, and his values. Even without religious belief, he found that his former way of life still held a positive personal and universal significance for him as it related to family, society and nation. He also had a familial, societal, national and scientific explanation for religion itself, for its commandments, customs and symbolism. Some of these appeared to be superfluous for anyone who had ceased to be a believer; others were no longer appropriate and required adaptation or transposition. Nonetheless, he could respect all the mitzvot, some because he identified with his own past as well as his family's and his nation's; some out of a conviction that through historic inquiry one could discover a sufficiently cogent rationale for them, particularly if they were adapted to contemporary life. Of no small interest, his scientific observations showed him that while religious society is conservative and inflexible, ready only with difficulty to change its views and behavioral norms, its claim that it is never selective, innovative or amenable to change is not completely accurate. Indeed, religious society has its own ways of adapting to time, to change, and even to innovation without giving the appearance of questioning the authority of eternal religious commands. Regardless of the differences between his scientific and religious postures, Ahad Ha-Am did not deny his Judaism and entertained hope that the religious society would grow closer to him in its own way and at its own pace.

The scientific assumption underpinning this thinking was that religion is a component of human society. It is the spiritual creation of those who believe in it. Although they, of course, believe otherwise. They understand religion to be the product of divine revelation, and that human input only contributes a limited interpretation to the content and performance of religion. But a man of scientific propensity understands where belief originates. He respects belief and knows that there is an essential difference between conceiving of religion as revelational and regarding it as a human product. A believer could not accept Ahad Ha-Am's scientific views or perceive of himself as the scholar saw him. This did not undermine Ahad Ha-Am's conviction; as an intellectual, he saw the truth as empirically grounded in objective analysis. Since it was the *truth*, it was also the correct interpretation of the religious behavior of those without scientific understanding. That is to say, as a scientific interpreter, Ahad Ha-Am laid down the assumption that there was always a human truth or need beyond religious belief — whether psychological, spiritual, or ethical, and of personal, family, communal, national, or universal scope. In any case, his role as an intellectual who identified with his people's culture out of national feeling was to interpret the truth he discovered about religion in his own way, to interpret and apply it within the historic continuity of national culture.

In order to fulfill this role with the appropriate exactness needed, Ahad Ha-Am distinguished between two modes by means of which human values are found in religious creativity: the direct mode, elucidated by the accurate classification of religious content, and human content which, in and of itself, is not religious; and the indirect mode, revealed through scientific study of the phenomenon of belief.

Ahad Ha-Am considered the first mode, the direct one, to be broader and more important. A study of comparative religion shows that most religions, including the Christian version of monotheism, make a pronounced distinction between the spheres of truth and the religious way of life and between the spheres of knowledge, creativity, and human life outside religion. Jewish monotheism was unique in its aspiration to have its truths and commandments apply to all spheres of man's activity, directing them all toward a single goal. Halakhah is comprehensive, yet detailed. It deals with all topics and every sphere of human activity from a religious point of view. But when the contents of both the Oral and the Written Law are examined in detail, point by point, it transpires that when they relate to the spheres of human activity — societal, economic, and political — the considerations are always considerations of relevance which derive from the internal structure of those spheres, or from values which inhere in the activity itself. These can be understood variously as civil law, ethics, etc. Furthermore, within the broad compass of the Torah — which in its totality is defined as religious — there is a wide variety of creations which directly express the values, the feelings, and the thoughts of human beings: the Wisdom Literature, scientific study at a level that was extant in earlier periods, poetry that is expressive of ordinary human feeling, politics, history, and so on. The overall framework was religious but the religious motifs were blended with temporal motifs, and it is clear that the content of ostensibly religious sources were not necessarily nor invariably religious. Therefore it is possible to relocate many of them, as they stand, without change in content or form, into the context of a non-religious world view and way of life.

The second mode touches upon actual religious content. Observation shows that if it is correct to assume that religion is a human creation, then a certain type of human truth ought to be found in the content of religion. Research that employs the appropriate scientific tools of psychology, sociology, anthropology or philosophy will reveal the human origins of religious truth. Consequently, even a non-religious person can find a reflection of himself, his quandaries, his aspirations to an examination of truth and his confrontation with the core questions of human existence within it.

We now turn our attention to a more detailed examination of each of the modes in which human content is embodied as part of the cultural-religious complex. Earlier, we alluded to the fact that Ahad Ha-Am believed halakhah to be most important because it was all embracing and comprehensive. Beyond the parameters of overtly religious ritual law, halakhah extends to all aspects of law and justice that human beings may have recourse to. Ahad Ha-Am did not regard himself as qualified to deal with the particulars of this issue, so that as a pragmatic thinker he related only to those topics which he saw as having immediate relevance. He avoided the topic that is now referred to by the term, *Mishpat Ivri* (Hebrew, i.e. national Jewish law). It should be emphasized, however, that the development of *Mishpat Ivri*, as a discipline, is rooted in Ahad Ha-Am's teachings. Rabbi Chaim

Tchernowitz (1870–1949), known as Rav Za'ir, a disciple of Ahad Ha-Am, was the first halakhist to devote himself to researching the evolution of this field. His goal was to demonstrate that in most respects the halakhah is not coterminous with "religious law" but has a much more comprehensive, developed and elaborate system of national law and jurisprudence. As such, it resembles the most highly regarded legal systems in Western culture, such as Roman and English law. It is dynamic and, if it is practiced, can prove applicable to the modern period with marked advantages over other legal systems.

Ahad Ha-Am himself chose to deal with an issue he believed to be more realistic for a historic period in which the Jews had no autonomous political framework in which they could apply their unique national law. In an essay called, "The National Ethic," he responded to the question of how a non-religious Jew could express *Jewish national feeling* in daily life by stating that the appropriate way was to live according to the values and norms of *Jewish ethics*.

How could Jewish ethics developed entirely in a religious framework be described as a national ethic? In order to answer, Ahad Ha-Am first had to elucidate the tenor of the relationship between religion and ethics. The issue was complicated because of the need to confront not only the traditional religious Jewish outlook which denied any distinction between religion and morals and held that the two concepts were inseparable, but also because of the need to confront the modern Jewish religious notion that rejected this distinction for an opposite reason, claiming that Judaism was in fact a religion of ethics (ethical monotheism). For Orthodox thinkers, the Torah does not have a separate category for morality; all its values and commandments are the authoritative revelation of God's will. All is religion. For modern religious thinkers, there is also no isolated sphere of religion in the Torah because everything is a moral commandment. God is the ideal of absolute good, and worshipping God by observing his commandments is behaving in accordance with values of the moral ideal which is an absolute universal ethic.

We shall see that Ahad Ha-Am appropriated certain elements of the latter approach in his work. In his view, too, there was a strong link in Judaism between religious truth and ethical truth. But as an intellectual and a national thinker, he could not agree to an absolute equating of ethics with religion, neither as espoused in the ultra-Orthodox or the modern versions. His claim was that, in and of themselves, religion and morality are separate, and that one can find religious and ethical content side by side in the Torah. The fact that there is reciprocal contact between them was important but it did not invalidate distinguishing between them. Moreover, Ahad Ha-Am found that morality develops in every nation as a human cultural product which takes many forms in the national ethic. In every people, ethics has unique characteristics that are rooted in other qualities of the people's culture.

It must be re-emphasized that Ahad Ha-Am confirmed the ultra-Orthodox religious outlook as representing a correct, authentic understanding of the phenomenon of religion qua religion. As such, religion is belief in a transcendental, divine Persona that reveals itself to human beings and commands them to enact certain precepts, some of which relate to the special relations that exist only between God and man. In dealing with Jewish religion, it is inconceivable that the relations between God and man could contradict morality; still, they do transcend morality whose province is the mutual relations between people. If this is so, then there is clearly a distinct area of thought, feeling and religious action whose rationale is exclusively religious. This is the realm which Rabbi Saadia Gaon defined as *shim'i*.* But the Torah does contain ethical commandments in the realm of relationships between man and man which Saadia Gaon distinguished from the *shim'i* and defined as "*sikhli*" (commandments amenable to human reason) because they are intended for the benefit of human beings.

Commandments of this kind are not difficult to find in the Torah. Especially notable are most of the Ten Commandments, and the well known Torah dictum, "Love your neighbor as yourself" which gained wide acclaim and universal acceptance. Since these commandments are amenable to human reason, and rooted in man's aspiration to that which is beneficial to himself as a human being, would it not then be correct to ask whether these mitzvot are not universal? If the answer is yes, it means that ethical commandments are indeed a component of any culture since culture is a human product; they do not specifically characterize a Jewish national ethic but are common to all cultures.

Is this really so? As a rational man of science, Ahad Ha-Am answered the question by pointing out several well known historical facts: it is a truism that there are some universal principles, values and norms of morality which appear in all national cultures, but if we observe culture by culture and compare ethical concepts, priorities and gradations of values, as well as the norms of ethical behavior, we discover that they differ widely among different nations. Moreover, even in the very same people, they are expressed differently from one period to another. The reasons are obvious. Morality is not a skein of abstract principles. Morality is applied pragmatically in specific conditions of societal and cultural life. When a culture develops and expands, its morality develops, expands and is refined. The greater

---

* "Auditory" — i.e., traditional precepts whose authoritative force lies in the bare fact of their having been commanded, without any explanation of why they must be observed.

a culture's development, the more complex and numerous are the problems that appear to have no single ethical solution, even when there is a general consensus about defining the principles of justice, love and mercy. Unique historical or biographical circumstances impel a society to prefer given values over others, and one solution over another.

Therefore, all the components of a national culture have an effect on its ethics. It goes without saying that religion too has an impact on morality, and there are religions which also attach a central valence to culture in the relationship between God and man. This is the case with Judaism. And being the case, there is no doubt that a *Jewish culture* exists which is expressive of the particular historic experience of the Jewish people. The uniqueness of the Jewish people's culture and religion impute a decisive value to morality in the relationship between God and man, expressed in the preference for a certain kind of moral values, a certain form of deliberation, and certain norms of ethical behavior. As a consequence, the morality of Jews is decidedly different than the ethics of non-Jews.

Ahad Ha-Am proffered a typical example when he sharply criticized Herzl who, in his opinion, had internalized a modern non-Jewish morality and attempted to popularize it among Jews. In one of his plays, Herzl glorified a rabbi's readiness to defend his honor by challenging an anti-Semitic opponent who had insulted him to a duel. Ahad Ha-Am protested that dueling was characteristic of the ethical concepts of Christian knights, a notion deeply rooted in Western culture. For Jews educated in the heritage of Jewish morality, dueling was an utter abomination. It would never occur to a rabbi to take part in a duel because for him this was nothing short of murder. What is the source of the difference? It is anchored in a preference for a set of values, and the manner in which these values are interpreted. A culture which ennobles dueling places a certain notion of chivalrous "honor" above the sanctity of life, whereas Judaism raised the sanctity of life above all other values, certainly above honor as a value.

Indeed, in this preference of one value over another, Jewish religion has a pronounced influence on morality. Jewish morality does carry a notion of honor, just as in Christian morality which has a positive regard for dueling there is a norm prohibiting murder. Judaism interpreted the concept of honor differently, just as it interpreted the concept of murder differently. Examination shows that Judaism is contemptuous of anyone who duels and so endangers himself and the life of another because of his "honor"; clearly, however, we are not discussing the specific instance of whether dueling is moral or immoral. It is rather the general situation which comprises two types of morality that come to the fore not only in response to insult and a challenge to duel by a non-Jew, but in the Jew's entire way of life. Judaism placed the values of justice, charity, mercy, self-control and restraint of anger in opposition to the values of gentlemanly honor.

This was the basis of Ahad Ha-Am's comprehension of the difference between morality and religion, and his determination that there are differences between the various forms of national morality. In his opinion, a non-religious Jew could extract a moral dimension from religious thought as it is practiced in an Orthodox way of life and in doing so, conduct a Jewish cultural way of life that was meaningful. This applied as well to social and national values which historically were closely linked to the national Jewish ethic: the Sabbath, holidays, and festivals, outstanding examples of cultural values that developed in a religious framework but whose content, in and of itself, was genuinely relevant to someone who was no longer religious. It is not difficult to show that through *national feeling* alone it is possible to find expression for the feelings, outlook and ethics of a Jew; the non-religious Jew could find a social message in the concept of Sabbath rest, and in the national, societal, and moral meaning of the holidays.

The relationship between morality and religion in Judaism might also serve as a point of departure for the way Ahad Ha-Am projected an inherent cultural, national, and universal meaning in religion. To that end, we must go back and examine the impact of the all-inclusive character of Jewish religion on the morality that evoked within it on the one hand, and the core influence morality had on religion qua religion on the other.

Ahad Ha-Am found that the impact of this all-inclusive character of religion on morality had both a positive and a negative aspect. He understood the positive aspect as granting each moral obligation an absolute force because — beyond the obligation which stems from an interpersonal and social network of relationships — the norms of ethical behavior were perceived as divine commandments whose abrogation would excite God's anger and retribution. He understood the negative aspect as a normative inflexibility which hindered the development of ethical thinking precisely because a norm that was declared to be a divine commandment was perceived as immutable, compulsory, and eternal. Despite this, Ahad Ha-Am saw an evolution in the ethical thinking of the prophets, the sages and the medieval scholars. As a striking example, he proposed the sages' interpretation of monetary compensation in the primary Biblical norm, "An eye for an eye." He believed that once the sages concluded that a norm sanctified in the past as a divine commandment was unjust, they would simply reject the possibility that God could have decreed such an injunction. Detaching it from the realm of literal meaning, the sages would declare that their new interpretation was God's original intent. But it is obvious that such a process is slow and more complex than the procedure of unconstrained moral thought.

The significance of subjecting ethical thinking to meta-rational religious authority appears in a different light if we attempt to find out why Biblical monotheism motivated the prophets and sages to superimpose divine legislation on all spheres of human activity. Or why they invested the ethical commandments with a primary meaning for relations between God and man.

How does Biblical monotheism differ from all other religions? Ahad Ha-Am's treatment of this issue was based principally on the prophets, somewhat on the sages, and most particularly on Maimonides and the impact of Rabbi Nachman Krochmal's *Moreh Nevukhai ha-Zeman* ("Guide for the Perplexed of the Time") which was derivative of Maimonides. The key, of course, was in an understanding of the prophetic phenomenon. The prophet testifies to having experienced God's meta-rational presence as a compelling truth of absolute authority, yet the content of what the prophet says remains rational. This implies that beyond the psychological phenomenon of prophetic vision, prophecy is itself the revelation of reason in man. Monotheism that is based on the Bible is essentially "a religion of reason" — an absolute aspiration to know truth in the cognitive sphere and to achieve justice in the spheres of values and deeds. This makes it impossible for monotheism to run counter to any judgment of truth, or any judgment of justice, which man perceives as a scientific-empirical or philosophic-cognitive certainty.

Following in the steps of Maimonides and Krochmal, Ahad Ha-Am drew a methodological construction for Biblical interpretation: the criterion of truth supersedes literal meaning in philological interpretation. Ahad Ha-Am had to contend with the same obstacle that Krochmal found: as a critical scholar he could not accept Maimonides' allegoristic interpretations because they subjected the text to a rubric of scientific or philosophic meaning which the text did not originally possess. Ahad Ha-Am believed that it was necessary to admit and recognize that later rational interpretation was both creative and innovative. It was the outcome of the interpreter's cultural development. It was valid interpretation from the spiritual-religious standpoint and it was justified even when the interpreter was completely aware of the arbitrariness of his interpretation. He was entitled to interpret differently because he employed an authority which religion granted him as a religious leader. As a scholar he knew that there was a progression in the knowledge of truth and the understanding of justice; as a religious leader, he knew that the essential aim of the Torah was absolute truth and justice. Therefore, he must set forth truth and justice as he conceives of them using scientific and rational criteria exclusively devoted to that objective, faithfully presenting them as the true content of the Torah. Admittedly, the prophets and early sages did not view truth as he does, but their objective was identical because they aimed at the same truth.

In light of this, Ahad Ha-Am concluded that if Biblical, prophetic mono-theism is defined in essence as absolute adherence to the values of truth and justice, one is not outside the sphere of Jewish thought even when scientific developments bring one to a conviction that contradicts the basic truisms of the Bible and the sages, or the writings of philosophers such as Maimonides; namely, that the world was created *ex nihilo*, or that God is a metaphysical entity who controls nature and rules history, or that the Torah was given, as we now have it, by a personal God at Mount Sinai. In other words, even when the validity of the tenets and institutions of monotheistic religion are totally rejected, what is retained underneath the institutionalized religious shell is the essential, eternal, prophetic meta-institutional content of monotheism which is the aspiration of man's spirit to truth and justice.

These thoughts were expounded at length in *"The Supremacy of Reason,"** the essay Ahad Ha-Am devoted to Maimonides' system. And in the context of the present discussion, his influential essay, *"Moses"*** warrants attention. It is of programmatic importance because it was written as the ideological platform for the *Benei Moshe* Order. Elected the movement's leader by its members, Ahad Ha-Am wanted to shape their thinking and entrust them with a mission. Whether consciously or not, he took on the mantle of a prophet as he placed himself on the pedestal of a spiritual leader. What he wrote was an attempt to present a new prophecy, and its authority, in the context of the meta-religious thinking of modernity.

The essay opens with a methodological hypothesis that resembles Maimonides' approach as Ahad Ha-Am understood it: in the scientific ex-ploration of history, one has to distinguish between historic truth and archeological truth. The question of whether a man called Moses, who was described in deeds and traits which the Torah attributed to him, existed in reality or not was in Ahad Ha-Am's view, an archeological question. Conceivably he existed as conceivably he did not, conceivably he was a man who differed from what is recounted in the Torah. But as far as Ahad Ha-Am was concerned, statements such as these were historically meaningless because they had no influence on the real course of history. There is true historic significance in the fact that the prophetic figure of Moses as described in the books of the Bible was, over the generations, considered to be the personage that founded the Jewish people, gave it the Torah, led it in the desert for forty years, and brought it to its land. If research shows that the figure of this sublime prophet was projected this way as a result of

---

 * Translated in *Nationalism and the Jewish Ethic: Basic Writings of Ahad Ha-Am*, Scho-cken, 1962.
 ** Translated in *Selected Essays* and also in *Nationalism and the Jewish Ethic*.

an extended process of literary design, generation following on generation, then the interpretation is all the more that Moses was, is, and shall be the ideal figure created in the spirit of a people who believes in his leadership and his message; the actual historical truth is that the literary figure of Moses shaped the self-image of the people, its world view, its belief, its way of life and its historic fate among the nations. In other words, Moses is the ideal embodiment of the Jewish people's spirit, or the ideal embodiment of Jewish culture as it developed throughout the generations. Ahad Ha-Am, therefore, set out to reshape this figure as an instructive paradigm for his own generation.

As a prophet, Moses denotes that prophecy is the ideal spiritual attribute of Jewish culture. What then is prophecy in terms that a contemporary Jew can recognize as the truth? Ahad Ha-Am's answer was that the prophet is a radically moral person, uncompromising, demanding of himself and others an absolute fidelity to truth at all levels: feelings, thoughts, speech, behavior and deeds. The prophet demands an uncompromising assessment of reality, a recognition of the obligations that stem from that appraisal and their immediate realization in action — *without compromise*. The difference between the prophet and the priest can be found in the measure of fanaticism and utter devotion to such realization. The priest is a typical establishment man, a pragmatic politician, a man of compromise; the prophet is the man who institutes the establishment but is always above it. He represents spirit that will never become institutionalized because it cannot ever compromise. This means that one cannot equate living religious truth, dynamic and developing, with religion because the latter is the establishment, and the establishment seeks stable authority and permanence. Religious truth always transcends religion.

What is the content of prophecy? What is its primary message? Ahad Ha-Am directed his readers to the story of Moses' life. Here was a man who, from the outset, demonstrated an unwillingness to countenance injustice in everything he did; a man filled with a sense of justice; a man who immediately rises against every injustice he encounters and is prepared to forfeit his life if need be. These were the principles to which Moses dedicated his life when he fought against Pharaoh, taking his people from slavery to freedom, imparting the Torah and leading the people according to its precepts. What is justice? Ahad Ha-Am defined justice as the enactment of truth, and from this he proceeded to a description of the personality of the prophet and an overall definition of the essence of prophecy: an unswerving loyalty to the value of truth both as knowledge and as its realization in deeds. In Ahad Ha-Am's view the conclusion that stemmed from this was simple and decisive: the true spiritual content hidden beneath the changeable shell of institutionalized religion is winnowed out by the Jew who is loyal to truth to the best of his ability to perceive it using the means available to him (in the contemporary period through science); by the Jew who accepts absolute responsibility (which stems from a recognition of the truth) to act justly and to demand justice; by the Jew who studies the truth and lives it in accordance with the ethical principles of Judaism.

To summarize: Judaism as a modern culture must be based on the national feeling as its form of historic consciousness. The culture includes the people's historic memory; knowledge of the Hebrew language as a language of instruction, creativity and speech; knowledge of the principal content of the original national literature in its broadest historic continuity, within its historic context; the Bible, the Mishnah, the Babylonian and Jerusalem Talmuds; the prayer book; the variety of medieval literature; and modern Hebrew literature. In practice, all this embraces behavior in accordance with the norms of Jewish morality and loyalty to the values of truth and justice.

Ahad Ha-Am did not restrict himself to articulating his philosophy. He grappled with the preparation of the tools required to continue cultural creativity based on all these sources. His proposal to set up a "spiritual center" in Eretz Israel was a long range political-educational goal. To achieve it, he devoted his energies to promoting modern Hebrew literature which could then be applied to the advancement of a broad spectrum of educational goals: directing research in Judaic studies so that appropriate contents could be prepared for school curricula; consolidating educational programs for national schools; developing modern pedagogical techniques for teaching Judaica. Because of this approach, from the very start, Ahad Ha-Am had an unusual impact both on his supporters and opponents. Indeed, his approach was so pervasive that it was absorbed imperceptibly, reaching many by means of their education and the atmosphere that prevailed in their environment. His influence continued to grow even after his death, and remains to this day so that, without fear of exaggeration, it can be said that Ahad Ha-Am's teachings became one of the most notable components of modern Jewish culture, actively disseminated in the world of education.

A clear indication of the extent of Ahad Ha-Am's impact on contemporary Jewish thought is the sharp polemic that followed on the publication of his work. A number of modern, Jewish thinkers — it will come as no surprise to learn that they were predominantly Orthodox thinkers such as Baruch Kurzweil and Yeshayahu Leibowitz — claimed that essentially he was not a philospher; that he was merely an ideologue or a superficial polemicist who dealt in issues that really required a better honed intellectual apparatus than the one he used. If this is so, how does one explain his lasting influence which extended to even such widely acclaimed thinkers and philosophers as Ḥayyim Naḥman Bialik, A.D. Gordon, Martin Buber, and Mordecai Kaplan — all of whom regarded Ahad Ha-Am as their mentor in Judaism and Zionism? It is true that Ahad Ha-Am knew the secret of lucid, accessible writing which imparts the thrust of ideas in a popular fashion; however, simple writing is not necessarily simplistic or superficial. One could, of course, give it such a reading; indeed those who angrily disagreed with his views claimed just that in their rebuttals, casting him as a shallow thinker.

One cannot overlook the possibility that in some aspects of his understanding of religious belief and a religious way of life — particularly the experiential aspect of belief — there was some shallowness in Ahad Ha-Am's thought. The emotional life that he so valued is found in his discussion of the spheres of nationality and humanism, whereas he does not reveal much insight in the sphere of religious experience. It appears he was put off by his impression of vulgarity in Hasidism. In any case, his attitude towards religion remained intellectual and scientific rather than emotional, with the result that modern, national Jews who did want to absorb the experiential, emotional messages of belief in Jewish culture found Ahad Ha-Am's concept to be missing a basic dimension.

Three influential modern Jewish thinkers attempted to deal with this deficiency and round out the teachings of Spiritual Zionism with regard to Jewish culture: Ḥayyim Naḥman Bialik, A.D.Gordon, and Martin Buber.

Chapter Nineteen
SANCTITY AND THE JEWISH NATIONAL MOVEMENT

Ḥayyim Naḥman Bialik (1873–1934) was an eminently versatile, creative personality. Primarily a poet, he was also a story-teller, essayist, thinker, and researcher in several fields of Judaic studies. His work is evocative of the great diversity of Jewish culture beginning with the Bible and going through modern Hebrew literature. Drawing on these sources, he not only contributed to the realization of his own cultural ideal, but he also exemplified the very process through which Jewish culture had been transmitted over the generations by means of the re-utilization and renewal of original sources.

A lasting ideological affinity and partnership existed between Bialik and Ahad Ha-Am. At the beginning of his career, Bialik considered himself the older man's disciple. He took direction from him even in the poetry he wrote; indeed he dedicated two poems full of admiration to him. Though in a later period Bialik had critical reservations about his mentor, he remained a follower of Ahad Ha-Am's Spiritual Zionism, espousing a definition of Jewish culture that included the element of national sentiment, Hebrew as the national language, Eretz Israel as the national homeland, a commitment to the continuity of literary sources from the Bible through the literature of the Hebrew renaissance, an appreciation of Jewish ethics, and the symbols of the Jewish calendar. All these figured in Bialik's cultural thought. He did not expand the theoretical content of Ahad Ha-Am's doctrine yet, in his day, he contributed more to the advancement of national Jewish culture that did Ahad Ha-Am, and added a much needed dimension of depth to its fundamental thought. It would be difficult to imagine the development of modern Jewish culture without Bialik's contribution. His writing, and that of the generation of authors inspired by him, produced an entire stratum of modern Hebrew classics organically linked to the original cultural sources of the religious canon that preceded it. Considered to be Zionism's poet laureate, during his own lifetime Bialik's work entered the canon of national literature. His work became a conduit through which students and writers joined the continuity of the traditional sources.

Ahad Ha-Am sought a similar status for his research efforts, anticipating that they would be seen as functionally analogous to Maimonides' two great undertakings, the *Mishneh Torah* and *The Guide to the Perplexed*. His essays were written as a rehearsal for an all encompassing philosophical study modeled on Rabbi Nachman Krochmal's work, *A Guide to the Perplexed of the Time*. He also undertook the editing of *Otzar ha-Yahadut* ("Encyclopedia of Judaism"), a project for the scientific teaching of Judaism. He got only as far as indicating the direction the enterprise should take without actually bringing a single segment of it to fruition. In contrast, through his poetry, essays and scientific editorial work (primarily in *Sefer ha-Aggadah* — "The Book of Legends") Bialik achieved a cultural creativity that surpassed that of Ahad Ha-Am. His writing, not unlike the very Biblical texts, legends of the Sages, prayer book, ethical literature and liturgical poetry of the medieval period which it embodied, had staying power and continuity. He was able to put Ahad Ha-Am's theories into practice through works that communicated the emotional and cognitive force of their Jewish sources while imbuing those sources with the experience and thought of contemporary nationalist Jews. In the process, he emphasized creative elements of culture that could not have been achieved without experiencing the spiritual creative phenomenon itself.

Bialik was regarded as the poet laureate of the modern Hebrew renaissance. His Zionist contemporaries found his poetry consummately expressive of their national sentiment in the sense that Ahad Ha-Am had used the term: a historic consciousness which connects one to the past, which makes one responsible for retaining a memory of that past and for realizing a vision of the future. How did Bialik accomplish it? Without question, his direct and pathos-laden eloquence, his overt call and exhortations for national revival and Zionist realization played a crucial role in shaping his figure as a national poet. In his poems, he epitomized the prophet, and many of his contemporaries saw him as a prophet of wrath and pity. But the national and Zionist ideals which he championed would not have had the impact they did were it not for his talent to make them part of the organic national memory. Bialik reshaped the historic myth of a Jewish people on its path through destructions and exiles toward redemption in its own land.

Given the crisis of agnosticism and assimilation, his task was difficult and complex. The religious myth that had formed the collective historic memory of the Jewish people throughout the generations was undermined by the modern historic consciousness, which was secular and scientific. It was a myth that had been nurtured by the Bible, the legends of the sages, the prayer book, the poetic hymns and kabbalistic literature of the Middle Ages. Bialik reworked the myth in terms of the contemporary crisis of faith. He saw the decline of the *Beit Midrash* (House of Study) as yet another destruction, the destruction of a Third Temple. The curse of exile was exacerbated because of the people's lack of faith in itself and its national destiny on the one hand, and because it wandered among enemies, persecutors, and oppressors in the wasteland of foreign nations on the other hand. The desperate rebellion against the decree of exile (which had its origins in the Biblical story about Israel's attempt to "ascend" to Canaan in spite of God's decree) was imbued with tragic elements of apocalyptic destruction on the way to a vision of redemption; it was an image integrated into a renewed personal and national myth, inspiring that redemptive vision as an expression of individual identification with the destiny of the people.

In his poems, Bialik was not only able to recapture the meaning of the religious myth, but to revitalize its motivating force. Even the revolt against religion assumed the force of a galvanizing and turbulent religious experience. The quasi-ritual status given to many of his poems is illustrative of their significance in Zionist life. Among the best know are *El ha-Tsipor* ("To A Bird"), *Ba-Sadeh* ("In the Field"), *Levadi* ("Alone"), *Al Saf Bet ha-Midrash* ("On the Threshold of the House of Study"), *Lifnei Aron ha-Sefarim* ("Facing the Bookcase"), *Im Shemesh* ("At Sunrise"), *Teḥezaknah* ("Be Stalwart!"), *Meitei Midbar* ("The Dead of the Wilderness"), *Megillat ha-Esh* ("The Scroll of Fire"), and *Be-Ir ha-Haregah* ("In the City of Slaughter"). These poems and others like them were studied in Diaspora Jewish schools with a nationalist orientation, and in youth movements both abroad and in Eretz Israel. They were committed to memory, recited at public events and ceremonies, sung as an anthem and a vow. While Ahad Ha-Am spoke of the centrality and importance of "national feeling," Bialik created, fashioned, and brought the concept up to date for his own peers and for two or three later generations.

There is an essential connection between the creation of a myth and the way language functions as a conduit of emotion and pageantry. Like Ahad Ha-Am, Bialik too identified language as a primary resource on which the creation of a culture depends and from which it is derived. Ahad Ha-Am explained this in a precise, fluent Hebrew which was equally available in translation to other languages. Bialik enunciated the same thoughts but expressed them in a poetic Hebrew in which all the strata of the language reverberated so that they took on a much more profound meaning.

In "The Sin Against the Language," Bialik's essay criticizing the Science of Judaism, all the powerful components inherent in employing language as a personal and national means of communication came to the fore. Beyond an initial agreement with Ahad Ha-Am, an examination of the essay indicates his differing conception of how language operates. For Ahad Ha-Am, language was instrumental, a means for transmitting ideological intent as well as emotional and sensual messages. Language itself was of no essential importance. For Bialik, language had an additional dimension through its physical presence and symbolic qualities, and in Bialik's view it was primarily experiential and emotive, penetrating beyond and through ideas and information. In its very functioning, language was, for Bialik, the core experience of the human spirit — the experience of expression which is, in and of itself, a penetrating activity of emotional, spiritual identification that transcends ideas and information.

Further examination shows that expression takes on qualitative variations in every language in ways that are not communicable through translation. The unique resonance of words, their tonalities and syntactical rhythms, and the intrinsic connotative associations of memory set one language apart from another. One finds that even without reference to ideational content, a person experiences a consciousness of spiritual individuality and ego-identity through the language in which he articulates his primary relationship to his environment and to himself, or in which he fashions the observations and emotional posture that ultimately determine his world outlook. Moreover, even before one considers the content of an individual's thought, by the very fact that a person speaks Hebrew, thinks Hebrew, feels Hebrew, senses and imagines Hebrew and lives a Hebrew life, the individual becomes a Hebrew person.

It would seem that only in appreciating what is communicated by the language itself can one grasp the deeply religious implications of the Hebrew word "sin" in Bialik's "The Sin Against the Language": that is, an action that injures the pure essence of the personality. "The covenant of language" is thus conceived in reality, and not just rhetorically, as "the most sacred of covenants." It embodies the cultural identity of each individual on the most intimate, primary, personal and existential plane; the plane at which the national spirit is found, the spirit which is the secret of creative continuity in the culture. Individuals contribute directly to it, but they do so by means of an energy that they discover in themselves yet is derived from a spiritual reservoir beyond themselves, the reservoir of language.

This difference between the poet and the philosopher in approach to language finds its direct functional expression in the rebirth of the Hebrew language as the infrastructure for the creation of a modern, national Jewish culture. Hebrew was not a "dead" language in exile; it was preserved as the language of prayer, of study and of religious thought. For it to become a spoken language and a language of literary creativity, a language that would be expressive of the full range of contemporary, national reality, it was necessary to augment and enrich the vocabulary, no less than to provide a greater flexibility and variety of structure, grammar, and syntax.

How could this be achieved? Ahad Ha-Am's answer was: "embellish your thinking." Precision of thought — its enrichment, depth and compass — would be the natural outcome of coining words and phrases which would serve as instruments for enhanced cognitive content. Bialik held the opposite view. It was the language itself that had to be directly embellished so as to enable thought that was richer, more profound, more exact and of greater scope. Thoughts could not be articulated, could not even occur, if they were not preceded by a language capable of expressing them. Language is not only precognitive, it is the mother of thought. All thoughts are potentially present in language, and the richer the language, the greater will be the creativity of thought.

Bialik concluded that the creation and development of language was an art form that demanded unique talents and abilities. The scholars of language and its artists (poets and writers) needed to collaborate in unlocking Hebrew. They had to make the language more flexible while remaining loyal to its original characteristics, being careful to prevent a schism between the linguistic expression of previous generations and the linguistic expression of the modern generation. This was Bialik's great fear. Left to their own devices, the people — even educated individuals and thinkers — would spontaneously revamp the language. This could spawn a new jargon that consisted of transposed foreign words, syntaxes and grammar grafted into Hebrew. The result would be a schism between ancient Hebrew and the modern language, something that had happened to several peoples for whom the tongue of their cultural sources became a foreign language which needed translation, so to speak, from the past to the present tense.

Bialik sensed this talent in himself and took on the vital task of renewing and expanding the language. In doing so, he became one of the innovators and leaders of *Va'ad ha-Lashon*, the Council for the Hebrew Language. In the final analysis, Bialik's contribution to the organic development of the Hebrew language was invaluable. He was instrumental in making it a language of contemporary communication and a continuing exposition of ancient Hebrew sources. Indeed, an entire stratum of Hebrew expression is clearly "Bialikian."

There is an obvious connection between the singularity of a culture's national language and the uniqueness of its literature which is a product of the language. Ahad Ha-Am's program called for maintaining the canonical Jewish sources from the Bible through modern Hebrew literature as a normative cultural and educational function. He regarded these sources as indisputable reservoirs of important identity-defining content: the historical narratives, laws and ordinances, commandments, ethical norms, beliefs and principles, symbols, imagination, visions and feelings. For Bialik, too, all these were repositories of content, and as such he considered them to be of great value. But, once again, one discovers that beyond the meaning of the specific content, he saw their significance in that they constituted a national literature. What he had in mind was the particular quality that written sources have as a *national literature*. There are various types of literature and they are of varying degrees of literary quality. At the highest level, one finds the distinctive characteristic of religious experience — the quality of sanctity — and from the perspective of quality, national literature belongs in this category.

Bialik was referring to the canonic quality of the sources, their classification as "sacred writings." But to be precise, this was not simply a question of an authoritative, institutionalized status; more importantly, it was the cultural force that radiated from the writings when they were tapped as the inspiration of a renewing, spiritual creativity. To the question: "What gave these rather than other sources their canonic status?" — one could assume that Ahad Ha-Am's answer would be that these were the religious ideas acceptable to the authoritative religious leadership who were responsible for their canonization. Bialik thought otherwise. It was their unique creative quality that was the basis of the decision to institutionalize them rather than the other way around. It sometimes happened that certain sources imposed themselves on those responsible for sanctification, overcoming dogmatic opposition in the minds of some of the sages (for example, the "Song of Songs" and "Ecclesiastes") because their inherent property of sanctity radiated to the people.

We are dealing with a literature whose expressive energy or whose potential for cognitive, emotional, sensual, visual creativity is so much greater, infinitely greater, than any content anyone may have found in it at some previous time, and from which subsequent generations were able to extract additional meanings. No exhaustive interpretation has ever been offered, nor can possible interpretations ever be exhausted. The sources can yield more than anything yet found by scholars, interpreters, or writers. Something of this essence is present in every linguistic product or work of art. Every human expression is possessed of a certain multifaceted energy that derives from fundamental qualities of language, the history of previous literary uses, or the shifting associations made by every literary study. But sources that are classified as sacred writings have, in Bialik's opinion, a specificity that stems from a unique creative meta-personal, supra-cultural dimension. Such works withstand the test of time and never wither. The people return to them again and again proving that they enfold the national spirit. It is such an understanding of the special cultural quality of sacred writings that underscores the difference between Bialik's cultural affinity to the sources and that of Ahad Ha-Am.

The significance of the divergence between the two men can be seen in an examination of Bialik's most important programmatic essay on the issue of Jewish national culture, *Ha-Sefer ha-Ivri* ("The Hebrew Book"). He raises a simple yet surprising idea. To confront the problem of Judaism's transition from a religious classification to a national-cultural one, the process of canonization, ostensibly a clearly religious action, must be reenacted so that the Jewish people can make a new start with a non-religious source for their culture that enjoys the authority that comes from the attributes of Scriptures.

The title that Bialik chose for his essay was calculated to such a goal: he avoided the use of words that exhibited an overtly religious connotation — neither "Torah," certainly not "Scriptures" but *sefer* ["scroll, book"], an apparently culturally-neutral word. Admittedly, literary association makes an immediate link to *Am ha-Sefer*, the "People of the Book," a obvious reference to the Book of Books (a Hebrew approximation of the word "Bible" for Christians [and English-speaking Jews]). In any case, the main thrust was abundantly evident: the People of the Book can exist and maintain its spiritual uniqueness only through "The Book" which for Bialik meant that it had an *a priori* cultural meaning. This being the case, the question to be determined was whether the People of the Book still had The Book by means of which it had become a people and by means of which it had continued to exist throughout the generations.

This was the question with which Bialik opened his essay, making an obvious effort to remain at a level of practical educational writing. He looked at the Jewish people's crowded bookcase and saw the painful paradox that confounded Jewish educators: it was a bookcase filled to the brim with Jewish culture — wisdom and knowledge, law and ordinances, ethics, art, and poetry. Yet when one sought *the one book* by means of which a modern Jewish nationalist educator could acquaint his pupils with their nation's culture unimpeded by the barrier of alienation, one discovered that there was no such book. The books from which the educators themselves had studied in the traditional *ḥeder* and yeshiva — The Five Books of Moses, with Rashi's commentary; the Talmuds, with all the interpretations and commentaries; the homiletic literature of the sages, and the ethical and philosophic literature of the Middle Ages — were all highly appropriate for their time, but now appeared to be totally remote and unavailable to the student of a modern Jewish school. These students, who had become accustomed to new pedagogical techniques and modern scientific and narrative modes, were incapable of reading the old books, let alone finding them of interest.

The fact that Bialik kept the discussion at the level of practical education rather than on the plane of ideology and principle should be emphasized. What was the basic difference between studying in a *ḥeder* or yeshiva and studying in a modern elementary school, gymnasia, or university? Initially, Bialik side-stepped the difference between the authoritarian religious approach and the open secular method. He chose instead to note the qualitative-literary and linguistic-stylistic differences among the various texts that were taught. In his search for a pragmatic solution, he thus avoided a head-on confrontation with the issue of belief and philosophy that would have closed off discussion had he tackled that aspect of the educational problem first.

Was Bialik overlooking the crux of the problem? Further on we will see that, on the contrary, this was precisely the way in which he attempted to deal with it employing an assumption that will become increasingly evident. But first we turn our attention to the divergence between the pedagogic and literary solution offered by Ahad Ha-Am, and the one offered by the author of *Ha-Sefer ha-Ivri*. Ahad Ham-Am had proposed a scientific, modern replay of Maimonides' method: a scholarly, theoretical book offering a modern historical interpretation of the traditional sources, and parallel to it, a scientific text book, *Otzar Ha-Yahadut* (*Encyclopedia of Judaism*) as a kind of Maimonidean *Mishneh Torah*. In such an encyclopedic work, the modern student would find a condensed, scientific overview of all the important themes in Jewish cultural history. Ahad Ha-Am proposed to overcome the alienation of the modern Jewish nationalist student from Jewish sources with a scientific exposition of Judaism done in a contemporary style. After this introduction, the student could be assisted in crystallizing his outlook on Judaism and the vital significance of contemporary study.

Bialik did not contest the necessity of such a book, but he regarded it only as a helpful tool, certainly not as an adequate substitute for the Book which had been studied in the *ḥeder* and yeshiva. It was not something about Judaism that was called for, but something that embodied Judaism itself, and Judaism itself consisted of certain books — "The Sources." They could be selected and interpreted scientifically, but they were not merely science. Moreover, in their vital, creative essence they were not science at all, nor were they philosophy, but, in truth, literature. Therefore, it was "The Book" itself which the people had to have; "The Book" would be a living, literary embodiment of Judaism, and would serve the needs of a modern, nationalist Jewish student. The sources had to be presented, the books themselves in up-dated form. Therefore, a modern canonization was required offering a totality that could be accepted by the people as an authoritative source work for the teaching of Judaism.

What texts did Bialik want to see included in "The Book" he proposed in his essay? First, the primary works that had already undergone canonization and which had the highest degree of authority because of their constitutive status. They enjoyed a pre-eminent position both from the religious standpoint (the Torah) and from the national one (the Hebrew Bible in its entirety but accompanied by modern, popular commentaries). Second, the Mishnah, (also with modern commentary) and a representative selection of the Aggadah found in the Talmud and the Midrash. Third, the prayer book, followed by an appropriate choice of liturgy; the religious and non-religious poetry of the Middle Ages, and the ethical and philosophic literature of that period which would, of course, include the works of Maimonides and Judah Halevi; and finally a selection of the best of modern Hebrew literature which had already achieved the status of classics. Again, all these would be accompanied by introductions emphasizing the historic aspect, along with concise scientific explanations whose purpose was to overcome obstacles that a typical modern student might encounter. Care would be taken to remove unnecessary dichotomies between the reader and the work. This was the essential and intended change, advanced by Bialik, from a traditional interpretive approach to a modern one. A modern interpretation would avoid the traditional creative homilies, opting instead for unmediated contact between text and reader by surmounting the historic separation between them. It would enable the reader to return to the reality of the work at the time it was written in order to understand the work in its own cultural context. Bialik obviously wanted to include the more important traditional interpretations (such as the legends of the rabbis, or Rashi's commentaries) as well as literary examples representative of the pre-modern period because it was important to stress the link between those interpretive works and their sources.

The plan did not call for a detailed obligatory course of study. Stipulating such a curriculum would have run counter to Bialik's plans for a Book which could gain the status of a national canon. His goal was to produce a concrete illustration of his concept so that it could begin to be implemented. How does one crystallize a program and make it real? Again we note that Bialik raised the issue only on the pragmatic plane, intentionally bypassing questions of principle. What he intended was a process in which the new "Hebrew Book" would achieve a status that paralleled that of the Bible, the Mishnah, the Talmud, and the prayer book in religious tradition. Can a religious institutional process be constituted on a national free-thinking plane? Is it possible to constitute a parallel authority in cultural terms?

Bialik's pragmatic answer came as the result of conclusions he drew from observing history. When at the end of every age it became clear that the books taught in the past had become insufficient for the spiritual needs of a younger generation, great sages and teachers whose authority was accepted by the people because it was rooted in their scholarship (a profound and all-embracing knowledge of the sources) and their wisdom (an understanding of the particular problems and needs of their age) came forward to provide what was missing. Their first step was one of selection. They re-examined the literature that had been sanctified in the past, and then examined the literature that had accumulated between the previous sealing of the canon and their own time. From the accumulated material, they selected what appeared to have best withstood the test of time and retained a vital spiritual message. The material that did not earn such a distinction became part of the archives, which means that it was removed from the curriculum and was no longer taught in schools or institutions. The selected works were first edited so that they would be suitable for instruction, then given the stamp of approval which meant that they could be added to the pedagogic process. In and of itself, this was a process of commentary. Through authoritative inclusion in the curriculum, these sources achieved a status of religious sanctity. In Bialik's opinion, the educational achievement was twofold: first, by such canonization the people were provided with the book that filled their spiritual, educational needs. Secondly, relegating other material to the archives eased the burden of learning. Attention could be devoted to new creative endeavors meant to forge a link between the tradition-bearing sources, already canonized, and the life that was constantly being renewed. In time, of course, a subsequent canonization would draw on newly accumulated literature.

This was Bialik's perception of how the Bible was canonized by the early sages who decided to assign the "apocryphal"* works to the archives. The Mishnah was canonized in the same way, winnowing out material that seemed extraneous. The process was repeated in editing the Talmud, and it was applied in such works as Maimonides' *Mishneh Torah* and the *Beit Yosef* of Rabbi Joseph Caro. It is self-evident that every canonization project had its own unique character, a singularity that was evident in the type of works anthologized, their sweep, and the diverse degree of sanctity assigned to them. It was this very diversity that clearly showed the cultural, historic character of the process. Each canonization was responsive to the spiritual condition, state of mind, concepts and opinions that prevailed among the people in any given period. Every canonization perpetuated the tradition and assured the future by addressing the particular needs of its time.

---

* In several places in the rabbinic literature, we are told that the rabbis sought to "hide away" certain books — i.e., relegate them to the back room where they would not be studied. What is now called "the Apocrypha" consists of those books excluded from the canon by the rabbis but preserved by the Catholic Church. (LL)

There was an obvious conclusion to all this: a period in the Jewish people's history had come to an end and a new one had begun. The spiritual needs of the Jewish people had changed. Studied as they had been in the past, the Books of the past were no longer pertinent. It was time to repeat the same process in keeping with the contemporary spirit, which of course was unlike that of previous periods. A new kind of sage was called for, not prophets, not Sages of the Mishnah or Talmud, not even rabbis. Bialik spoke of a different mode of scholarship, a different design for assessing the value and importance of books, their editing and explication. Everything was different. In his essay, "The Hebrew Book," Bialik added a positive demand to an earlier critique of the Science of Judaism: scholars of a modern Science of Judaism, from among the foremost scholars of Judaica, would meet together with outstanding writers and educators to settle on a comprehensive, fully articulated program committed to clarification and proper editing which would render a scientific interpretation that suited the modern period. At the same time, these modern sages would imbue the project with a national spiritual authority that flowed naturally from their recognized wisdom and scholarship. To summarize: the first and foremost duty of a modern Science of Judaism would be to endow the people with *The Book* that was missing.

On the face of it, this was a necessary and practical proposal. Just how necessary and practical Bialik tried to demonstrate by a work that was inspired by the spirit of its sources, and an impressive contribution and model in its own right. Together with the writer Y. H. Ravnitsky, he collected, edited, composed and explicated *Sefer ha-Aggadah* (*The Book of Legends*). "Collected" — in the sense that from the sea of Aggadic literature in the Talmud and the extant collections of legends of the Sages, he assembled and selected what he considered to be the material that had best overcome the test of time; the criterion was based on ideational content and narrative, on form and style. It was "edited" in the sense that each of the legends was arranged by categories representative of the full scope and variety of Aggadic literature. It was "composed" in the sense that the categorized legends were melded on a topic-by-topic basis in such a way that they constituted a thematic continuity. The continuities were narrative, historic, chronological or philosophical. Finally, the work was "explicated" by winnowing out extraneous material, proofing corruptions of the text and correcting them so that the original character was retained. Scientific and relevant explanations, for the most part linguistic, were added in order to afford the non-scholar a fluent and more readily available reading of the text. Since, as they appear in Talmudic and rabbinic literature, the legends of the Sages are outside the grasp of a modern reader who has not studied in a yeshiva, one is easily convinced that by harnessing all the talents needed,

Bialik achieved the goal that he had set for himself. In practice, then, Bialik's *Book of Legends* became a popular text that presented the legends of the Sages in a way that remains germane for the modern Hebrew student to read, enjoy and find interesting.

Ultimately, however, the original question re-emerges. When Bialik's words are carefully studied, one realizes that what he proposed was an institutionalized and authoritative edition of the "classics" which would be taught in Jewish nationalist schools and read by the general public. All the national movements of Europe created classics in such a way for their nations. Every nation sought to promote its archetypal literature for the purposes of national education. There could be no reason, therefore, not to create a parallel nationalist Hebrew classic. But, could such a nationalist-educational endeavor be distinguished as the creation of a *canon*? Could a classic literature take the place of The Book in its original religious sense? Would such a literature have the authoritative status of *sacred writings*?

At the end of his essay, Bialik answered the question that he had ostensibly avoided. Had he not said earlier that every canonization in the past had its unique character that was responsive to the needs of the time, employing concepts that were current at that time? Had he not said that the sanctity of the Five Books of Moses was not same as the sanctity of the Prophets, and that the sanctity of the Prophets exceeded that of The Writings; that the sanctity of the Mishnah and the Talmud was not equal to that of the Bible? Clearly, there was a qualitative and essential difference between the national project that Bialik proposed in his essay, and between all the previous undertakings. Unquestionably there were great differences in their standing, degree of authority, and extent of sanctity. Concluding the essay, Bialik explicitly stated that he was dealing with a national rather than a religious endeavor, such as the *Mishneh Torah* of Maimonides. But that was exactly the point. That was how it should be. His work was intended for the free-thinking nationalist school rather than the Orthodox one. Readers of the essay, however, realized that consistently Bialik did attribute an aspect of sanctity to the national, non-religious endeavor he was proposing. And typically, he called it, "national sanctity."

The question then arises: What is the significance of the term "national sanctity" that Bialik equated with the religious sanctity which he believed typified Jewish culture from generation to generation and made it unique? Admittedly, in "The Hebrew Book" this question remains unresolved. One can only infer that Bialik assigned an element of sanctity to any work that had the special quality which he believed to be characteristic of works representative of the people's "spirit" and which were granted the status of "timelessness." Furthermore, he equated the spirit of the people with holiness; in his writing he even used such religiously charged terms as "providence," "prophecy," and "godly." But he did not spell out his warrant for doing so. In order to find such an interpretation, we have to shift our attention from the theoretical essay to other works in which Bialik had recourse to religious terminology, openly and unambiguously. These were works in which he sustained the "national feeling" by the use of myth; that is, in his poetry. Bialik's national poetry was an artistic expression of a religious stratum for which Ahad Ha-Am proposed no alternative.

A close reading of Bialik's poetry as the modern embodiment of the Jewish national mythos serves to sharply underscore the difference between him and Ahad Ha-Am (and his affinity to Berdyczewski.) Ahad Ha-Am had also used the term "national feeling" as an explanation for the over-all individuation of varying national cultures. In his essay, "Moses," Ahad Ha-Am pointed to the prophets, particularly Moses, as the personification of Jewish national feeling that he characterized as fanatic devotion to absolute truth and to absolute justice. It was in just such fanatic devotion that Ahad Ha-Am saw the eternal, spiritual content of monotheism. But it must be stressed again that by placing Moses, the greatest of the prophets, as the personification of the people's feeling and the manifestation of the monotheistic ideal, he maintained a rigorous and consistent distinction between "national feeling" and the godly presence; certainly between the monotheistic ideal — which was a human spiritual ideal and as such that of the prophets and their followers, and monotheistic religion insofar as it was an institutionalized religion based on a belief in a transcendental godly presence. Ahad Ha-Am did see the prophetic spirit of the people manifested in the shell of its religion; nonetheless he continued to regard religion *qua* religion as a separate external shell, stressing that in the secular age spiritual continuity was only possible by maintaining a clear distinction between the human spiritual content of monotheism on the one hand, and religious faith and its institutions on the other hand. The age of religion had passed.

Like Berdyczewski, Bialik consciously crossed this dividing line. As far as he was concerned, attributing a dimension of sanctity to national feeling was nothing more than equating national sentiment with the transcendental godly presence in which the people believed. He believed that continuity was to be found not only in the ongoing application of monotheism in terms of human spirituality, but in the very belief in a transcendental godly presence. This presence was manifested in the people through their prophets, and in the practices of the religious establishment from which a transcendental religious sanctity flowed as in the recurring process of canonization and archiving.

What enabled Bialik to ideologically justify and experientially enact the crossing of the boundary that separated human spiritual ideal from religious belief? In the approach to myth in the poetics of Berdyczewski and Bialik, mythos possesses an emotional, simulating presence of great force and of absolute tangibility. Indeed, Bialik and Berdyczewski were as aware as Ahad Ha-Am of the difference between a naïve believer who related to myth as the direct revelation of a transcendental deity on the one hand, and on the other hand a thinking believer who consciously related to myth as myth, i.e., as a sublime emanation of the national feeling present in the soul of each individual as the collective "ego." Transcending individuals, it was this that united the people — a consciousness that did not diminish the actual force nor detract anything from the fullness and authenticity of the religious feeling expressed in it. In their view, whether the response was thinking or not, it was the very same feeling. When one lives the myth as a powerful presence of prophetic feeling and imagination, cognitive reflection disappears from religious consciousness so that it becomes all-inclusive. Indeed, this was how it appeared in Bialik's national poems, enabling him to hear God's word, or speak to Him, in the same religious parlance that a naïve believer used.

This pertains to how strongly one feels a religious presence and the reality of the experience. A second observation, however, shows a different expressiveness, convoluted and embroiled within itself: a naïve religious feeling that is no longer so naïve. Of course, there are times when even the innocent believer argues with his God. The guileless belief frequently expresses itself precisely in rebellion and as a protest to a heaven that is silent in the face of malicious evil. But in Bialik and in Berdyczewski, the quarrel and the outcry reveal a modern crisis of faith that was occasioned by a reflexive concept that regarded experiencing the divine presence as a myth that stood for national feeling rather than transcendental presence. Again, as distinguished from Ahad Ha-Am, the cause for their crisis of faith was not the challenge posed by modern science, it was rather the traditional challenge of coming up against malicious evil: the perception of having being abandoned and betrayed, the helplessness of the individual and of the Jewish people, the sense that there is no divine, providential delivery from the spiritual and physical dungeon of exile which becomes ever more onerous, persecuting and threatening. The outcome is that consciousness becomes strengthened, and it is consciousness which, ostensibly, is the mother of all religious rejection. It is, as well, the root of the Zionist idea: only the Jewish people itself can extricate itself from the exile into which it has been thrust, and in which it has remained to its devastation for so many generations. This is true whether it is through its own deficiency, perhaps through God's, or perhaps through both its and God's deficiency — which is ultimately the same thing.

When the language that the poet uses in his quarrel with God is examined, we find that the argument is merely a metaphor for the poet's controversy with himself and his people, for their ineffectualness, nullity, and despair. Supposedly the people await the mercy of the heavens; they refrain from doing anything that they ought to demand of themselves in order that they may be redeemed and thus sanctify the name of their God, their spirit and themselves. This is the construction that must be put on Bialik's cry of disaster and protest against the "silent heavens."

Seemingly it is a re-enactment of a naïve believer's feelings of despair, but in truth it borders on heresy: the God that should have been with the believer at this hour is not, so he hurls the cry of His non-existence in His face! Is there any positive religious significance to such a cry? Ahad Ha-Am's answer — rational and consistent — would certainly have been negative. In his view, religion had come to the end of the road, and the Jewish people had to recognize that it alone could redeem itself. They had no Redeemer outside themselves. But rather than a rationalist response to the absence of God, Bialik gave an experiential, emotional answer because of a different creed — the faith of a believer which is apparently reborn out of despair: only by virtue of great faith can the people redeem itself! From this standpoint, therefore, to remonstrate against God for His absence holds an inherently religious significance despite its being paradoxical. Indeed, the outcry carries within itself the emotional force that had once been present in the naïve faith before its collapse; and since this is so, it has the potential to save itself from despair by means of an experiential transposition that will awaken the believer's consciousness to the source of his belief deep within himself and his soul, and in the redemption that it carries within itself through the force of his will and his strength as a believer to act and change historic reality.

The responsibility now falls on him. The "absence" of his God is nothing more than his own weakness, the "impotence" of God is merely his own. It is for the believer, and for his people, to uncover the strength of spirit that remains in them in order to save themselves; they will be redeemed from the narrow straits of exile and rediscover that their God is still with them! In Bialik's religious myth, the concept of a historic present repeatedly reflects precisely that moment of a believer's crisis, of extreme despair and disillusionment in himself and his God when belief is renewed, and a divine presence on the experiential plane of historic realization is discovered.

This is Bialik's version of the "sundering of the heart," and one recognizes in it a certain closeness to Berdyczewski. Bialik, too, rebelled against the despotic, national deity that had decreed exile for His people. Bialik, too, was embittered by the exilic character of rabbinic halakhah, and he, too, searched for a pantheistic alternative to a supernatural deity. Nonetheless, there was a great difference between the two men.

First, it is important to reiterate that in the paradox of a shattered faith, Bialik struggled to find spiritual, religious affirmation. This was true even when his lyric phrases were charged with negative, critical utterances that bordered on violent cruelty. Even in poems such as "The Dead of the Wilderness" and "The City of Slaughter," all the more in the mythic work "Scroll of Fire," his spiritual goal was not to dislodge religion in order to destroy it but to shake it up so that it could be preserved through a Zionist transformation. It was a supreme, spiritually creative effort to confront the crisis of faith in order to overcome it. In other words, the aim was to escape from the distress of the spiritual crisis, not simply from the threat to the people's survival in exile (in Bialik's view as in Ahad Ha-Am's, the two were linked to one another). It was clear to Bialik that without renewing the people's strength of belief, there could be no salvation from exile because exile was first and foremost the alienation and assimilation of the national spirit. From Bialik's perspective, the rebellion against God was not intended to break or obliterate religion. It was a cry "for the sake of God," a revolt that stemmed from a desire to enable the modern Jew who rebels against the fate of his people and their cultural, spiritual reality to express his defiance and rebellion in a familiar, religious language; to mobilize the ancient source of religious energy to reform the people's spirit so that it could persevere and be redeemed, to renew the religion as of old when the people lived on its land.

A quotation from the closing lines of one of Bialik's early poems of revolt will serve to illustrate his rebellious position. The content of *Ha-Matmid* ("The Talmud Student") is reminiscent of Berdyczewski's hostility to rabbinic Judaism with its exilic religiosity and despotic God. Following on a lengthy Berdyczewski-like lament over the fate of a Talmud student who sacrifices his natural life — both physical and spiritual — in the name of a religious ideal, decimating himself on the altar of Torah, the poet casts himself in the role of one who has forsaken the yeshiva, saying —

And I remember, too, how strong, how sturdy
How strong the seed must be that withers in those fields,
How rich would be the blessing if one beam
Of living sunlight could break through to you;
How great the harvest to be reaped in joy,
If once the wind of life should pass through you,
And blow clear through to the yeshiva doors...

Bialik maintained this basic stance in all aspects of his work — neither to neglect nor abandon, but to pave a vital pathway to the very doors of the yeshiva! Which brings us to the second difference. Bialik moved away from Berdyczewski and grew closer to Ahad ha-Am's when he, too, sought a unifying continuity for Jewish cultural heritage in which the full range of the culture's resources would be utilized.

We recall that Berdyczewski distinguished between two contradictory cultures and religious concepts: one, a prophetic-halakhic religion and culture that were fanatically devoted to the ideal of divine unworldly sanctity; and the other, a natural-mundane culture and religion that aspired to an ordinary national life of a people in its land. Berdyczewski revolted against prophetic, halakhic, rabbinic culture and in its place sought only the renewal of a mundane, natural culture with its attendant pantheistic religion. A similar expression is found in such poems of Bialik's as "The Talmud Student," "The Dead of the Wilderness," "Facing the Bookcase," and others in which there is a rejection of rabbinic-prophetic Judaism and the claim that Judaism sacrificed the down-to-earth life of the people on an altar of ideal sanctity. One also finds a richly expressed, enthusiastic support for pantheistic religiosity in his poetry that yearns for the fullness of the mundane life ("The Pool," "Splendor," "In the Field," and "Alone and Unseen"). Unlike Berdyczewski, however, Bialik believed that both aspects of religion could be found in the self-same sources, that there was no conflict between two opposing cultures or religions; rather, two ideal poles (transcendental and mundane sanctity) co-existed. The inner tension between them was the source of creativity and continuous renewal — in the same culture and in the same religion. In his view, the two religious stances could exist only through a proper balance, and only when they complemented rather than negated one another.

The two groups of poems cited above fall into two distinct categories of Bialik's poetry, the "nature poems" as compared to the "poems of the Beit Midrash." As an adult, the longing for the religious-sensory experience of his early childhood, found in the nature poems, was clouded by the phenomenon of alienation and rupture. Spirituality was banished from the sensory religious experience leaving only a sense of earth-bound materiality and alienation. What was its source? Could it be that the crisis was not connected to the disappearance of a transcendental, spiritual sanctity so explicitly sensed in poems of the Beit Midrash?

No more than Ahad Ha-Am did Bialik accept Berdyczewski's argument that the rabbinic-prophetic element in monotheism was essentially an exilic creation. On the contrary. Bialik regarded prophetic monotheism as the authentic root of Jewish national spirit. In its essence, prophetic monotheism did not reject down-to-earth life; indeed, it sought to sanctify mundane life by means of an abundant spirituality. It was the Exile that had brought about the conflict between transcendental sanctity and the desire for an integrated religious-mundane way of life. Consequently, the adjustment ought not be achieved through the cancellation of one of the elements accompanied by a unilateral imposition of the other, as Berdyczewski would have liked, but through the discovery of a renewed balance between the two elements. It is here that one finds the meaning of Bialik's aspiration to pave a living path to the very door of the yeshiva.

In any case, it is apparent that in all his work — literary, scientific and intellectual — Bialik looked for constancy and fusion. There is reason to believe that he attempted to bridge the dichotomy that one finds in his poems between mundane, natural phenomena and the phenomena of transcendental spiritual sanctity. In his epic narrative poem, "The Scroll of Fire," he begins with a description of the Destruction and Exile whose impact on the spiritual life of the people created a break between two concepts of divinity: a vengeful and destructive deity, and a loving and comforting God; as well as between two prophetic notions: an ideal of destructive revenge, and an ideal of a spiritual yet down-to-earth love. The parallel symbolic story that then unfolds speaks of the frustration of both the personal and national goals caused by the fatal exilic rupture between spiritual sanctity and natural, mundane life. Only a re-institution of unity within a single culture, and a single way of life, can redeem the nation and its individuals from the dilemma of spiritual and physical exile. Still, as a work representative of Diasporic reality, "The Scroll of Fire" ends with a far off, ambiguous hope shrouded in a sense of perpetual tragedy: is the people capable of mobilizing its spiritual power to break the curse of exilic disunity and duality? The undertaking in the Land of Israel was intended to provide the answer.

Undoubtedly Bialik regarded the ideal of religious sanctity as a primary concept to be re-instituted in the culture of modern, Jewish Eretz Israel. This would be accomplished first by re-uniting the two religious ideals that had diverged to their mutual disadvantage in Exile; and second by transmuting spiritual sanctity to a perception of national sanctity in order to create an authoritative, inspirational source which would place the full responsibility for the redemption of the people in its land on the people and on its individuals.

Ultimately, the passion to realize this cultural ideal in the Land of Israel explains Bialik's reassessment of another issue concerning the renewal of Jewish culture: his attitude towards halakhah. An instructive change is apparent between his work in the period when he wrote in Eretz Israel and the previous period in the Diaspora. The Diasporic period was marked by an almost biased protest against rabbinic Judaism and Halakhah which he projected as despotic and rigid. In that early period, like Berdyczewski, he sought an unbroken continuity with the sources, particularly with the lenient, almost dreamlike Aggadah with its talent for speaking to the hearts of despairing people, reinvesting them with belief. At that point, Halakhah symbolized for him the dungeon of exile and its excessive decrees, whereas the Aggadah bespoke a vision of redemption and solace. It was precisely the encounter with Eretz Israel which forced Zionism to face the harsh challenge of reality and brought Bialik to an opposite judgment: the dream-like Aggadah was suited to the Diaspora while the pragmatic realization of Zionism required a halakhah!

This was the background for his well known essay, "Halakhah and Aggadah." Initially, Bialik speaks categorically about a unification of opposites within the Jewish sources. While he admits there is a qualitative difference between how Aggadah and Halakhah relate to one's personal way of life and historical reality, he maintains that the difference is only apparent. These are merely two aspects of a single spirituality. Aggadah is the vision; Halakhah is its realization in practice. Nothing can be realized without a normative creativity that is tested in actual practice, in the reality inherent in details. Admittedly, Halakhah without Aggadah is a body devoid of spirit, but Aggadah without Halakhah is sterile.

Bialik felt close to the pioneering workers movement of Eretz Israel because it was a movement of realization. Indeed, he wrote its anthem, *Teḥezaknah* ("Be Stalwart!"), a song that faithfully expressed the halakhic norm which was the leitmotif of settlement and social realization — *the ideal of labor*. However, just as Bialik was an enthusiastic supporter of pioneering realization, he was critical of the labor movement's way of life, a way of life that was meant to express spiritual values in the land which was assumed to be the "spiritual center" for the entire nation. The literature written in Eretz Israel, Bialik claimed in his essay, displayed a great deal of vision, a great deal of Aggadah, but it was devoid of an implementing, educating Halakhah that would shape the individual's way of life, and that of the community and the people. Bialik feared the dangers of forgetfulness, of deterioration and decline. The spirit to vitalize the realization process, the spirit of belief, and the spirit of national identity could only sink into materialism if they remained without a focused halakhic expression to define and order the way of life. Consequently, he concluded his essay with an emotional, prophetic call to the writers of Eretz Israel not to make do with Aggadah alone. He called on them to renew a strict, unyielding, binding Halakhah that would save the Sabbath and the holidays thus ensuring a renewal of the spiritual life of Jews in Eretz Israel.

Did such a Halakhah ever emerge? Indeed, could it have been created? Though at the conclusion of his essay Bialik was forceful, even blunt, it would appear that the sharpness of his words were a cover for deep frustration. On a personal level, he attempted to engender a new Halakhah and carry it out in the Jewish spiritual life of Tel Aviv. The Oneg Shabbat gathering which he initiated and conducted there is an outstanding example. But this only partially filled the spiritual void and touched but a small segment of the country. Bialik's signal contribution to a creative culture, it should be emphasized, was primarily in the sphere of Aggadah rather than Halakhah. Even in his Hebrew Book Project referred to earlier, Halakhah was restricted to the Mishnah. Was it, therefore, an accident that the example through which he illustrated his entire project was the Book of Aggadah? Indeed it was not. True, after Bialik's death, a draft for a Book of Halakhah was found among his unpublished manuscripts; the question remains, was this simply because he had not finished the work? Be that as it may, in his essay, Bialik's demand to the younger writers of Eretz Israel was directed to their undertaking the role of "masters of a spiritual Halakhah."

From the standpoint of developing a Jewish culture in Eretz Israel of the pre-state era, the important issue is to what extent Bialik's "Aggadah" shaped the image of the Yishuv, and to what extent it called forth a response to its fulfillment through the creation of a new Halakhah that would be binding.

Chapter Twenty
THE DIMENSION OF SANCTITY IN PIONEERING LABOR ZIONISM

The Spiritual Zionism of Ahad Ha-Am and of Hayyim Nahman Bialik had wide-ranging ideological impact within the Zionist movement and beyond. Indeed, the works of both, particularly Bialik's poetry and *Book of Legends*, were regarded as core texts of modern Jewish education. Essentially, this is still true; one cannot imagine Jewish culture in the State of Israel without them. Each of the three major streams of Zionist ideology interpreted Ahad Ha-Am's and Bialik's work according to its own ideological bent, generally through a process of selecting the particular works to be read and taught in its educational institutions. Ahad Ha-Am's impact on social Zionism was transmitted primarily through essays such as "The Wrong Way" and "Truth From Eretz Israel" which aroused a pioneering response to settle the Land of Israel. His essay "Slavery in Freedom" reinforced abhorrence of assimilation and strengthened notions of national identity, spiritual independence, and indigenous creativity among the younger generation. It engendered a reaction against the Territorialists and in favor of Zionism in the land of Zion, against Yiddish and for Hebrew, against traditional education and for a modern Hebrew education that rejected the "religious shell" in favor of a selective approach to Jewish heritage and secular, national content. Each of these concepts was compatible with Berdyzewski's thinking.

Bialik's influence had a similar impact, particularly his national poetry which was found not only in the curriculum of nationalist Hebrew schools in Eretz Israel and the Diaspora but in the social, ceremonial fabric of the adult Jewish community as well. These were the poems that most overtly expressed Bialik's "negation of exile": poems such as "The Dead of the Wilderness," "Poems of Wrath," and "In the City of Slaughter;" or, by contrast, poems that spoke of a longing for the wholeness of natural life and a return to nature: "Aftergrowth," "Splendor," "At Sunset" and "The Pool." Once again, these are the very works in which Bialik's affinity to Berdyczewski is so evident.

Within Socialist Zionism, a small but influential group had misgivings about the implications for Jewishness in the Marxist version of socialism; they rejected the anti-religious and anti-spiritual outlook that had taken root within it. And they also had reservations concerning what they considered to be Herzl's simplistic political Zionism. At the same time, they were open to the cultural message of spiritual Zionism and saw Ahad Ha-Am and Bialik as guides to Jewish education and renewed cultural creativity. The younger socialist Zionists embraced their mentors' original and unique approach to solving spiritual questions that sprang up in the wake of pioneering endeavors in Eretz Israel.

From its inception, the Labor Movement in Eretz Israel focused on a social utopia: the creation of a new Jewish society which, while utopian, was a society predicated on radical pragmatism. The critical decision that the movement made was to begin everything anew, to build on solid foundations and, in so doing, to develop the infrastructure for a comprehensive society beginning with its economy and settlement through to the content of its spiritual life. Any individual who aspired to such a goal was expected to undergo a thorough personal revolution, to effect an almost complete reordering of all the elements of his previous way of life, perhaps even to the extent of changing his personality as though reborn to a life of "realization."

An orienting philosophy evolved against the background of such a personal revolution; confronting the problems of spiritual existence, it drew its ideas from spiritual Zionism. One cannot totally transform one's personal life without a belief in something. Those pioneers who recoiled from the tenets of Marxist faith or from Brenner and Berdyczewski's despairing faith because of their Jewish education, sought to ground their belief in the Judaism that persisted within themselves; even as they devoted themselves to secular realization, they felt themselves impelled to return to the notion of religious faith and sanctity. This was the reason for what seemed to be a paradox: spiritual Zionism embarked on a religious awakening precisely against the militantly secular background of the pioneering labor movement's settlement and societal program. It seized on the experience of divine revelation which burst from cultural-national sources that were both primal and personal: the archetypical experience of encountering the ancient landscape of Eretz Israel; the fundamental experience of speaking Hebrew; the primal experience of physical labor, of creating a collective society in which human interaction discovers unsuspected emotional depths in man; the authentic experience of returning to the starting point of the people's history which was also a return to the Bible that had *mediated* the encounter with the actual landscape, with the Hebrew language and with the history of the people in its land. From all these primary sources, a Jewish religiosity was renewed which incorporated a revelational, prophetic dimension.

The most influential and prominent theoreticians of the Labor wing of Spiritual Zionism were A.D. Gordon and Martin Buber. Each created a comprehensive philosophical system at whose center was the restoration of religious belief. They each related to the full range of Hebrew culture: the national sentiment, the sense of belonging to a generations-long continuity of the people, the historic memory that was embodied in it as a mythos, the affinity to Eretz Israel, the link to the Hebrew language and literature, and the affinity to religion and tradition. Each proposed a singular interpretation which was influenced by his own religious world view. To review the full range of their concept of Jewish culture would require a discussion of all of these issues, but for the matter at hand, we will restrict our focus to their understanding of religious revelation and the way in which their approach to prophetic religion shaped the process of social realization. It was an original contribution, and it had a palpable impact on the creation of the new Hebrew culture in Eretz Israel.

A. D. Gordon (1856–1922) was considered by both his comrades and opponents as the founder of a new kind of Jewish religious movement, indigenous to the renascent Eretz Israel. His contemporaries characterized it as the "religion of labor." It bears noting that this curious notion was far from Gordon's own thought. Not only did he not coin the expression, he strenuously objected to it. Yet, there is no doubt that his world-view was founded on an immediate religious experience, and that labor was at its core.

In the way he lived, and in his writing, Gordon personified the significance of aliyah to Eretz Israel that was undertaken in order to devote oneself to the actual realization of Zionism, expressed by settling on the land and working in agriculture. His aliyah was sparked by his closeness to the Spiritual Zionism of Bialik and Ahad Ha-Am. Though he rejected Jewish life in the Diaspora, Gordon did not wish to reject the precepts of the religious education in which he had been raised. Indeed, already an older man at the time of his aliyah, he saw himself as religious, even Orthodox. His arrival in Eretz Israel demanded that he undergo a transformation. As an Orthodox Jew he could have found his place in the old Yishuv of the Orthodox community, but as a pioneer who made aliyah in order to realize Zionism, having chosen a life on the soil, he had to find his place within the pioneering community. It was a community most of whose members shared Berdyczewski and Brenner's dim view of religion and tradition. Because the precept of Zionist realization was paramount for him, Gordon opted to be among the pioneers of the Second Aliyah; as a result, he had to forgo many Orthodox mitzvot. Even without ritual, however, he remained a believing Jew. The difficulties and hardships he confronted in his adjustment to the new environment reinforced his need for belief as a source of inner strength; therefore, he had to find a surrogate for his earlier faith, both in thought and way of life. What could replace traditional religiosity? The solution, of course, had to be found in work, the content of his new life as a pioneer. Work sustained him and through it he forged his social ties; through it he participated in the redemption of the country and its people. Gordon's profound contemplation of the relevance of labor thus became an expression of his underlying relationship to his environment; it was the focal point of his religious outlook and work itself, actual work in the fields, became the center of his religious way of life, a veritable worship of God.

Before discussing his "religion of labor," it is important to note that first and foremost Gordon meant agricultural labor; only afterwards did he refer to all other types of creative physical labor which directly process the resources of nature. Certainly, in so far as they were required for human life, he included spiritual, scientific, theoretical, artistic, and even organizational creativity in his definition of labor, but only secondarily. Labor, in its primary form, was the effort needed to extract the earth's material bounty and, along with it, the emotional-experiential and spiritual sustenance which is the result of man's active involvement in the surrounding nature on which his physical-psychic life depends. In Gordon's view, spiritual creativity, too, was a product of physical labor: the spiritual richness that manifests itself in philosophical, artistic, and scientific creation flows from the inherent spirituality of nature, to man's soul, in a coalescing experience.

Obviously Gordon regarded tilling the soil as the fundamental and formative fulfillment of Zionism: re-establishing the people's rootedness in their land. There cannot be a genuine taking hold of the land without settlement, and there is no true settlement of land without its cultivation. Working the land would inspire spiritual blossoming and it, in turn, would mature as a full and unique culture.

With these two considerations in mind, Gordon enunciated his basic, pragmatic standard: *hagshamah atzmit* was the quasi-halakhic norm required from both the personal, human standpoint and the Jewish, national standpoint; this *self-realization* would be accomplished through agricultural labor in Eretz Israel. Gordon derived all the other norms for structuring a Jewish society and for the renewal of Jewish culture from this rudimentary demand.

What was self-realization? It was the prescriptive, ritualized standard of pioneering Zionism — almost halakhic in nature — that began in the period of the Second Aliyah. Neither the term nor the notion were coined by Gordon. He adopted the simplest meaning of the term from his younger comrades. They had used it as their incisive critique of the majority of Zionists who were eloquent Zionists while remaining in Exile. To set themselves apart from such Zionists, the pioneers of the Second Aliyah demanded that every individual who came to the conclusion that Zionist realization was indispensable for the salvation of the Jewish people take upon *himself*, directly and immediately, the duty of *hagshamah*. Such a Zionist must come himself to Eretz Israel and settle on the land rather than wait for others to realize the goal for him. To this uncomplicated meaning, Gordon added an additional, more profound insight whose importance was underscored by his own life experience in Eretz Israel: it was not enough for a pioneer to carry out the *Zionist* task through his deeds, he also had to realize *himself* in the process. Gordon emphatically rejected the notion of *self-sacrifice* that his comrades, the young pioneers, had embraced largely because of the *Zeitgeist*, the prevailing mood which was a mixture of enthusiasm and depression. To counter that temper, Gordon claimed that a people's redemptive endeavor could not be achieved by a short-term volunteerism similar to the patriotic fervor of enlisting in an army. The endeavor had to be a life-time commitment. In any case, even if one's people could be saved though sacrifice, they could not be redeemed by it in the sense of renewing life and its reconstruction. Sacrifice is death, not life. Individuals who sacrifice themselves neither create nor build. Only individuals who regard the realization of Zionism as an act of redeeming themselves, who make it the entire content of their lives, will devote themselves to *hagshamah* and achieve its goals. Moreover, only if self-realization in the first sense is coupled with self-realization in its second meaning can it be societal, cultural, and spiritual rather than limited to the national, political plane. Thus *hagshamah* becomes an enterprise for the economic, social and cultural settlement of the land.

Though the initial "halakhic" norm was formulated by Gordon's predecessors in the Second Aliyah, the development of the theory of labor was engendered by enlarging on the intricacies and inferences of *hagshamah* and articulating its complexities. It was broadened until it became an all-encompassing world view and belief system. The religion of labor was envisioned as guiding an entire way of life. In the philosophy of labor, Gordon identified directives that applied to all spheres of creative culture — the various aspects of national as well as personal life. The multiplicity of ways in which labor created the gamut of creativity was not self-evident, and the workers had to be sensitized so that they could experience work as a spiritual dedication. Understanding this can serve as a key to Gordon's teachings which developed as an interpretive observation about his own personal experience and that of his comrades as they worked.

Gordon was a systematic thinker. His method was to consider every facet of human life "From The Foundation" (the name of one of his better known and more influential essays). He believed that the foundation was nature; that is, the relationship between "Man and Nature" (Gordon's theoretical, systematic, and widest ranging essay). His initial grounding assumption, based on universal experience, was that man is a creature of nature. He is a descendant of nature, lives in nature, and is dependent on its resources, but he also contributes to it and elaborates it. Consequently, work is man's most vital effort from the standpoint of his active union with surrounding nature. Man's primal sense is the experience of birth and procreation, and the natural bonds with a human environment that are their outcome: parents and family that carry on the nurturing of the newborn until it becomes self-sufficient. The second experience that a person has is physical labor which connects him to nature as the source from which all material, psychic, and spiritual needs are derived; that is, in maturity a person discovers that, after his own birth and the procreation of his offspring, physical work is the direct and most significant link he has with surrounding nature. This link, which channels the flow of nature's energies, must be tapped for his very existence, growth and development, so that he can raise his children, educate them, and engage in social and cultural activity.

What then is the significance of work as a means of fusing with nature? Gordon's answer was expanded by two concepts which he used systematically: "connection" to nature, and "creation" based on nature. Man's union with nature is a connection in the same sense that one speaks of a stream joined to a fountain by the waters that flow through it, or the flame of a lamp connected to its wick just as the wick is connected to the oil. In each case there are two essences, each one distinct from the other; if, however, the connection between them is severed, the stream will disappear, the flame will die. In the same way, if man's connection to nature as his source of energy is broken, man will die and disappear. Consequently, connection is a form of continuation; work is the connection because it is the direct physical process by which man extracts nature's resources in order to create the energy that sustains his physical being in all its spiritual functions.

Still, there is a difference between man and all the other living and growing things that are also connected to nature. The others consume only what nature provides directly for them, adding nothing of their own, with the exception of their essence which, after their death, returns to nature's cycle of energy. Man is unique in that for him to exist as a human being, he requires more from nature than she directly provides. Therefore, he takes more than is offered but also returns more than he took, and in so doing insures that the source of energy does not diminish. In this sense, work is a process by which man energizes nature to increase its bounty in accordance with man's needs thus augmenting the resources by his own creative contribution. Since man accomplishes this by his connection to nature — and as an undifferentiated component of nature — he becomes a most intensive factor in nature's predisposition for the creation apparent in the progression from mineral to vegetable, from vegetable to animal, and ultimately to man. It is through the intermediacy of labor that man creates culture, the additional sphere of human nature. Culture expands nature, raising it to a more sublime form of perfection.

In considering the fusion of man's connection to nature through work, we discover the cosmic, pantheistic meaning that Gordon ascribed to labor: through procreation of offspring and through spiritual growth, human beings differentiate themselves as uniquely distinctive individuals and groups in nature. Each person is distinguished through individuation, and human society sets itself apart from nature through the cultural environment that it fashions for itself. Yet man remains inseparably connected to nature, which gave rise to him out of the amplitude of her vitality. Consequently, in order to persist in his individuality, man must be all the more strongly bound to nature because of the increasing resources he consumes. Labor is the only positive solution to the problem of individuation. The laboring man reconnects to his source over and over again, and constantly reinvests his vigor in the forces of nature. He initiates or reinforces a creative role within nature, thus the laborer secures his achievements and broadens their scope, raising nature to a more sublime human sphere, perhaps even to a transcendental one.

Such was the religious significance that Gordon attributed to labor, a dimension of sanctity in which he determined that nature is a limitless repository of creative, purposeful energy which Gordon identified with the Divine. In these terms, then, labor is a means of uniting with God in order to heighten and develop the life force. Worship of God is found in precisely the simplest of tasks — physical exertion which man invests in order to increase the fruitfulness of his environment. "Communion" occurs when such labor is consciously invested in full awareness of its cosmic significance. This communion is a kind of worship in which personality is focused on expressing itself in the language of conscious gesture and task; nature responds by bestowing on man the fruits of his labor. In such a case, worship is the creative expression of a union intended to intensify life as one's most sublime and perfect experience of religious sanctity. It is the quintessence of human existence vis à vis the procreative source which sustains it and nourishes it. Along with the physical yield that the laborer reaps for his sustenance and that of his family and society, work is also the storehouse from which spiritual creativity in all spheres emanates.

This is, of course, a description of the universal condition. It applies to all individuals, societies, and nations. But along with universality, Gordon placed equal emphasis on the absolute and separate nature of each individual, specific society, and nation. How could he claim the absolute value of each of these divisions without detracting from the universalist value, and how could he sustain the universalist value without detracting from the autonomy of each of the divisions themselves? The most economical and yet most profound answer to the question is found in self-realization as a value: that is, how man lives his life in accordance with the volitional realization of his values. In this universal sense, realization is the implementation of general ideas (inextricably related to abstract concepts that arise in our minds) by means of concrete objects that serve to represent them in our actual environment. In tactile reality, only concrete objects exist; these have some relationship to one another, possessing not only unique characteristics but individual existence. True, conceptual abstractions can be useful for they establish a general orientation, but we would misrepresent reality were we to equate it with abstraction. According to Gordon, actual reality derives from a unifying source hidden in its depths (God) but it becomes manifest in the infinite multiplicity of individual essences, each of which is uniquely singular. We relate to actuality as individuals to other specific individuals whom we encounter, to such societies as we encounter, to such nations with whom we have contact, rather than through an undifferentiated and all embracing attitude to *man in general* or *humanity at large* as abstractions.

In concrete terms, the implications of this Gordonian "return to nature" is not to nature in the abstract but to a particular and unique quintessence in a particular and unique environment. Every *autonomous* individual reverts to his own nature, every *autonomous* family, tribe, and nation must revert to its own unique selfhood through the nature into which it was born inasmuch as every individual, society, and nation has its special place in nature — literally, the homeland in which it was born. This is the definitive touchstone from which, and only from which, one can draw the relevant resources of one's unique selfhood so that autonomous existence is maintained and developed in keeping with its singularity.

Gordon interpreted the link between all nations, and all the individuals that comprise the nations, in their natural homelands, according to this model. Naturally, what he regarded as the duty and right of all nations, he saw as the duty and right of the Jewish people and of individual Jews; Jews pined for their homeland and should be expected to return to it — thus, reuniting with the nature of their land. It was on this primary and most profound logic that he predicated the Jewish people's return to its homeland, to Eretz Israel, rather than emigration to any other country. It was, as well, his rationale for resettling Eretz Israel through agricultural labor as the enabling means for the people's return to their unique national life. First and foremost, in his particular religiosity, he regarded their original national experience as an expression that flowed from the special character of the people and the special nature of its land. Gordon believed that through labor on the land of Eretz Israel — labor in its simplest yet most profound sense — the Jewish religion in its full polychromatic nature would be revitalized, and from this fountainhead of creativity the entire national culture would be renewed.

At this stage, the question is: What differentiates the religious experience of the Jewish people from all other religious experiences? Ostensibly, the answer could be found through recourse to such commonly known abstractions as "monotheism," "Torah," "mitzvot," or "holiness" as the central Jewish experience. (It should be noted that Gordon posited holiness as the core experience of Judaism, drawing upon Leviticus 19:2 "You shall be holy; for I the Lord your God am holy.") But, again, these are abstractions. Although they are precise from a conceptual, abstract standpoint, they do not divulge the experience at their core, for experience is not amenable to understanding in abstract terms. In order to know it fully, one has to actively participate in the experience, to feel, and to apprehend it through the senses. With experiential certainty, which he did not attempt to articulate, Gordon indicated that the religion of every people is an embodiment of its autonomous, original experience which originated and emanates in the natural features of its own land. On the other hand, Gordon indicated that one could identify what is unique to each religion through its particular informing patterns: values, pragmatic norms, and symbols; in other words, by means of the culture that each religion engenders. According to Gordon, in this initial sense, culture is the concretization of religious experience in every sphere of human activity — material and spiritual. Consequently, if one compares the values and norms of one culture to that of another, by means of these patterns one discovers what individuates each culture.

To support his assertion that culture, in its broadest interpretation, is the crystallization of all peoples' religious experience as it develops and is renewed, Gordon pointed to the fact that the creation of culture, in all aspects, flowed from religion — society and societal ethics, the essential approach to natural resources, science, the arts, and philosophy. At a later stage, these elements separated and were "liberated" from religion; this liberation reached its peak in the modern era. But, in Gordon's opinion, the authentic experiential motivation and the cognitive spiritual source for the creation of a culture was still to be found in religious experience as the primal experiential awakening of a spiritual emanation. The separation from religion was perhaps justified by the institutional decline of religion, which made it obsessive, mechanical, and fossilized to such an extent that religious experience had become bereft of spontaneity. In the short run this enabled European culture to develop, but in the long run separation from religion caused impoverishment, distortion, and the degeneration of culture. This was particularly apparent in the spheres of ethics, emotions (art), and the spiritual life (philosophy and thought). In consequence, only the aspects of domination found in science, technology, and material production prospered and moved ahead rapidly, but these developed in an avaricious and aggrandizing direction that would destroy both the human spirit and the natural environment.

From this, it is clear that Gordon sought the renewal of a direct link between religious experience and the totality of cultural creativity. He believed that this should be expressed primarily in social life; that is, in the network of interpersonal relationships. We return to the notion of labor as the primary form of creation: How is human society created in the first place? Gordon believed that historic observation repeatedly pointed to two natural sources: birth and progeny (family), and work.

Birth and procreation are the outcome of the union between a male and a female; where human beings are concerned, however, for their issue to be truly human, it is not sufficient for a man and woman to copulate. The parents must also unite in the full societal sense, establishing a permanent family for an entire life-span so that together they can raise their progeny, educating them to become genuinely human. Undoubtedly, this is a social process which finds its expression in the relationship of the parents and the children. A society of family is established which expands organically into the extended family, the tribe, and the people.

Here, one must examine what occurs when the link that extends beyond the organic family is maintained as a network of permanent social relationships. The answer to this is found in labor, the second natural source for the creation of a society, whose task it is to sustain and provide for the human family in the fulfillment of its functions. Indeed, labor is essentially a social process. More exactly, it is the daily ongoing association of human beings. For the most part, human beings cooperate in their labor and the enjoyment of its products. Consequently, one can find in labor the orienting norm for a natural, healthy society that is in consonance with that society's aims. When one examines the essential character of labor as a social process, one discovers the type of social relationships to which it gives rise, and this is the beginning of the culture that provides an infrastructure for the family as well.

There are two aspects to the societal character of labor. First, productive: the cooperation of individuals in such a way that each one functions according to the best of his ability in concert with those working alongside him. In the absence of a norm of cooperation and mutual reinforcement, labor cannot be developed to the qualitative and quantitative levels necessary for making tools, or employing those tools at the level of the complementarity needed between tasks, so that each operation achieves its goal. Second, consumption: labor is meant to provide for people's existential needs, initially on the physical level, and then on the sensual, imaginative, emotional, and intellectual planes. It may be said that man works in order to provide for his own needs, those of his family, and of the society with which he cooperates when he labors. But, in Gordon's opinion, satisfying human needs through labor is not only a means of consuming (in the sense of taking what nature provides); it has a more fundamental meaning. It is a kind of giving: an investment of creative effort in order to enhance nature's ability to give. It is man's gift to nature, and through nature to society, thus enabling nature's bounty to enrich society. In other words, properly speaking, labor is not a selfish exploitation of either natural resources or human resources. The laborer must exploit neither himself nor his fellowman. The norm of mutuality with nature is maintained by orienting labor to give, not simply to take, for whatever man takes for himself is also a product of what he and his comrades have given in their continuous, creative enterprise. It must be emphasized that in Gordon's view, this is not a case of "altruism" versus "egoism." In giving, one neither diminishes nor sacrifices himself; on the contrary, the individual constructs and creatively expands his own selfhood. Labor requires resources, but in essence it is a process of expansion directed at the other!

It is obvious that Gordon's theory of labor was a normative, value-laden directive for structuring a true society that would be achieved through special ethical teaching intended to guide the spontaneous relationships between participating individuals. The dilemma faced by individuals who create a laboring society is the same ethical problem from which all other ethical problems of interpersonal relations stem. The problems are embodied in the question: What should be emphasized in the network of productive relationships, as well as the network of consuming relationships, which individuals establish between themselves? Should such a society be based on taking selfishly for oneself? Or should it be based on giving to the partnership that creates a collective? An emphasis on the first orientation sets up a competitive, aggressive, dominating, compulsive society that exploits and enslaves all its individuals by one another, turning power into such a regnant goal that the fulfillment of human life itself becomes secondary to the aims of the regime.

The opposite emphasis creates a society based on morality, justice, cooperation, the equal value of all people, and the desire to raise and cultivate life to a loftier stage. Gordon calls the first type a "mechanical" society, whereas he regards the second as a natural, authentic, "organic" society which furthers the creative disposition of divine nature. Each of these societies has its own set of morals. The first is marked by a tendency that Gordon defines in terms of "restriction" which focuses on the power-hungry, isolating ego drives. The second he defines in terms of expansion. It enlarges the life of the individual by attachment to others and to the group, in this way enlarging the level of creative experience. Consequently, according to Gordon, these are the ethical norms that are derived from the ethics of labor. In the actual functioning of labor, their application sets up a process of appropriate social relations and sustains a society that expresses the affirmative and authentic nature of every individual rather than an organizational, compulsive, mechanical mold.

On the spiritual plane, when one discusses social relationships designed for labor and shaped by it, what emerges is the deep-seated affinity between social relationships and the religious experience that pulsates in labor. In and of itself, the social significance of labor expresses man's fundamental orientation vis à vis nature from which the laborer draws his sustenance (whether exploiting nature or enriching it), and vis à vis the society in which the worker labors, and toward which he directs his endeavors (whether exploiting others and society as a whole or enriching them). It is not difficult to imagine what, in Gordon's view, the proper approach should be, with which Jewish credo he identified. Gordon believed that the social significance of labor was a direct continuation, and a direct articulation, of the religious experience achieved by means of creative physical endeavor in which workers provide for their own material consumption, for that of others, and for society at large; and for spiritual creativity as well, which is another kind of socially significant labor.

Just as society issues from nature by means of birth and progeny, and through the labor of men and women, so too society's cultural and spiritual creativity originates in procreative, nurturing union that is facilitated by labor. It is commonly recognized that language is the infrastructure of cultural creativity. In an even more primary context, language (which is interpersonal communication) is itself the primary social relationship, not simply a necessary tool without which societal relationships are impossible at any level or in any sense. Gordon believed language to be the natural, spiritual potential of people who share an inborn kinship. They develop this potential along with other emerging natural relationships between each other. In other words, the initial languages of ancient peoples are natural languages, rooted in the unique human landscape of a specific society and in its natural environment. Every people has its own innate natural language, just as it possesses a natural homeland. Moreover, all these languages have a dimension of religious sanctity that is rooted in the very nature of their environment.

The enabling and accelerating element in the development of a language and the attendant unfolding of its cultural creativity is once again labor as a form of communication between man and nature, between individuals, and between individuals and society. Labor requires communication that calls for increasingly precise and detailed expression. Relationships of mutual exchange based on labor dictate that language also becomes increasingly intimate so that the most profound human needs can be understood. For that very same diversity of reasons, labor mandates the development of science, technical skill, trades, arts and thought. According to Gordon, the innermost meaning of this creativity is nurtured by the religious experience that inspires labor.

This assumption was the foundation for his unwavering belief that the return to the original natural surroundings of Eretz Israel, the return to Hebrew as the natural national language of the Jewish people in its land, and the reawakening of the Biblical heritage and the Hebrew literature of the Jewish people throughout its generations, would together herald a natural, spontaneous renewal of the totality of cultural creativity that so characterized the Jewish people.

Unlike Ahad Ha-Am and Bialik, Gordon saw no need to spell out or define more precisely what he believed to be the components and unique characteristics of that cultural product which was deserving of the term "Jewish culture." On the strength of his own religious experience, he thought that such normative definitions which made an *a priori* determination of what was to be included in Jewish culture and what did not belong in such a classification were not only unnecessary, they were harmful. A spiritual creation should directly express the untrammeled spontaneity of the creative experience whose origin is in religion. It was sufficient that the Jewish people return to live in its own land where they would speak their own language in order for the creative drive to emerge from out of its original religious recesses, and conditions of complete freedom would assure that whatever was expressed in that creation would be uniquely authentic to the Jewish people. The requisite norm for culture was, therefore, a life of labor in Eretz Israel, in a free and independent Jewish society that was Hebrew-speaking and conversant with Hebraic sources, particularly the Bible. Everything else would result from spontaneous creativity.

It should be stressed again that Gordon believed that spontaneous creativity was a direct expression of the experience of holiness manifested in uniting with nature, which itself was a kind of prophecy. Gordon's conviction was simple and absolute: renewed spontaneous creativity in Eretz Israel — mediated through the Hebrew language, the Bible and other canonical sources of Hebrew literature — would again become original Judaism. This conviction was contingent on a full and unambiguous renewal of Jewish religious experience and consciousness. In this, his statements were as uncompromising as a halakhic decree. If materialistic heresy persisted, and if hostility and alienation grew between the pioneers and the Jewish belief system (particularly as expressed through the Sabbath and Yom Kippur), then even a life of labor in Eretz Israel and speaking Hebrew would not stanch the flood of assimilation.

As against the rebellious atheistic option advanced by Yosef Haim Brenner, Gordon presented the labor movement in Eretz Israel with an alternative of religious constancy.

There are significant differences between A. D. Gordon's overall teachings and those of Martin Buber, many of which will be discussed below. However, on the central issues of the renewal of Jewish culture in Eretz Israel, there was such great affinity that one could describe Buber as Gordon's disciple. Buber regarded his mentor not only as a source of wisdom but as a role model of Zionist realization. Through his aliyah, Gordon had acted out beliefs drawn from the most deep-seated strata of his personality: the organic link of the Jewish people to Eretz Israel and the Hebrew language, the accomplishment of a social utopia in Eretz Israel, the revitalization of Hebrew culture based on the profound, prophetic Biblical experience of the Jewish people and its affinity to the sources. Buber saw in A. D. Gordon the ideal representation of the pioneer who validated his credo by carrying it out in practice.

Nonetheless, Buber did not concur with Gordon's teachings on physical labor's cosmic religious significance. As we shall see below, this stemmed from a substantive difference in their philosophical approaches. In no way, however, did this detract from Buber's championing of "self-realization" as a normative value, nor of its applicability in social relationships. It was only regarding the primacy of the spiritual significance of agricultural settlement that Buber dissented, and he oriented his educational process in a different direction. In what follows, we abbreviate Buber's views on the modern renewal of Jewish culture in Eretz Israel in order to deal with the special perspective he added to the concept of social realization, without spelling out his broad-ranging and multi-faceted teachings which deserve a thorough-going examination in their own right.

In the early stages of Buber's quest for a renewed contact with spiritual, religious Judaism, he was caught up in the same Hasidism and pantheistic, mystical Kabbalah that Gordon had found so appealing. Subsequently, however, he dissociated himself from mysticism and pantheism, and in a later formulation of his approach to Judaism, he embraced Hasidism only as a social ethic and an educational mode. In their place, he proposed a theory of dialogue. It was a theory based on the prophetic experience as recounted in the Bible. According to Buber, God is perceived by man as a meta-natural persona who has will, is creational, regnant, and directs the world. Man turns to God as the absolute "Thou." God is therefore the Spirit that transcends both man and the universe, and exists in a sphere of absolute sanctity. Still, there is an encounter between God, man, and other living creatures. God is the Creator, and He turns to man requiring of him a life of sanctity. When man responds, a wondrous meeting occurs between the human "I" and the divine "Thou."

It is instructive that Buber applied the norm of self-realization to this encounter that occurs between the human "I" and the divine "Thou." According to Buber, man is expected to *realize* God in his life through the encounter. Man is commanded to *instill* God into his life by devoting himself to fulfilling His commandments through man's actions on earth, particularly in his relation to his fellow man. Whenever a genuine relationship of love occurs between man and his fellow man, the presence of God is evident. It should be noted that Buber believed one can observe nature in such a way that God's presence as the Creator is manifest. By this, he meant an experiential, meta-scientific, mytho-poetic scrutiny which discloses the dimension of beneficent wonder in the Creation. Such observation reveals the evidence of God's beneficent will in the very fact that the world exists rather than the condition of an absolute void. But Buber dissociates even such descriptions of the materialization of God in nature from pantheism. The divine "Thou" retains absolute transcendental distance from the created universe. The divine *Essence* is a perpetual mystery which man is incapable of plumbing, hence man must not have delusions of penetrating its depths for in this he mimics the attempts of pagans or mystics. In Buber's language, man can converse with God and be certain that he is heard, but there is nothing he can say *about* God. Therefore, one can refine one's understanding of the demand to realize God in interpersonal reality: thus, what is realized is God's word. The word represents the speech of the persona. It is the actual presence by which the "I" perceives the "Thou," just as genuine attention is the actual face that the "Thou" presents to the "I." The word emanates from the Interlocutor's essence and enters the Selfhood of the Listener, yet the separation between them persists.

From this it is clear that nature, in and of itself, including man as a natural creature, is *material* rather than spiritual. Nature is not incorporated in the Godhead. Nature possesses its own reality and its own characteristics and, although nature is open to an encounter with the spirit that emanates from God, nonetheless it differs from, and may even be alien to, the spirit. In material nature, there are physical, gravitational forces which give rise to isolation, alienation and even to intentional evil; these are the consequences of the alienated spirit which so characterizes the sphere of human reality. As a result of the duality between disaffection from God and openness to God's command, the history of mankind is a story of the relations between man and spirit; it is the unending struggle between man's responsiveness to the encounter with the divine "Thou," and man's physical alienation. History is the tragic conflict between aspiration to realize God in human society, and between the alienation and surrender of the senses to the *gravitational pull* of physical nature.

According to Buber, tension and conflict are unremitting, nor will they ever end. The significance of man's existence, his mission and role are derived from this. To exist as a human being means man must seek to repair and ennoble his own nature, and elevate the nature of his environment to the spiritual sphere through deeds, relations, and creations that signify an aspiration to ethical holiness. It is the aspiration to redemption that gives human history its thrust: "to repair the world in the Kingdom of God." Still, the achievements are always merely partial, and each incomplete achievement is valid only for its time. Contemporary accomplishments can only help by providing an orientation for the achievements of tomorrow, but in no way can they assure tomorrow's achievement. If we rely on what we have already accomplished without further efforts to continue and maintain these accomplishments, we will lose what has already been achieved as well. Consequently, the norm of self-realization is the perpetual obligation incumbent on human beings. To believe that we have arrived at the ultimate reformation, or even to assume that some day that will be achieved, is but false prophecy. The significance of man's existence is the creative struggle for redemption. In every *here and now*, man must ask the question anew: What can be done, and what more is called for, given the conditions of reality that pertain to this time and this place, in order to repair the network of relations between man and man, and between man and nature or, minimally, to narrow the gap between what exists and what ought to be? To this end, one needs to study the heritage of the past, to draw conclusions and an orientation from it. Yet, the heritage must be applied and the unique obligations which are valid for the present defined in order to assure a more perfected future. Belief is actually the hope that the effort invested in our actions will bring that-which-should-be and that-which-is closer together than they were yesterday or than they are today.

It is obvious that Buber understood the role of the Jewish people in human history — a people founded by the patriarchs, Moses, and the prophets — against the background of the development of humanity as a whole; it is as clear that he interpreted the role of the Zionist enterprise against the background of the Jewish people as a *covenantal people*. Like Bialik, Buber sought to refashion the Jewish people's national memory as historic myth, the center of which would be the Chosen People's aspiration to self-realization as its redemptive goal; like Gordon, Buber wanted to direct the realization of the pioneering endeavor in Eretz Israel so that it would be in keeping with that spirit.

From this point onward, Buber's philosophy rejoined the thrust of Gordon's thought: Buber believed that the labor settlements were the focus of Zionist realization, the fundamental tenet of which was to renew Jewish society in keeping with Biblical prophecy as a requisite of Eretz Israel in the first half of the 20th century. His term for the ideal Jewish society that had begun to take shape in Eretz Israel was *ḥevruta* (fellowship). Relying on the model he observed in various communal frameworks of the labor settlements, particularly the kibbutz, he made great efforts to describe the qualities that ought to characterize the ḥevruta. Yet Buber considered the components of kibbutz structure as transitory; whereas, in fact, the message for subsequent generations was embodied in a commitment to maintain the prophetic *covenant* through interpersonal and national deeds.

To that end, the *organic*, communal norm that Buber adopted was, in effect, the same norm of social realization that Gordon had propounded. It goes without saying that Buber also accepted the demand for "self-labor" and the rejection of exploitation of others: every person must be self-supporting through his own labor which would contribute to the welfare of all. Nonetheless, the substantive difference that arose between Gordon and Buber regarding the religious-cosmic significance of physical work called for conclusions about the quality of the societal-cultural process.

We have seen how Gordon rooted culture in labor, labor being the source of any spiritual renewal. Buber did not attach spiritual significance to physical labor. Rather, he returned to an explanation of the spirit's own modes of expression as well-springs in which the spirit originates; that is, in literature, art, philosophy, particularly in the unbroken sources of religious thought. Thus the need arose to pay greater attention than Gordon had to the issue of educational curricula with theoretical study at its center. In this, Buber drew closer to Ahad Ha-Am and Bialik though, in fact, his attitude to the traditional sources exhibited greater selectivity than did theirs. His approach to the sources could be summed up as follows. Like Berdyczew-ski, he too revolted against the rabbinic heritage, particularly against cut-and-dried, institutionalized halakhah as mandatory dogma, but like Ahad Ha-Am, Buber drew upon the prophetic heritage as the basic foundation of original Judaism. Despite the fact that he rebelled against rabbinic halakhah, he replicated its obligatory norm of implementation, an approach that sought to integrate the totality of the individual's way of life, and of society, directing them both towards an ideal of ethical holiness.

On the one hand, Buber needed the notion of theoretical study as a living process which posited the intrinsic value of study for its own sake or of study as an expression of the spiritual life in thought, image, and spirit; on the other hand, he promoted the instrumental value of study for orienting the process of Zionist realization as a way of life. Such an approach challenged the concept of humanist education which had taken root in the Jewish people in the wake of the Enlightenment Movement and the Science of Judaism, proposing the culture of Zionist realization as the appropriate alternative. Buber's critique of 19th and 20th century Science of Judaism was even more trenchant than Ahad Ha-Am or Bialik's had been. As Buber saw it, the cardinal sin of *Wissenschaft Des Judentums* was its very *academic* one-sidedness that pursued absolute objectivity while totally disregarding the subjective aspect of any learning process, and the need for all learning to be guided by vital, realistic significance.

Buber did not question the importance that the Science of Judaism placed on knowing the content of the sources as they had actually been articulated by their authors. Indeed, he agreed that objective philological tools were necessary for this. But Buber believed that modern Jewish society also had an interest in relating the sources to itself in order to orient its stance in contemporary culture and history. Just as the authors of the sources expressed their own contemporary orientations and aspired to transmit their teachings to future generations, the present generation had to transmit a coherent teaching to its children. Traditional religious education accomplished this through its own means; Buber, who had accepted the modern critique of traditional homilies, looked for educational ways to teach the sources which would be consistent with modern philological criticism but would not turn the latter into lifeless, archival texts. Instead, they would be presented as they had been taught in the past: as vital contemporary documents, as objects with which to identify and internalize precisely because they were relevant to the historical moment.

Buber devoted a notable part of his studies to issues of humanist and Jewish education, but his most important contribution to education, based on Jewish sources, was his research documenting what he defined as the

Jewish people's "way of holiness"; this began with the epoch of Biblical prophecy and continued through the period of Zionist social-pioneering. The reference here is particularly to his dialogical studies of the Bible and of Hasidism: *The Prophetic Faith, The Kingdom of God, Moses, The Origin and Meaning of Hasidism,* and *Hasidism and Modern Man.* These studies researched the sources with an explicit educational-religious aim: to transmit the original spiritual message of the prophets and Hasidism and, through them, to renew the spirit that should pulsate in the social renaissance of the Jewish people returning to its land.

In summation, it may be said that Buber's and Gordon's impact in shaping Jewish culture in Eretz Israel was at best partial, but persists nonetheless. Gordon's religion of labor did pattern the social ethos of Zionist labor settlements in their initial stages during the periods of the Second and Third Aliyah. Buber's teachings were primarily absorbed in shaping the educational concepts of some national schools in Eretz Israel, and in shaping the outlook of a number of important educators and writers who tried to influence their students. But it can be unequivocally stated that the aspect of religious belief that both men wanted to transmit by their teachings was absorbed only by the few, and in limited circles. The extent of their influence did not go so far as to impact on a modern social-religious movement; consequently, their thought remains only a profound heritage, a legacy which gave rise to a great spiritual aspiration. Although that aspiration was a significant part of the cultural atmosphere of the founding fathers, they encapsulated it within themselves, failing to give it voice. Now, as it resurfaces in this generation, it awaits a movement that will bring the notion of sanctity to realization.

Chapter Twenty One
ORTHODOX ZIONIST CULTURE —
SANCTIFYING MODERNITY

The Orthodox Zionist movement regarded Zionism as the enactment of a Biblical commandment and the consummation of an ancient vision, rather than as an innovation of modernity. In fact, the legitimation of its endeavors was based on these revered sources. It would have been disingenuous for the movement to claim that its decision to actualize the vision of redemption by joining a movement of national independence did not fly directly in the face of tradition, a tradition upheld by rabbinic leadership since the defeat of the Bar Kokhba rebellion. Perhaps the modern age presented propitious circumstances for such an initiative that had been missing in the past. In any case, Orthodox Zionist support of Herzl's secular political Zionism, not withstanding the extreme opposition found in ultra-Orthodox circles, underscored the point that fulfillment of the ancient dream constituted a revolutionary departure. Embarking on a national-political initiative signified that one was fully prepared to apply the practical, functional, political, economic, social, intellectual-scientific and technological tools of the modern secular system. It was tantamount to admitting that the Jewish community and the Jewish state that were to be established through the use of such instruments would necessarily be modern; that is, in many respects the community and the state would be modeled on prevailing national cultures that characterized the enlightened countries of Europe. The objective was already clearly seen in the latter stages of the *Hibbat Zion* movement under Pinsker and Lilienblum. Even earlier, in the mid-nineteenth century when the movement was led by rabbinical figures, there was a call to adapt tools borrowed from non-Jewish modern political entities to achieve the "Return to Zion."

In any case, identifying with the goals of modern Zionism was, in and of itself, a tacital — if partial — acceptance of the modern culture that underlay the establishment of a state. A measure of technological-scientific education, certainly fluency in foreign languages, took on crucial importance alongside traditional Torah studies. To that end, it was necessary to adopt the concepts of *Torah Im Derekh Eretz*, the educational bi-culturalism available within

Central European modern Orthodoxy. Originally, because of its allegiance to the Emancipation, modern Orthodoxy had been non-Zionist, and later this scruple developed into anti-Zionism. Adapting modern Orthodoxy to Zionism required neither educational nor structural changes; only the ideological message that pointed in the social-national direction had to be re-oriented. It could be said that Orthodox Zionism began by defining itself as a *national* version of Modern Orthodoxy. Its adherents believed that they could better attain the original goals of modern Orthodoxy — a totally integrated, undifferentiated fusion of two types of culture, Jewish and general — goals which anti-Zionist modern Orthodoxy had aspired to but had not achieved. In central Europe, the shift to Orthodox Zionism originated in communities with an orientation to modern Orthodoxy. At the same time, in eastern Europe, the modern Orthodox trend began precisely in religious communities that had Zionist tendencies. The educational approach of two educators, Rabbi Yehiel Michal Pines (1843–1913) and Rabbi Isaac Jacob Reines (1839–1915) are illustrative of this. Both these prominent figures devoted the major thrust of their work to reforming religious education, to making it receptive to essential universal, scientific knowledge as an adjunct to traditional religious yeshiva studies.

Furthermore, it appeared that the culturally cohesive blend of Judaism which would be possible in a national-religious culture of Eretz Israel was a more attractive model than the bi-culturalism that modern Orthodoxy proposed in central Europe. A mutually respectful dialogue between Ortho-dox religiosity and general European humanistic culture was crucially different from the acculturation process of Orthodox religiosity to a Jewish national culture of Eretz Israel. For acculturation in Eretz Israel, another kind of religious legitimation was needed and, in the same way, there was a need for a different perception of national culture which would enable the new synthesis to become the core of a culture that placed religion as the highest, overall authority. An integrated national-religious culture would not separate the humanistic component from the Judaic one. Instead, it would *consecrate* the *secular* elements thereby broadening the scope of what was considered sacred. It was this that had made it possible to accommodate the notion of *Torah Im Derekh Eretz* (adherence to the strictures of Halakhah along with acculturation to secular European culture) in the Diaspora. In Eretz Israel, the confrontation of the religious Zionist movement with the Jewish free-thinking nationalist public (a community that had begun developing modes for its national culture) required the Orthodox Zionists to advance their own educational models in keeping with the Orthodox-nationalist world view.

Three Orthodox nationalist models evolved to parallel those of the "free-thinking" sector: the schools of the *Kibbutz ha-Dati* Movement (Orthodox kibbutzim) resembled those of the Labor Zionist stream; the General National Orthodox educational institutions were analogous to the Spiritual Zionism of Ahad Ha'Am's followers; and Rabbi Abraham Isaac ha-Kohen's educational views corresponded to the Spiritual Zionism of Bialik's and Gordon's adherents. Though Rabbi Kook's approach was never put into practice as a comprehensive school system, it became the dominant influence in the world-view, ideological and educational emphases of nationalist-Orthodox schools in Eretz Israel. Indeed, one could say that the model to which all Orthodox educational streams in Eretz Israel aspired (an aim they never quite achieved — perhaps never endeavored too earnestly to attain — realizing that what is ideal is, by definition, utopian) was the model propounded by Rabbi Kook. Consequently, his view became the ideal self-image of Orthodox Zionist culture. The Orthodox Zionist concepts that were put into practice were projections of that culture.

But before assessing these diverse concepts, it is useful to describe two earlier notions. The Orthodox kibbutz movement adopted, without qualification, the Socialist-nationalist notion of *hagshama* (Zionist self-realization) of the Labor Zionist pioneers. They had no reservations about such socialist principles as self-labor, non-exploitation of the labor of others, full equality, communality of ownership and use of public land. They believed in self-rule and direct democratic governance. Nor did they make changes in the agro-economic system, administrative structures, or forms of collective education. The social ethos and cultural forms that evolved in *Kibbutz ha-Dati* were almost indistinguishable from those of secular kibbutzim on which it was modeled. Yet this model had no negative impact on the fulfillment of traditional Orthodox halakhic norms such as family purity, marriage, kashrut, the prescribed observance of festivals and the Sabbath, as well as daily prayers and benedictions. Questions that required specific halakhic solutions did arise but they did not impinge on the realization of social values, only on some agro-technical practices (observing laws of the Sabbatical year, milking cows on the Sabbath, etc.), and halakhic solutions were found for all such questions.

Therefore, despite the sense of counterpoint in *Kibbutz HaDati* settlements between ways of realizing national, social, or egalitarian values (which did not originate in religious precepts and were not sanctioned by halakhah) and between the halakhic way of life, there was also an understanding of the complementary quality of these strands which permitted them to be blended into a common culture. One set of values stemmed from the religious traditional Orthodox Haskalah — Torah study was observed in Orthodox kibbutzim no less than in any other modern-Orthodox society. The other set of values was absorbed from the *Zeitgeist* of universal enlightenment.

Consequently, dedication to the realization of a social-national ideal as one component of the overall religious ideal made certain demands on its followers. It called for a Hebrew-speaking, personal and societal way of life in Eretz Israel which would bring about an integrated, unified culture. The culture's self perception was that it was authentically Jewish from both the national standpoint and from the standpoint of traditional religion. The fullness and perfection of the integration was enabled by A. D. Gordon's non-Marxist, Jewish interpretation of kibbutz life. That interpretation underscored the Jewish-religious essence in even apparently "secular" or "universal" aspects of the kibbutz, and certainly in such extra-halakhic facets as physical labor and the egalitarian collective ethos. Through the intermediacy of Gordon's philosophy these fundamentals of kibbutz life were regarded not as "extra-halakhic" ideals but rather as "supra-halakhic"; that is, a desire to achieve the ideal values of religious morality on an even higher plane than that which the halakhah had intended for the majority of Jews but one which was definitely in keeping with the spirit of religious idealism.

Hence, one can say that among the various streams of labor settlements, *Kibbutz HaDati* most closely approximated A.D. Gordon's vision without actually embracing his religious philosophy because ultimately they preferred the teachings of Rabbi Kook.

The general educational approach of Orthodox Zionism practiced a Zionist bi-cultural version of *Torah Im Derekh Eretz*. On the ideological plane, this was expressed in a call to realize Zionism through active participation in the Zionist enterprise in Eretz Israel; on the pedagogic plane, it was expressed in preparing and transmitting curricula which promoted settlement of the land; and on the linguistic plane, it was expressed in improving language skills so that Hebrew could be both a holy language and the national language with which to meet life's needs. Thus, cultural integration meant fulfilling the value of living in Eretz Israel, and in teaching all subjects in Hebrew whether they were identified as *Torah* (sacred subjects) or as *Derekh Eretz* (secular ones.) Both were perceived as constituting a single national culture, or as the total product of Jewish intellect and civilization. There was yet another ideal: the synthesis of culture by means of halakhic creativity; that is, making halakhah responsive and applicable to the full gamut of Jewish national life in Eretz Israel; so much so that all aspects of Zionist realization — whether modern economy, statesmanship, social policy, security, or politics — would be in accord with the Torah. The primary motto of *Mizraḥi* (the Orthodox Zionist party) was "Eretz Israel is for the people of Israel, governed by the Torah of Israel."

The most fully articulated and consistent educational model of this national-religious culture is found in the work of Rabbi Haim Hirschensohn (1857–1935). An Orthodox-national thinker of bold sweep, he placed the pursuit of modern halakhic culture to be practiced in Eretz Israel at the center of his studies. Though he was not recognized as a leading spiritual authority within Orthodox Zionism, more than any other philosopher, his tenets reflect the pragmatism of the educational-cultural process that evolved in that movement.

The core concept in Hirschensohn's national-Orthodox thinking was the need to distinguish between nationalism and Orthodoxy with the intention of subsequently reconciling them. He viewed these two strata, the national and the religious, as being initially disparate with autonomous etiologies. Furthermore, the earliest, underlying tier was the national stratum which was secular and temporal. In the beginning, the Jewish people had emerged in a natural ethnic process, as had all other nations. Then, by means of a constituting *covenant*, the Israelite tribes were established as a national-political entity which was, and remains, intrinsically *secular*. In this aspect, too, the Jewish people resembles other peoples. Hirschensohn believed that the *brit* (the religious covenant) could be enacted only if predicated on an ethnic foundation and a political covenant. Ultimately, Jewish national existence would be infused by the *brit* with a totality of spiritual-religious content.

The conclusion inherent in this historical-ontological assertion is remarkably like that of Ahad Ha-Am's statement that Jewish identity was originally determined by the content of the people's temporal national life. Therefore a national Jew could be considered a Jew in the full sense of the term, even if he was non-religious, while a religious Jew, even one who was ultra-Orthodox, could not be considered a Jew if he excluded himself from the national contract. The substantive difference between Hirschensohn and Ahad Ha'am was, of course, their assessment of religion. Hirschensohn did not regard religion as a mere shell whose only function was to fasten together and grant authority to national-cultural content; rather, he saw it is the *purpose*, source, and supreme meaning for whose sake the national "shell" should be maintained. A national Jew who is not religious is still a Jew in every sense, but his nationality is devoid of underlying Jewish content and is consequently fragile, feeble and easily undermined. It is doubtful whether such Judaism can be transmitted to subsequent generations, for the content the children inherit will not originate in the sources of Judaism but from the modern sources of other nations — even if the process unfolds in Eretz Israel and is communicated in Hebrew.

In any case, Hirschensohn's assumption that Jewish culture has a temporal, secular base which determines one's nationality implies that there is more than a mere framework which binds secular and religious Jews in a common identity. An entire cultural stratum is involved and, even when it is not spiritually sufficient, it is a vital, necessary component for independent Jewish existence which, in turn, is the foundation of a full spiritual life. Moreover, this stratum of secular, national culture underlies the arena in which all the positive political, social, scientific and technological elements of progressive Western culture can interface. All these elements are admissible, even necessary, from a national standpoint. It becomes a quasi-religious mitzvah to accommodate them to Jewish life.

If this is the case, what is it that synthesizes the religious stratum — which relies on the absolute authority of internal sources — with the national stratum, which is predicated on external universal sources? Hirschensohn's answer was: Halakhah. He believed that *a priori*, as *Oral Law*, the role of halakhah was to harmonize Judaism's immutable values of spiritual idealism and religious ethics with the components of a constantly changing historical reality. It should be emphasized that the harmonizing function of halakhah was necessary not only to provide for the people's vital, existential needs — enabling them to live according to halakhic requirements — but also, and primarily, from the standpoint of realizing the inherent meaning and logic of positive temporal values and attributes. They were neither to be overlooked nor fought against. Democracy is a case in point. Democracy, as interpreted by the progressive, political consciousness of modernity, is the best system because of its internal logic and the functional morality of the political regime. That is precisely why halakhic validation of democracy is required in keeping with democracy's own principles. Democracy is desirable and right from a halakhic-religious position that flows from the fundamental recognition that it is inherently good and promotes progress.

From this point forward, Hirschensohn's wide ranging theoretical halakhic work took two complementary avenues of thought. The first amplified a halakhic philosophy and methodology that allowed for restoring a creativity suited to the cultural requirements of modern national life; the second devised detailed halakhic solutions to fundamental issues that could arise in the modern political, cultural and social life of a future Jewish state in Eretz Israel. He dedicated *Malkhi BaKodesh*, his magnum opus, to these issues. However, since neither the halakhic proposals nor the methodological approach in that work gained acceptance, it is not germane to the present discussion. The Orthodox Zionist movement disregarded his solutions, remaining constant to Orthodox halakhah. They opted for Rabbi Kook's idealized and unrealized utopia as well as for his halakhic outlook (which will be described below). There is no question that from the Orthodox viewpoint, due precisely to their realism and applicability, Hirschensohn's insights and solutions appeared too daring. Consequently, it could be said that had Religious Zionism hazarded putting its own ideal national-cultural-religious model to the test, and attempted to implement it in a consistent way, they would have adopted Hirschensohn's proposals. It was the only path open to blending the stratum of Torah with that of *derekh eretz* within the context of an integral Jewish national culture which would rigorously maintain the distinction between the sacred sphere with its absolute immutable affirmations and the temporal universal sphere marked by constant change and development.

Rabbi Kook's philosophical doctrine embodied a cultural-religious synthesis which emphasized the composite sources of that synthesis. It can be typified as a kabbalistic teaching with great affinity to the thought of Rabbi Judah Loew Ben Bezalel, the "Maharal" of Prague. Rabbi Kook "updated" the notions of the Maharal using prototypes of modern Jewish idealistic philosophy such as Rabbi Nachman Krochmal's historisophic and dialectic insights, or Moses Hess' conception of Jewish nationalism. Conversely, Rabbi Kook's philosophy can be described as modern Jewish idealistic philosophy (of Krochmal and Hess) *reinstated* into its earlier origins in Kabbalah. These ostensibly opposing characterizations complement each other in a doctrine primarily intended to demonstrate that Jewish religious culture is a distillate that retains essential attributes of all cultures joined to their divine origin, just as the Jewish people combines the ideal of humanity in itself. Rabbi Kook illustrated this when he stated that the totality of true knowledge — scientific as well as metaphysical — the aggregate of conclusions regarding truth and justice, and the sum of positive cultural creativity in all spheres of western society, reach the acme of their impressive achievement in the modern era; all these stem from the self-same infinite Source whose presence and leadership in history is attested to by the Torah of the Jewish people.

Four main ideas coalesced in the proof, exposition, and application of this comprehensive outlook. Together they posit an absolute union with an all-inclusive universality:

1. A kabbalistic-pantheistic theory of emanations interpreted by idealistic-philosophic means, according to which cosmic reality in all its ramifications emanates in staged structures from the sublime, divine Source beginning with spiritual spheres of eternal indivisibilty, and extending to spheres of atomized, corporeal tangibility. The latter exists in a perpetual cycle of becoming and extinction.

Knowledge of truth, too, its assessment, and the motives for every thought, feeling, speech and deed issue from divine origins flow through all the emanated spheres. They are unified at their source, becoming separated and antagonistic in the sphere of materiality. The Torah, as the totality of truth and morality that are transmitted in it, in both concealed and revealed forms, is the knowledge, the measure, and the guide to reality as a whole.

One concludes from this that all types of knowledge, thought, and feeling manifest in human beings apply to a sector of reality for which they are true, and that all assessments and all deeds have an inherent specific, binding, necessitating and justifying attribute. Consequently, conflicts, contradictions, arbitrariness and malice also originate in the sublime source and are intended to heighten, complete and unify. There is another important methodological religious conclusion that springs from such a notion of divine cosmic unity: in every world outlook, and in every way of life, even those that the Torah defines as mistaken, evil, and malicious, one can find a core of truth and justice, and it is this dimension which places them in reality. Of course, when one examines such views in the context of the reality that precipitated them, and at the level of life experience which this reality attained, the mistake, the malice, the evil and the denial of such sublime truths as belief in the unity of God, as well as the rejection of morality, can be seen from a higher and more inclusive perspective which exists beyond them differently than it appears to the perpetrators themselves. False, unjust, wicked outlooks and behavior which the Torah condemns may stem from mistaken judgments which err on the side of too inclusive an interpretation of motives that, in and of themselves, are correct and proper. What sinful people want to attain is often based on an injustice that was done to them or on a valid, personal need that they have; it is a kind of partial truth and partial justice that they seek which then collides with the partial truth and partial justice of others. The error which turns partial justice into wrong-doing is, therefore, an excess of generalization. The wrong-doers turn their partial justice into absolute justice and, in so doing, deny justice to others. Therefore one can arbitrate between the parties and bring them together by means of a more inclusive, hence limiting, point of view which defines and balances matters anew.

When we try to deal with such outlooks and behavior in order to correct and elevate them, we should ferret out the partial truth and justice from which they stem, pointing it out and acknowledging it to the other. Only subsequently can we attempt to raise these partial truths to the level of reality and the plane of elevated Torah discernment in order to enable the other to apply the core of their own truth and justice in a valid, just manner which reinstates the partial to the whole. But we must also be aware that inevitably human knowledge and human judgment are partial. They may appear mistaken from the standpoint of a higher and more universal truth to be found in the latent recesses of the Torah whose time for revelation has not yet come.

This approach was the dialectic methodology which Rabbi Kook perfected and applied in his teaching, particularly in his confrontation with secular humanism, humanistic religiosity, Marxism, the varieties of socialism, and streams of Zionism — secular ideologies and world outlooks that had proliferated among Jews. He found a core of partial truth and justice in each of them which qualified them for redefinition from a higher religious perspective. Clearly, he was striving to refine, elevate, and unite all these models of Jewish culture by uncovering a more sublime sphere of religious-Torah truth in them than had previously been imputed to them by the religious tradition. In fact, Rabbi Kook subjected Orthodox and ultra-Orthodox Jewry, too, to a dialectical critique in his effort to find the most elevated, inclusive sphere of religious thought in order to unite all the contending movements and spiritual streams of contemporary Jewry into an all-encompassing, harmonious cultural whole.

2. The flow of sublime emanations descends, is atomized, and becomes material so that it may act in the temporal world to reveal God's wisdom and beneficence in man's progressively enlightened cultural creativity. But refinement is finite, and it is limited by the material "vessel's" ability to absorb and express these emanations. Therefore, a precondition for each new stage in the development of nature and culture is the strengthening and repair of the "vessels." The flow of beneficent sublimity expands throughout nature, but it is concentrated in the life of human beings and their social-cultural creativity where a true continuous development and progress is revealed, whereas nature has already reached its full perfection. Cultural development in all peoples comes to the fore gradually, but this is particularly so for the Jewish people who serve as the connecting conduit that channels the divine emanation to the entire human sphere. At this point, it is important to place special emphasis on Rabbi Kook's notion of the development that occurs in the intellectual-emotional experience of belief and knowledge of God which Rabbi Kook believes to be man's sublime goal.

Generally, kabbalistic mysticism expressed itself in an aspiration to reunite with the sources of divine emanation in their most sublime spheres through various means of internalized contemplation or ecstatic theurgy. The mystic shuts his eyes to the external material world. He looks inward and aspires to reunite with the divine source from which his soul emanated. When he makes contact with the sublime sources, he can direct the divine emanation and cause it to flow to temporal spheres, refining it. It must be emphasized that the autonomous activity of the mystic is not directed at the worldly sphere but rises above it. In this respect there is an instructive reversal and transvaluation in Rabbi Kook's teaching. In his thought, the activity which engenders devotion and elevation is in the opposite direction, joining the descending direction of the flow of God's emanation, and paralleling the direction found in A. D. Gordon's philosophy. This is what brings about the closeness of these two men. One can define the form devotion takes in the teaching of both these modern religious thinkers as a mysticism of *self-realization*, or a mysticism of creativity which extracts divine beneficence from the higher spheres. It channels this beneficence into the material vessels of mundane life in a desire to fill them with the fullness of divine wisdom and love, insofar as it is possible for these vessels to withstand such fullness. The exhilaration and religious fervor found in Rabbi Kook's thinking, both in terms of content and mode of presentation, was the enthusiasm of creative expression addressed to the individual and the whole of the Jewish people in order to imbue them with a determination to elevate themselves through spiritual creativity; in other words, the enthusiasm of *hagshamah* (realization through materialization) rather than the enthusiasm of *hafnamah* (internalization) and *bittul ha-yesh* (negation of corporeal reality).

It also applied to the personal and national redemptive experience which is central to Rabbi Kook's thought. It was perceived as a progression in which personal and national life would gradually be perfected and fulfilled, expressed through an unfolding cultural creativity.

3. The tendency to *hagshamah* is, of course, the inclination toward development and progress in human history, particularly that of the Jewish people. This development proceeds in a staged progression from the creation of the cosmos to the fulfillment of man's role in temporal life. In this, Rabbi Kook accepted the assumption of idealistic historicism which defines history as a progression in accordance with an intra-historic systemized pattern, except that in Rabbi Kook's kabbalistic perception that undeviating intra-historic regularity reveals the flow of emanations into temporal "vessels"; these then act in and through the vessels, just as man's spirit and soul act through the body, bettering it and enhancing its functions.

The most important principle in Rabbi Kook's concept of the unfolding dialectic which directs the history of the Jewish people within the history of all other peoples can be defined as follows. The extent of divine beneficence which can be "encapsulated" in temporal reality depends on the sturdiness and absorptive capacity of the temporal vessels. The more functionally healthy and stalwart the body is, the greater is its capacity to absorb and express the life of the spirit and the life of the soul. Similarly, the broader, more highly-developed the economic, political, social and cultural institutions of a people are from an ethical and functional standpoint, the better able they are to absorb the flow of divine wisdom and beneficence, and express them in a temporal life that is graced by redemption. Commensurately, of course, the more brimming with divine beneficence the mundane institutions are, the stronger they become, and the more enhanced are their functions.

According to Rabbi Kook, this is the key to understanding the import of great struggles, wars, and crises in the course of history. It is certainly the key to understanding the fate of the Jews as a people faithful to its teachings, and in terms of its relationship to other peoples. Preparing the material vessels so that they could fully absorb the divine wisdom and beneficence intended for the repair of temporal life required an extended, complex process of development, as well as a myriad of hard and painful "trials." Initially, the Jewish people fashioned its tools of sovereignty and national life in their native land. However, they were subjected to exile so that the tools could be honed in preparation for the spiritual perfection that is unique to the Jews, so that each individual Jew would *realize* a Torah way of life. At the same time, the Jews were expected to disseminate the divine light, the wisdom and goodness — which is the knowledge of God's truth and Torah — among the nations. Consequently, when the hour of redemption comes — the hour when religious practice is perfected, the hour of the ethical elevation of all the peoples — the Jewish people will be able to return to a life of full national sovereignty, in its land. At such a time, it will put into practice that which, through painful trials experienced in exile, it perceived as spiritual-religious perfection. Perfection will be manifest in the cultural religious life of the people, and in its relationship with the surrounding peoples.

4. The Jewish people refines the vessels of realization needed for its religious, spiritual perfection as a nation of Torah while, simultaneously, it propagates the knowledge of God through the example of its life dedicated to His service. Here one must take note of Rabbi Kook's special developmental dialectics which become evident in Israel's relations with other nations on the cultural plane. It is obvious that while in exile, the improvements and advancements of civilization's temporal vessels — the sciences, technology and arts, statecraft, etc. — occurred precisely among the other peoples rather than among the Jews because Jews devoted themselves exclusively to maintaining their uniqueness as a people devoted to God. At the time of the redemption, when the Jews return to their land and to their sovereign life, Jews will discover that they must "borrow" from the material civilization and the temporal wisdom of the people among whom they had lived. However, an analysis in depth shows that, in Rabbi Kook's view, the Jewish people exiled among the nations served as a conduit that provided the nations with the spiritual strengths necessary for the creation of their material cultures. Everything was channeled through that conduit because the source of all wisdom that the Jewish people dispersed among the nations is the divine, bounteous emanation which flowed by means of the Torah. Non-Jewish civilizations merely extracted from it the elements they required, and developed them for their own circumscribed needs. Consequently, the cultural "borrowing" from others is merely a restitution of temporal cultural creativity to its original owners, into its rightful place.

Reinstating temporal culture to its rightful place was needed because other peoples saw material civilization and its values as their goal, certainly not as a means of dispersing divine light in the world. Therefore, at the expense of spiritual elevation, the non-Jews expanded the bounds of their civilization, imbuing it with a material aspect that concealed the divine light and detracted from its brilliance. The basic feature of such "idol worship" is that it perverts the means into an end. This was clearly the root cause of the opposition and hatred which other peoples felt toward the Jews (who had only dealt well with them) exactly as it was the cause for the evil, pagan corruption which marked the life of other peoples. Therefore, the Jews are obliged to accept only those parts of other cultures which are positive and proper, and which constitute the means to an ethical, religious end. A limitation and a reformulation must be superimposed on to these foreign elements so that every stratum and sphere appropriated into the temporal creativity of the Jewish people will serve to fulfill God's commandments in all the ways of life. Thus the Jewish people returns to a normal functioning of full temporal, national life only so that it can uncover the spiritual quality specific to itself, thereby continuing to serve as an example to all other peoples in the sanctification of temporal civilization, reunited with its source.

The heart of Rabbi Kook's teachings attributed a supreme religious importance to the creation of a Jewish national culture in all its human, temporal aspects. The more that national culture expands and improves in terms of quality, function, ethics and expression, the greater the extent of devotion to religious, spiritual life, to Torah and mitzvot. It was because of this that Rabbi Kook affirmed the great cultural aspirations of the secular Zionist movement. This was true not only with regard to land settlement, agricultural and industrial development, political and social organization, defense and security, and the like, but with regard to the inauguration and advancement of sports, art, literature, and science. He gave his enthusiastic support to the establishment of the Maccabi Sport Organization, the Bezalel School of Art, the opening of the Hebrew University, and other such enterprises. Moreover, stressing the significance of positive elements of culture to a believing religious way of life, he looked for organized, gradual ways with which to open religious, national educational institutions to the teaching of such elements. He also dreamed of establishing a "higher yeshiva" where the junction between temporal, scientific knowledge on the one hand, and sacred wisdom on the other, would be pursued.

He believed that the full development of temporal culture would uncover the complementary harmony that exists between scientific truth and spiritual religious truth (a problem Rabbi Kook dealt with in depth in the philosophic strata of his teaching), between humanistic-socialist morality and religious morality, and between the refinement of artistic expression and sublime emotional, religious spirit. In other words, he believed that a fully articulated temporal culture which would be developed in Hebrew in Eretz Israel would serve as the vessel in which the divine emanation would be collected. That culture would obey the discipline of sacred commandments; it would find the adaptation and proper relationship between the vessels and temporal, material functions, and between spiritual, religious goals and meanings.

The guidance that will assure that, at its fullest, national temporal culture reaches a stage of sanctity, stems from the Torah both in theoretical and normative halakhic dimensions. A culture that sanctifies temporal creativity is a halakhic culture. But at this stage in Rabbi Kook's discussion, one is confronted by the difficulty he had in crossing over from the vision to its realization. He wanted to propose theoretical solutions. As noted, he wanted to create a bridge between scientific truth and "*Hokhmat ha-Kodesh*" (sacred wisdom), between the highest aspirations of humanistic, socialist morality and religious morality. He invested great efforts in explicating the reasons for the mitzvot and their relationship to fashioning a fully perfected, progressive life at the national, social level so that the secular public could comprehend the reasons for keeping the commandments by virtue of their positive values.

In projecting a Halakhah that proposed norms acceptable to a people experiencing a full economic, social, political and cultural life in their land, he collided with a major obstacle. He met with a systemic resistance to innovative forms which stemmed from halakhic patterns of thought that had crystallized during the period of exile, from the stubborn devotion of ultra-Orthodox Jewry (from which he himself originated and within which he served). Ultra-Orthodox Jewry showed no readiness to admit that the dynamic of historic development mandated a parallel dynamic in patterns of halakhic thought. They refused to recognize the need for the creation of an overall national culture and the forging of a halakhic system which would reconcile the scientific rationale of production in a temporal civilization with the spiritual rationale of religious "sacred wisdom." In the ultra-Orthodox view, a dynamic approach to halakhah was illegitimate in principle, a kind of "reform," heaven forfend. In other words, a breach of the religious fortress.

The collision with this obstacle brought Rabbi Kook to a daring theoretical differentiation between the exilic Torah and the Torah of Eretz Israel. The former is a formal, halakhic deliberation informed by unbending principles. It operates on the strength of rabbinic scholarship and determines halakhic norms in accordance with authoritative precedent alone, functioning without need for religious-ethical intuition to directly set halakhic norms for spiritual, moral, religious values or the circumstances of historic cultural time. In contradistinction, the Torah of Eretz Israel is a direct, moral, spiritual, religious deliberation. It operates by the authority of a dynamic, renewing prophetic revelation. Rabbi Kook departed from the teachings of Maimonides which he saw as representing the exilic Torah viewpoint when the latter stated that prophets have no halakhic authority. According to Rabbi Kook's view, prophecy would reassert itself in the rebuilt Eretz Israel; it would fashion a halakhah which was self-renewing and adapted to the reality of a redemptive age.

But as a scholar and a responsible man of halakhah, Rabbi Kook regarded his Torah of Eretz Israel as a vision for the future, only possible when historic circumstances would permit. To this end, it was necessary for the entire Jewish people to unite under the aegis of the Torah. First, a whole-hearted repentance on the part of free-thinking national Jews had to be inspired so that they could recognize that the soul of Torah pulses within their national endeavor. A whole-hearted repentance was needed in the other camp as well; ultra-Orthodox Jewry had to be awakened toward an acceptance of the totality of Israel, and to the vision of its re-establishment. Only then would a consensual authority unite the entire people, even as the rabbis weighed and promulgated Halakhah in keeping with the Torah of Eretz Israel.

It is unnecessary to belabor the point that Rabbi Kook believed that his generation was at the crux of the redemptive process and at the initial stage of repentance. The settlement and rebuilding of Eretz Israel were certain testimony to that fact. Complete repentance would surely come, and the entire Jewish people would indeed unite under a single Torah-inspired halakhic authority which would then expand and proliferate in a prophetic direction. But until that time, it was crucial to maintain two parallel courses: national, cultural, material creativity, especially as practiced by the free-thinking sector of the population; and spiritual-religious creativity, as conducted by the national religious sector. All this in order to prepare for the great hour when divine emanations would reign over temporal life, and the two streams would be able to join and unite.

The picture presented is a clear-cut Messianic, utopian vision of a culture that blends within itself a national, temporal normality with metaphysical, spiritual singularity. Yet without a qualitative change in a temporal reality that would elevate itself to the level of spirituality, the vision was unattainable. The transformation is slow to come; indeed, it has not yet been realized. But it would appear that it was precisely its utopian character that empowered an unattainable vision to become the authoritative source for the ways in which Orthodox Zionism put the Torah of Eretz Israel into practice. As they approach the envisioned horizon, which they strive constantly to realize, Orthodox Zionism sees the two cultural strata uniting; in the reality of the present, they remain separate.

Chapter Twenty Two
JUDAISM AS A CULTURE IN THE DIASPORA

The Zionist variant of Jewish national culture was created in Eretz Israel, for life in Eretz Israel. The ideological foundations of the culture were, however, laid in the Diaspora and its initial implementation (revival of the Hebrew language, modern Hebrew literature, art, education, preparation for pioneering life, even self-defense) began in the Diaspora. Nonetheless, everything that was done was done with an eye towards immigration to Eretz Israel. It was in the Land of Israel that a Jewish national presence would be created whose language, literature, education, societal institutions and patterns of social life were essentially both national and Jewish. Eretz Israel quickly became the major center for spoken Hebrew, for literature, and for education, and it was from here that cultural material was disseminated to the Diaspora. Thus a cycle of cultural feedback was generated, making Ahad Ha-Am's "spiritual center" a reality for those sectors of the Jewish people who identified with Zionism, and who saw themselves as potential *olim.* Even those parties and movements which rejected the notion of a "spiritual center" as the *goal* of Zionism, engaged in activities that were consistent with the ideology of a spiritual center.

Leaders who guided the creation of a national Zionist culture found no practical distinction between the creative processes in Eretz Israel and those in the Diaspora. There was only one model: the one directed towards Eretz Israel. How, then, would Jews who decided to remain in the Diaspora play a part in the national Hebrew culture that would evolve in Eretz Israel? Ahad Ha-Am had no practical answer to the question, and made do with statements that were either general or vague. Apparently this was because the question of Zionist realization in the Diaspora was not an immediate concern. Ahad Ha-Am did not regard the life of eastern European Jewry with which he was familiar as existing in a "Diaspora"; rather, he saw it as an "exile" whose existence he "negated." The mass migration from Eastern Europe to the free diasporas of America and other Western countries was already at its height. As for the Jews that remained in central and Western

Europe, the majority were being drawn — rapidly and irreversibly — towards assimilation. Along with most leaders of Spiritual Zionism, Ahad Ha-Am believed that this assimilating Jewry did not have the spiritual potential necessary to create an independent national culture, and this meant that the question would become germane only after the creation and stabilization of new diasporas, assuming these would still have the capacity for Jewish national identification.

Historical developments were such that it fell to the American Zionist movement to deal with shaping the image of Judaism as a national culture in the Diaspora by articulating the application of the spiritual center idea for life in the Diaspora. In this the Zionist movement differed from modern religious movements which had simply transplanted the identity models of central European Jewry. How would a secular national Jewish culture find its institutional expressions? What would the characteristics of such a culture be? How would it draw on the spiritual center in Eretz Israel while retaining an independent socio-institutional infrastructure of its own? Mordecai Kaplan (1881–1983), the founder of the Reconstructionist movement and the father of the Community Center movement, was the most prominent thinker to address the problem. He proposed both a philosophy and a program, and worked towards their implementation.

Mordecai Kaplan was born in Russia and, together with his family, immigrated to the United States as a youth. He considered himself a disciple of Ahad Ha-Am and, to a certain extent, also of Simon Dubnow (1860–1941). Dubnow had projected a concept of "autonomism" in the Diaspora which paralleled that of Ahad Ha-Am's Spiritual Center in Eretz Israel. At the same time, one can easily discern, in Kaplan's solution to the problem of Jewish existence in the Diaspora, the influence of the new political, social and cultural circumstances which he found in the United States, as well as the impact of external philosophical and religious elements. Several differences immediately stand out between Kaplan's approach and the theories of Ahad Ha-Am, Dubnow, and Ḥayyim Naḥman Bialik:

1. A departure from the mind-set so characteristic of revolutionary secularism, both from its pessimistic view of the Jewish people's fate in the short run, and from the standpoint of its radical confrontation with institutionalized religion;

2. A reaffirmation of the optimism of 19th century European liberalism, i.e., a revival of faith in the inevitability of historical *progress* which would alleviate the plight of the Jewish people;

3. Acceptance of the influence of pragmatism, a philosophy that developed as a leading theoretical movement in the United States, replacing Ahad Ha-Am's dogmatic European positivism in Kaplan's thought;

4. Adoption of the American notion of religious-cultural pluralism, created in the wake of the mass immigration of disparate ethnic groups to the United States;

5. A secular assessment of religion which stressed its vital, positive factor in shaping culture from within itself.

What stands out prominently about these ideas is the fact that they precisely mirrored the cultural experience of the New World at the beginning of the century. As a totality, they fueled hopes for shaping a uniquely Jewish sub-culture which would find institutional expression in socially cohesive communities. This would be accomplished without restraint or interference, with the complete integration of Jews into the cultural-social fabric of the burgeoning American nation. In contrast to Europe, it was clear that at least on a theoretical level, America held out the possibility that the two national cultures — Jewish and American — could co-exist without either friction or mutual rejection. Indeed, in a land where every immigrant group developed ethnic, or religio-ethnic, sub-cultures of its own and preserved a cultural connection with its country of origin, peoplehood-oriented American-Jewish communities could thrive and support a spiritual center for the Jewish people in Eretz Israel, though they themselves had no intention of immigrating. These communities would direct their educational efforts and cultural-national creativity towards the implementation of Zionism's cultural-national message in the Diaspora.

Mordecai Kaplan began his career as a teacher in New York at the Jewish Theological Seminary of the Conservative movement. There he found a positive attitude towards spiritual Zionism and an affirmation of the totality of Jewish tradition which encompassed the specific cultural life of a community, not its religion alone. When, however, he observed modern religious attitudes against the background of assimilatory, social openness in the American environment, he found these attitudes to be inadequate. This drawback was particularly true of Jewish identification as espoused by the Reform movement in America, though there, too, there were signs of Zionist tendencies — along with a more conservative approach to religious revision than had been the case in central Europe. Kaplan saw the basic approach of both modern religious movements to the continuity of Judaism in the western Diaspora as fundamentally flawed. The approach was too narrow. Like Orthodoxy, the Conservative and Reform movements based the continued existence of the Jewish people on religion as a faith and on a network of ritual commandments. The Conservative movement tacked on tradition, customs and ceremonies, and a few nationalist sentiments. Could the life of a people be founded on such principles? Could such principles provide an answer to social and spiritual needs that were diverse and complex? Could such principles maintain Jewishness in the face of the seductive pull of a culturally rich environment that provided most of the material and spiritual requisites that went beyond religion and tradition?

Kaplan's negative answer to these questions stemmed, in the first instance, from an assessment of the place which a religion based on the concept of a supernatural God and aspiring to a supra-terrestrial spiritual life could hope to hold within modern reality; there was, as well, the increased level of achievement and consequent rise in the level of expectation and gratification that was provided by a material culture grounded in science and advanced technology.

Regarding the first issue, Kaplan concluded that in the face of scientific progress, conventional versions of monotheism — whether the traditional concept of Orthodoxy and of Conservative Judaism, or the liberal-Idealistic concept — were on their way to being refuted. He believed that the humanities and natural sciences unequivocally discredited belief in a super-terrestrial sphere of spirituality which controls nature from above. He did not, however, believe that as a consequence monotheistic religious faith was invalidated or had become superfluous in the modern era. Nor did it follow that the denial of a separate, supernatural spiritual sphere meant there was no purposeful, value-laden component within nature itself. On the contrary. Influenced by American pragmatism, Kaplan recognized a valid distinction between science which deals with the laws of nature, technology which deals with the practical application of these laws for the benefit of man, and the ethical values that must guide man in his social-cultural setting as he functions within nature for his own good and the good of the natural environment. Such values are not scientific. They are the determination of a rational free will.

In Kaplan's view, this distinction defines the parameters within which a worldly religiosity can serve a vital function. It can provide value-laden ethical and spiritual guidance which science and technology, in themselves, cannot provide. It is clear that faith in a this-worldly, rational God who serves as a source of ethical guidance for a this-worldly endeavor, is a radical revolution in traditional religious faith. Such a revolution is required in order to reconcile religion with the conclusions of scientific research: natural, social and human.

As to the second issue: Modern secular society is focused on creating an articulated temporal cultural order which can provide for all its material and spiritual needs. Such an endeavor requires great creative physical and spiritual efforts to build a civilization in concert with the principles of nature. Since modern man wants the gratifications that such a society holds out, traditional religious ideals of Torah study and the observance of commandments lose their significance and their influence among the masses. An ascetic, spiritual life that aspires to an otherworldly sphere no longer appeals to the majority of people. Only if Judaism can offer its adherents a wide-ranging scientific, technological, social and cultural foundation for their creative national undertaking, can it continue to exist and sustain its people.

These two mutually supportive conclusions make it clear that the Jewish people can prevail in the environment of a modern culture only if they have a temporal "civilization" of their own. Such a civilization must be similar to that of the surrounding peoples so that the Jews can preserve their integrity while maintaining positive mutual contact with their neighbors and integrating into the common environment. At the same time, the Jewish people must ensure that they remain separate from all those aspects that other *normal* national cultures claim as unique to themselves. This is the fundamental truth that Zionism taught. With these factors in mind, Kaplan came to the conclusion that the idea of the "Chosen People" could no longer be justified or validated. It would be best to discard it. The Jewish people has a unique history and culture, it had and has a unique religion, but all peoples have their own cultural uniqueness and every people contributes its special creativity to mankind. Accordingly, from the standpoint of being a people with its own unique features, the Jewish people is like all other peoples. If it lacks any vital components of a normal, national "civilization," it is because of the conditions of exile. Thus endangered, the Jewish people must strive to become whole.

A simple and straightforward conclusion follows from this:

> Jewish identity that is based on supernatural religiosity along the lines of either modern Orthodoxy or ultra-Orthodoxy, or a Judaism that is conservative in its outlook, cannot long endure, and will quickly disintegrate. Neither will an identity long endure that is based on a modern religious system that has adjusted to scientific conclusions if it reduces the concept of Judaism to religion and religious tradition while seeking "civilization" only within the creative reaches of other peoples. A modern Jewish people needs a complete territorial, national culture as do the cultures of other modern peoples. Religion must be modernized so that culture becomes *one* of its components, one of the charac- teristics of its uniqueness. Only in this way can the Jewish people preserve its identity and contribute to general culture.

Kaplan's observations of the history of the Jews confirmed his views. Throughout the generations, Judaism had been a total life-experience of a people, not merely a religion. The basic components of the temporal aspects of culture existed and operated inside the established religious framework.

Even during the period of exile, a cultural framework, albeit a stunted one, was created in the religious system. During the modern era, the religious establishment collapsed, revealing beneath it the cultural heritage. Modern religious movements aspired to shake off the cultural background that had emerged, attempted to maintain only religious elements because of their aspiration to become integrated into the richer civilizations of other peoples. Kaplan believed this to be a prescription for an acculturation which would inevitably lead to assimilation. If religion itself was incapable of maintaining a people's identity, all the more was this the case for a religion emptied of the cultural content that had preserved and reinforced it in the Diaspora. The opposite was true: all the cultural components of the ancient heritage that were still valid (national historical memory, language, literature, ethics, etc.) had to be husbanded in order to recreate a national, temporal culture capable of competing with the richness of surrounding modern cultures. From its inception, Judaism had been a national civilization; only by strengthening and expanding it, only through its renaissance as a civilization, would Judaism have a continued existence in the future.

Kaplan preferred the concept "civilization" to Ahad Ha-Am's "culture." Civilization expresses a more radical aspiration towards national independence since it includes all the physical components of culture: a permanent territorial base, science, technology, a state. Clearly, the Jewish people could create all these components only as an independent national entity, only in its own land. In what sense could Judaism exist as a civilization in the Diaspora? Obviously, Jews in the Diaspora would be participating directly in the civilization of their surrounding environment! They could, of course, find added support in the fact that they also had a national state that functioned as a complete civilization, and it was Kaplan's belief that for the Jewish people to exist in the Diaspora, this was a vital dimension. Consequently the link between Diaspora Jews and their homeland needed to be organized, active and efficient so that Diaspora Jews could be true partners in their state's civilization. As for maintaining their identity in the Diaspora, they would have to make do with "culture" as explicated by Ahad Ha-Am.

In other words, with relation to the Diaspora, Kaplan intended the concept "Jewish civilization" to mean something similar to that which Ahad Ha-Am intended by "national culture" — that is, historical memory, active knowledge of the Hebrew language, familiarity with Hebrew literature from all sources and periods, creative participation in a revived national literature, maintenance of the halakhic national ethic, and maintenance and observance of communal-familial frameworks as the expression of a Jewish way of life. However, Kaplan's conception of national culture was much fuller and more encompassing than was Ahad Ha-Am's, even for the Diaspora. It was fuller because it included religion as a central, orienting component of the national culture. It was more encompassing and broader in its shaping of community and trans-national frameworks, and in the range of cultural activities that would provide content for these frameworks.

Kaplan agreed with Ahad Ha-Am that modern science had discredited faith in the existence of a supernatural divine entity that creates, leads, commands, and rewards. This meant that religion in its traditional sense was irrevocably undermined. But in contrast to Ahad Ha-Am, Kaplan felt that religion played a vital function in the life of mankind, that even in the modern era it continued to be vital to the same degree and in the same form. Simply put, there is a human need for faith in a God who commands and leads, to whom people can turn in their distress, in whom they can trust when facing forces of evil whether these stem from within themselves, from natural sources, or from human society; a need to draw spiritual strength from their belief so that they can hope and act in the fulfillment of man's purpose. It is a human need which no other cultural factor can provide. No other element can meet man's aspiration to a sanctity which reflects an absolute and eternal value structure. There is, therefore, no substitute for religion as a source of faith and hope and a feeling of commitment to the moral goals of mankind; neither is there a substitute for religion as a source for perceiving sanctity and for ways of appropriately expressing these perceptions: prayer and blessings, the symbols of Shabbat, the holidays and holy days, and the traditional commandments with their ethical, social and national meanings.

Man, the creator of culture, is conscious of his special place in nature. He knows that he has the freedom to act and create at his discretion and in keeping with his needs and values.

Where do man's values originate? Unquestionably from his nature as a human being, though not from any causal necessity implicit in that nature; rather, from the freedom to choose his goals and to make a commitment towards their fulfillment. It is not, therefore, science that is the source of values, but man's will to make choices. It is not science (which devises the tools for man's actions in nature) that can assure the fulfillment of values, but only faith and hope. What are faith and hope based on? Is it possible that man can depend on and trust in himself only, solely in his will and his abilities? Certainly not. Together with the awareness of his freedom and ability to create, man is aware of the limitations of human nature and of surrounding, natural conditions. He recognizes that both internally and externally there are forces in conflict with the fulfillment of his will, his goals, his values. No science can provide answers to the existential needs that stem from man's recognition of his unique state in nature. It is only faith in the religious sense and only modes of religious expression that can authentically and effectively satisfy such existential needs.

It should not be difficult to prove man's need for belief, or its ethical justification. Neither is it difficult to prove that faith is itself a type of spiritual strength that authenticates itself through the fulfillment of its goals. A believer can overcome external and internal difficulties where a non-believer may stumble. It is therefore possible to claim that faith is capable of verifying itself through its achievements and thus to justify, or "prove," its authenticity. Nonetheless, a major question arises — if the need for belief, in and of itself (or even the inherent value of faith as an existential move) is sufficient to sustain itself, if there is no scientific basis to ensure that man's faith, prayer, blessings and his hope for the future rely on Someone or Something beyond himself that is worthy of his trust — is human need enough to provide its own fulfillment? Kaplan's response is that need which stems from the ethical-rational nature of man (who is himself part of nature) testifies to the point that there are forces of various kinds within nature. There are forces of preservation which science discovers and that technology uses; there are mechanisms of breakdown and entropy that are the source of processes of withering, disease and death. But there is also a purposeful factor that can be identified in nature, which acts in an evolutionary progression. This factor is reflected in the appearance of forms that become increasingly more complex and sophisticated, especially in the appearance of man from within the chain of continual development, and it is reflected even more strongly in his cultural creativity. This is sufficient to prove that there is an autonomous force in nature that operates with a proclivity to values and progress. It is that force that man identifies in his own nature as divine. Since this is the force in man that has volitional and emotional expression, it is acceptable to relate to it as something he knows, to experience it, and to feel its creative and progressive power within his very being, as his personality. Man can pray in a personal language, and express his desires in a personal language even though the force in nature which impels toward progress cannot be identified as *personal*; it is rather a purposeful trend that develops and advances nature in contrast to the processes of entropy, deterioration and destruction.

Of course, these assertions do not amply justify traditional faith in an omnipotent God who intervenes supernaturally in nature, but Kaplan believed that they constitute an underpinning for a trust and belief that human action which stems from free will and is based on values can exist and be aided by nature; that, in the course of history, such action is capable of gradually overcoming obstacles. Faith contains ample emotional-poetic content to justify the use of traditional religious language, interpret its expressions and principal symbols, and even to prove the inherent worth and spiritual effectiveness of prayers and blessings.

It is clear that Kaplan considered religion a creation of human culture. Moreover, he declared that religion develops its beliefs, values, symbols and special rituals through its linkage to the totality of the entire culture within which it operates, and which it guides. In other words, every religion develops in concert with the particular value-laden characteristics of its culture. Kaplan had no difficulty in maintaining the universal value of tolerance towards all religions which are based on positive ethical values. He rejected the pretentious assertions of monotheistic religions that compete with each other for the position of the one and only true religion. And, of course, this applied to Jewish religion as well. In its defense, it should be said that initially Judaism had been intended for Jews alone, without an aim of converting other peoples or lording it over their cultures. Kaplan also rejected the arrogance of claiming the status of "Chosen People." While the Jewish religion is the virtue of the Jewish people and the treasure of its culture, it is not the treasure of other peoples. Consequently, a Jew has sufficient reason to prefer the religion that embodies within it the values of his special culture, just as any person who has internalized the values of another nation and culture into which he was born and in which he was educated, has sufficient reason to prefer the religion of his culture. But the preference for unique selfhood need not lead to rivalries or confrontations with the unique religions of neighboring cultures, certainly not with the cultures in which Diaspora Jews take part. Among other particulars, Kaplan's approach expresses an aspiration for full normalization in the relations between the Jewish people and its surroundings.

The expanding scope of Jewish civilization was depicted by Kaplan in his emphasis on the relevance of political-institutional and symbolic-ceremonial national aspects. The historic fate of the Jewish people was to be dispersed to several geographical centers. Even when a Jewish state was reborn in the historic homeland, Jews would remain divided between that main center and several large centers in the Diaspora. Like Ahad Ha-Am, Kaplan believed that it was neither possible, nor perhaps desirable, to change such a reality which had determined the image of the people's culture and religion and given them a universal dimension. But, he continued, if this was so, it was desirable to strive towards normalization of this unique national reality. In addition to its shortcomings and difficulties, such a structure also had great advantages. Each center of Jewish life would make its specific contribution to the common culture of the entire people, making it inadequate simply to cultivate political, cultural ties between each Diaspora and the center of the complete Jewish civilization that would arise in Eretz Israel.

To begin with, a framework should be established through which the national unity of all the centers would be expressed; such a framework would determine the legal-political nature of their relationships, their mutual and joint responsibilities, and the various political, economic and cultural activities through which such responsibilities would be translated from the potential to the actual. Within this united, national framework it would be necessary to stress the common religious-cultural denominator, giving it a prominent and impressive ceremonial expression at special times, both during life-cycle events of the individual (such as Bar and Bat Mitzvah, in which all individuals would express their desire to belong to the people and symbolically accept the commitment of loyalty towards it), and in the life of the community. Thus every Jew, no matter who, would be granted the status of full and equal citizenship in the Jewish nation. This would be expressed through defined rights and obligations: through electing and being elected to national and even international institutions, through taxation, and through various political, social and cultural activities on the supra-national level.

Obviously, in order for this sense of belonging to the entire Jewish people to be acted out operatively and institutionally, as broad and encompassing a footing as possible had to be provided on the local level as well. The nation state would serve as a base for the individuals who were its citizens. But even within the Jewish state, the connection to the Jewish people and its unique culture required communal organization. So much the truer for the centers in the Diaspora. In these centers, the local community would have to be the focus of belonging and the framework through which Jewish identity would exist as a suitably complete social-familial lifestyle. On the level of communal organization in the Diaspora, Kaplan projected a program broad enough for the concept "Jewish civilization" to be applicable. No longer was there to be merely a "holy community" that united Jews around the synagogue, the study hall, and other clearly religious institutions. While this was clearly of importance to Kaplan, it is understood that for a community whose task was to implement "Jewish civilization" in the Diaspora, it was crucial that a broad ranging variety of social, cultural, religious and educational activities be developed. All types of creative expression would be affected: adult education, the arts, sports, drama, entertainment. Lectures, artistic performances, study circles and creative workshops, etc., would turn the traditional religious community into a "community center" that would represent Judaism as a *national civilization*.

Of course, the participation of Jews within their surrounding culture would be reflected in such a community center. However, the institution would be independently Jewish and would facilitate participation in, and response to, the influences of the culture being created in the reborn Jewish

State. In addition, umbrella cultural institutions (such as colleges for Jewish studies and organizations for developing and advancing Jewish art and literature) would be established through which the Diaspora could make its contribution to the national culture common to the entire Jewish people, a contribution representing the encounter with the best of universal human creativity. Thus Diaspora Jewry would be enriched while enriching the creative activity that would emerge within the Jewish State.

In all these respects, the concept of Judaism as a civilization is the application of Zionist aspirations to the development of an organic national culture, introducing modernity and normalcy to Jewish existence through the preservation of the complexity of its national uniqueness.

It is difficult to evaluate the degree of success of the Reconstructionist movement which Kaplan founded in the United States as a branch of the Conservative movement. It was from the beginning, and it remains to this day, a movement that is active but limited in scope. Nonetheless, its ideological influence can be felt beyond the boundaries of its organization, especially in the establishment and operation of community centers. These centers have been successful, have expanded and have attracted Jews, many of whom have no interest in religion, to a socially affiliating framework. But have these "civilizational" activities succeeded in increasing the trend toward cultural assimilation in the Diaspora or in stopping them? Has a "Jewish civilization" commenced in the Diaspora, or is there a possibility that one can arise in the future? Is it possible for a pan-Jewish unity to be established at a level of cultural-political intensity that would provide a national *standard* for the Jewish people, both in Israel and the Diaspora? Do the trends that shape modern culture in western nations today allow for a development in this direction? The achievements racked up until now in the American Diaspora cannot justify a positive answer to these difficult questions. A "common" technological civilization whose goal is a universal village — strong enough to blur particularistic national identities — seems likely to overcome the impact of societal organizations which are only partial and particular. In the modern world, it would appear that Jewish "civilization" is capable of maintaining itself only in its own State.

Chapter Twenty Three
THE SECULAR JEWISH CULTURE OF YIDDISH

At the same time that a modern, national, secular Jewish culture was being generated in Hebrew, a popular Jewish culture — which was modern and secular — was being produced in Yiddish, first in the eastern European Diaspora and subsequently in North and South America. The vital interface between these two cultures was, in effect, an outgrowth of the common Jewish societies of the Diaspora in which they functioned; each striving to be representative of the people's life, values and Jewish identity. Nonetheless, a deep-seated competition existed between them as each language vied for recognition as the "national language of the Jews." Basically, it was an antagonism between an orientation that was national-Zionist Eretz Israel centered, and an exilic or Diasporic folk orientation. In any case, the dispute was over the nature of contemporary Jewry's unifying link to all aspects of its historic culture.

Throughout the generations, Hebrew was both the national and the sacred language of Jews. It served as a link between the diasporas, a continuity to the sources that bound the people to Eretz Israel. Hebrew was the language of the authoritative past and the language of a redemptive national future. By comparison, beginning in the 10th century, Yiddish was the language of daily existence; it was not only the on-going language of a major segment of the Jewish people, it also facilitated the interaction of Jews with the gentile societies of eastern and central Europe.

It was precisely because of this that, initially, Yiddish had a decided advantage over Hebrew despite its dismissal in the aristocratic early stages of the secular Enlightenment. When one speaks of the development of a modern, secular Jewish culture, one speaks of Yiddish. Yiddish, the day-to-day language of the entire people, was after all the language of secularity; the language of the home and the street; the language that bespoke life beyond prayer and blessings, Torah study and halakhic decisions; the language of sorrow and suffering; the language of both comedy and tragedy; the language of love and joy; the language of life's wisdom and humor. It was also the language through which Jews expressed their involvement in the physical, socio-cultural environment of the lands of their dispersion. What this means is that a thriving secular, folk culture already existed in the Yiddish language for eastern and central European Jewry. Manifest though this was in the folksy treasures of the Yiddish language itself, as well as in such literary genres as poetry and melodramas, it was a fact overlooked by those who were attempting to write a national literature in Hebrew. Yiddish bridged the sacred literature of Hebrew and the daily existence of Jews in their surrounding society; indeed, on the secular level, it was the link between Jews and their environment. Consequently, it was possible to identify the early folk literature and language of Yiddish as a kind of cultural heritage, even as a kind of unique tradition which could serve as one's Jewish identity.

For those authors, poets, thinkers, journalists and teachers who created secular Jewish culture, and who transmitted it (this was also true of artists and musicians), whose affinity to the Jewish milieu bound them to Jewish motifs in the Yiddish language and its literature, the clash between Yiddish and Hebrew signaled a difficult fork in the road. Certainly there were distinguished authors who refused to give up either of the two cultures, producing different kinds of works in both Jewish languages. But ultimately, the determining factor was one's ideological orientation with regard to national identity and a vision of the future. Hebrew led to a national future in Eretz Israel. Yiddish was bound up with the present in the Diaspora. Did the Diaspora hold out a future? Was there a chance that in the transition from exile to a free Diaspora, a foundation could be created for a society that would have an independent and tangible Jewish folk-character based on Yiddish? Could a Jewish society survive — for two or more generations hence — on the strength of Yiddish language and culture as its identifying characteristics and the texture of its life? The argument raged over this question as well.

Two political movements championed Yiddish culture as the future culture of the Jewish people, making it a fundamental principle. The movement for Jewish Autonomy advanced a national alternative to Zionism out of its belief that in the context of a solution to the problem of nationalities in Austria, Poland and Russia the Jews, too, could achieve cultural-social autonomy within communal frameworks. Such frameworks would set up independent educational and cultural institutions employing the Yiddish language. The second of these, the Jewish Labor movement, organized the Jewish working class in eastern Europe and America as independent segments within the broad movement for social revolution. Whether they aspired to Jewish autonomy in a classless society that would emerge after the revolution, or whether they sought integration in "tomorrow's world," each of these political movements regarded Yiddish as the most effective instrument by which to educate and motivate the Jewish masses. To that end, they developed a literature of persuasion and propaganda, and surrounded themselves with a wide-ranging network of cultural and social programs.

A fully articulated ideology of Yiddish culture was evolved, particularly by leaders of the movement for Jewish Autonomy. Notable among the leadership were Simon Dubnow (1860–1941) and Nathan Birenbaum (1864–1937). From their observations of Jewish history which they perceived as the people's exposure to the rise and fall of large, influential centers of creativity, both of them concluded that as early as 2000 years ago, the Jews transcended the "normal" needs of other civilizations which coalesced along national, territorial, political frameworks. The Jews matured to become a "spiritual people," a people whose unique cultural milieu is marked by its languages (Hebrew and Yiddish), its historic memory, its canonical and literary sources, and its humanistic ethos. Furthermore, they saw this as conceivable not only in the absence of a territorial, political context, but also in the absence of a religious context and content. Secular spirituality could sustain itself in the conditions of an emancipated Diaspora whose pre-conditions were peace and welfare, and in which communal frameworks and autonomous networks of schools and cultural institutions could function.

Still, one cannot regard either the ideologies of the Autonomists or their analogues in the Jewish Labor Movement (the Jewish Workers' Bund at one end and the Labor Zionists at the other) as programmatic positions that oriented or guided the development of Yiddish culture as a secular Jewish culture. In fact, that culture had developed in response to the spiritual, cultural needs of a mass Jewish society that was already functioning in the Yiddish language. The culture also developed in response to the need of creative thinkers — writers, poets, essayists, philosophers, critics, journalists, teachers, artists and actors — to express their cultural, social reality through the medium available to them and loved by them. Using Yiddish, they strove to match the achievements of the Western culture in which they also felt themselves at home. Here, too, Yiddish culture had a decided advantage over Hebrew and its literature. Yiddish did not need to create an enabling political and social infrastructure as a pre-condition for expressing itself in modern terms. Consequently Yiddish could evolve as a normative culture in keeping with the models it found within itself, or in its Western cultural environment. Within two or three generations, modern Yiddish literature attained impressive achievements that were clearly not inferior to the best of Hebrew literature in the period of its renaissance. Yiddish literature gave voice to a broad public and provided for its needs for as long as the society it portrayed continued to exist, and Yiddish culture was an autonomous living folklore.

Beyond an obvious affinity to the Jewish people and its language, did all this exhibit characteristics of a uniquely Jewish culture? The answer is decidedly yes. Against the tragic background of exile, Yiddish culture was filled with a self-awareness of Jewish worth, a consciousness that arose from the ongoing comparison between Jews and other peoples. Yiddish literature gave forceful expression to Jewish suffering throughout the generations, particularly in the modern era, but was devoid of radical Zionism's negation of the Diaspora. It confronted the meaning of Jewish suffering, not only or even primarily as a religious issue or as a national issue, but rather as an outstanding example of the moral-existential and universal suffering manifest in the human condition. But at the same time, Yiddish literature and culture underscored the uniquely ethical-humanistic outlook of the Jews, particularly the qualities of existential wisdom gained from daily life in the Diaspora which was marked by profound tragedy on one hand, and humorous self-criticism and self-acceptance on the other.

Thus it was that Yiddish literature maintained, structured, and embodied a tradition that identified the Jewish persona. Of course, this tradition reflected a religious way of life and its sacred literature as well, but generally the literature did not relate directly to the sources. Instead, its direct concern was the lives of people who experienced the religious life, interpreting it by means of their human faculties — their behavior, expressions, and practicality — the characteristics of Jewish mentality and of the spirit which set the "Jewish personality" and Jewish society apart. In this way, religion and religious values were reflected in the daily life of the personalities and the society which enacted them, and in their confrontation with life's tribulations. In their works, (with a variety of emphases), the three great classicists of modern Yiddish literature, Y. L. Peretz (1852–1915), Sholem Aleichem (1859–1916), and Sholem Asch (1880–1957) portrayed the tradition of the Jewish existential mentality, differentiating it from normative halakhic tradition. When contemporary Yiddish speakers identify the Jewish way of life as "Yiddishkeit," they use a linguistic term which has no equivalent in any language, least of all in Hebrew. The word is meant to set apart a singular, existential type of personality, or human species.

History has rendered its unambiguous judgment in the debate between those who championed Yiddish culture and those who advocated Hebrew. After the destruction of European Jewry in the Holocaust and the integration of Jews (who emigrated from eastern Europe) into the Americas to live in a "free Diaspora" that had ceased to be exile, secular Yiddish-speaking society disappeared. Only the ultra-Orthodox continue to use Yiddish, which they have adopted as the differentiating every-day language of their voluntary exile. The cultural life cycle that had maintained Yiddish literature as a modern, secular literature is gone. With the exception of researchers and academics, what remains is a great literary tradition, almost without heirs.

Chapter Twenty Four
THE TRANSITION FROM THE HEBREW CULTURE OF PRE-STATE ERETZ ISRAEL TO ISRAELI CULTURE

In the previous chapters, we have examined some of the central ideas in the thinking that influenced the creation of a modern, cultural alternative to the traditional, Torah-oriented definition of Judaism. As we have seen, the idea for such an alternative first arose at the end of the 18th century with the advent of the Enlightenment movement and the beginnings of Emancipation. We reviewed the development of this idea and the attempts to attain it by means of national, social, and political enterprises; institutionalized education systems; research; linguistic and literary renewal; various forms of social and political activity, and the ways in which all of these impacted on behavior — holidays and festivals, prayers and ceremonies, and social, cultural activities.

The Jewish communities in exile and in the Diaspora, as well as in Eretz Israel, attempted to implement models — partial or complete — of modern Jewish culture. However, though the theories were created and the efforts to implement them were begun in a specific exile or diaspora (and despite the fact that some of the theories focused on exile or Diaspora as a preferred, even inevitable reality), the most consistent effort to provide a full, complete cultural alternative worked itself out in the context of the Zionist movements as they attempted to secure settlement, economic, social and political objectives in the Land of Israel. It was here that the appropriate conditions emerged. It was here that the socio-political infrastructure was created that enabled a viable arena in which to fashion a multifaceted national Jewish civilization with all the material and spiritual components this term implies.

Jewish cultural endeavors in exile and in the Diaspora also focused on Eretz Israel where the greatest achievements were being made. Paradoxically, this applied not only to the Science of Judaism, which established its first and most important university center in the Land of Israel, but also to modern Orthodox Judaism which was amplified according to the formula "religious studies along with secular knowledge." And, despite its fierce opposition to Zionism, this was true even for ultra-Orthodox Judaism. The process of establishing ultra-Orthodox centers in Eretz Israel occurred contemporaneously with the unfolding of Zionism. In the wake of the Holocaust and following the establishment of the State of Israel, Eretz Israel effectively became the largest and most important Torah center of ultra-Orthodox Judaism. The modern religious movements (Conservative and Reform Judaism) were the last two movements to become part of the picture, though one might argue that they did have their national equivalent in "Spiritual Zionism." Immediately following the Second World War, a situation emerged in which there was an obvious division between the Jewish community in Eretz Israel that was absorbing the remnants of the European exile and that of the Arab lands, and Diaspora communities in the countries of the West, particularly the United States. A de facto global Jewish culture already existed in Eretz Israel — heterogeneous in nature, and riddled with internal divisions along political, socio-economic, socio-ideological and ethical lines compounded by the conflict between religiosity and secularity. In the Diaspora, various partial Jewish sub-cultures emerged, each isolated from the others and integrated, after its own fashion, in the dominant culture of the non-Jewish environment. Even the attempt to establish a Jewish "civilization" in the Diaspora, in the spirit of Kaplan's philosophy, did not, in the final analysis, move beyond the scope and depth of an American sub-culture: i.e. another component of American pluralistic civilization.

Accordingly, to further examine the philosophical and practical efforts of coping with problems of creating and maintaining a modern Jewish culture, one must focus on the place where a "civilization" was created for which the Jewish people bear exclusive and comprehensive responsibility: the State of Israel. To this end, we must assess the overall achievement of all those movements that together sought to create a national Jewish culture in the Land of Israel during the pre-state Yishuv period, and examine the ramifications and turning points brought about in them by the establishment of the State. This was the period of mass immigration (particularly from Arab lands), the entry of the Orthodox Old Yishuv into the political and social establishment of the New Yishuv, the concomitant rehabilitation of the ultra-Orthodox movements in the Land of Israel after the Holocaust and with the assistance of the State. There was also the vexing question of relating to the central position of American Jewry as a vital focus of contacts between Israeli Jews and Diaspora Jews, and between the State of Israel and the countries of the West. It hardly needs to be said that such profound transformations have changed the physical and cultural landscape of Israel almost beyond recognition, forging the entity that is currently known not as "Hebrew culture" but as "Israeli culture."

We begin this summary by recalling the contention that Hebrew culture in the Land of Israel was created as the result of a revolutionary impulse realized by leaving the Exile which represented the past, and settling in Eretz Israel which represented a new beginning founded on an ancient rock. "Negation of Exile" was the initial motivation common to most of the diverse streams of the new culture. Negation not only meant revulsion at an abnormal situation — subservience to foreign rule, persecution, humiliation and constant threats to the physical survival of the Jewish people — but also the rejection of cultural patterns that emerged during the process of adapting to conditions of exile. Aliyah to the Land of Israel, as it was motivated by Zionist ideology, also reflected the negation of the languages of the Diaspora, of its social structures, the occupations by which Jews made their living, their social and personal ethos, values, ambitions and ideals. At the same time, Zionist aliyah reflected a determination for the continuity of the Jewish people, and a desire to ensure its distinct identity. Eretz Israel was seen not only as a refuge from persecution and discrimination but also as a solution to the challenge of assimilation.

Zionism rebelled against exile and all it stood for; it sought an alternative that would ensure normal "selfhood" while maintaining national identity. To this end, all the Zionist movements drew on resources from within the Jewish heritage, as well as from external sources. The dialectical tension between the aspiration to transform the spiritual, cultural identity of the Jews and bring it in line with "normal" modern European models, and the aspiration to maintain national Jewish autonomy and the continuity of national Jewish historic consciousness, is the rationale for including all streams of national culture active in Eretz Israel from the 1890s through to the establishment of the State of Israel in the general category of "Hebrew culture."

The use of the term "Hebrew culture" was primarily a recognition of the victory of Hebrew in the "language war"; indeed, it was a Hebrew culture, rather than a Yiddish one or one using a foreign language. The decision that the culture would be Hebrew required *reviving* the Hebrew language as the most important and immediate cultural endeavor. There was an urgent need to develop the language from its role as a sacred tongue into a national language adequate for all the cultural needs of a modern nation, along the lines of European nations. The use of the term "Hebrew culture" underscored the assumption that language is the defining feature of any national culture, and that it is language that characterizes and identifies every national culture. It is through language that each nation is distinguished from other nations. In the Bible, itself, the word *lashon* ("tongue") is used as a synonym for "people" or "nation." In reiterating that the culture of the

Jews is defined above all by their national language, Hebrew, the intention was to emphasize the desired congruity between the Jewish people and other "normal" peoples of Europe — the English, French, Germans, Poles, Russians, etc. For each of these nations the name of the nation is the same as that of the nationality, and the name of the national culture is the same as the name of the language.

Thus, the aspiration to reconstitute the Jewish people's national existence as a condition of normality was concretely expressed by the use of the ancient national language to refer to the new culture that was being created in its ancestral homeland. From the national standpoint, language and land were the two primary traditional resources used in distinguishing this culture. In retrospect, it may be seen that no other language could possibly have been chosen for this function, just as no other land could have been embraced as a homeland. Hebrew was the only Jewish language that linked all segments of the people throughout the generations and in all parts of the dispersion. As the sacred tongue, it was the language of the religious sources — the Bible, prayers, religious literature and thought, Halakhah and the *piyyutim* [liturgical poems]. Hebrew had also filtered down through the other "Jewish languages" such as Talmudic Aramaic, Yiddish and Ladino. In these languages not only are the words that relate to Jewish faith and religious lifestyle taken from Hebrew, but the languages themselves are written in Hebrew characters. As a result, a thread of commonality was created between the various Jewish languages which characterized all of them as particular languages of a single people. It is significant that in the languages used by the Jews the national mother tongue was called by its ancient name "Hebrew," rather than "Jewish" or "Israeli." Yet it is ironic that it was precisely this loyalty to Hebrew (with its multiple strata reflecting the whole gamut of Jewish cultural history) that emphasized the highly abnormal nature of Jewish nationality and the scale of the revolution that was required to regain linguistic normalcy. After all, the name of the people (the Jewish people or the People of Israel) was not the same as the name of its national language — a situation unparalleled in the case of any other nation and language. Even the culture that developed in the Land of Israel was not able to change this exceptional fact: the culture was named after the national language, but precisely because of this did not share the name of the people itself.

This may be an appropriate juncture at which to note another inherent irony of this abnormal national phenomenon. There was a dissent to this consensual view. Only the zealous founders of the extremist movement that came to be known as the Canaanites demanded that the people being renewed in its ancient homeland adopt the name of its language and culture: Hebrew. The Canaanites overtly advocated a complete and irrevocable break with links to the Jewish people and Judaism in order to establish a new people in the Land of Israel, bearing the name of its ancient language. This demand, however, provoked fierce opposition from all streams of Zionism, including those who were fanatical supporters of the Hebrew language and who despised Yiddish. The constitutive Zionist consensus was that the name of the people whom Zionism represented was to remain unchanged — the Jewish people or the people of Israel. The Zionist movement saw the Canaanites' ideology as a threat which would rupture the bond between Jews who returned to their homeland and those who remained in exile and the Diaspora. In effect, such a disconnection would have deprived Zionism of its motivation, human resources, and purpose and would have led to the destruction of the movement.

It hardly need be emphasized that the problem reflected in the lack of congruence between the name of the language and culture and between the name of the people was not confined to the world of linguistics and semantics. The problem touched the core of national consciousness and the atypical cultural and historic memory of the Jewish people whose cultural identity in exile was not consonant with its linguistic identity stemming, as it did, from its earliest origins. This distinction between the name of the language and the name of the people, just as the distinction between the language that had united the Jews in their various exiles and the languages they had spoken there, effectively reflects the ongoing development of the people's culture through unrelenting waves of assimilation. Given such a historical backdrop, it should have been evident that the return to Hebrew as the cultural language of a people that continued to call itself Jewish would represent no more than another link in the chain of national identity, through a process of assimilation of a new type.

However, before addressing in depth the question of identity as symbolized by the return to Hebrew as the national-cultural language of the Jews, we should examine the full significance of the constitutive status granted Hebrew as the original primary definitive and characteristic factor shaping the content and essence of the culture. Retrospectively, one may state that this formative status that was granted Hebrew in the process of renewal made it the main creative force behind the content that was intended to replace religious content. In other words, the return to Hebrew effectively epitomized the process of cultural and national secularization undergone by Judaism.

A study of most of the secular Zionist ideologies examined earlier affords conclusive support for this assertion. All these ideologies defined Jewish culture in terms of European national humanism, as the renewal of the

Jewish national "spirit." This "spirit" is synonymous with "national ego" or "national selfhood." It is what represents the collective life experience of the people over the generations. Yet where was this elusive spirit to be found? How was it to be identified in direct and concrete terms? The only possible answer to these questions lies in the national language as it operated in all spheres and registers of expression. Speech and dynamic expression are the direct and concrete embodiment of the spirit that unites the people.

In the context of the present discussion it is not necessary to detail the distinct ways in which the Hebrew language was perceived as the embodiment of the national spirit. For our purposes, it is sufficient to note the fact that this "spirit" was understood as the creative, operative force that lay behind all strata of cultural creativity — not only those that exhibited it directly (culture in the narrow sense) but also in material creativity (civilization). Everything created by the people within the scope of its national linguistic communication, everything reflected in descriptive and vital terms in its literature as representing national social existence, everything expressed in the various art forms, all these directly or indirectly reflect the spirit embodied in language.

To be more precise, in the perception of culture as the expression of the "spirit" of the people, language plays a central role in terms of function, value and symbolism. Language is the pool of content the people draw on when expressing themselves. Language unites the members of the people whenever they act jointly and in all their joint functions. Language transmits cultural heritage from generation to generation, conveys historic memory, shapes the conscious and emotive affinity to the homeland, creates the image of the people as a collective entity by investing symbolic significance to its social and national institutions, and transmits and interprets the values and norms according to which the people lives.

This holds true for all nations and all languages. If one wishes to understand the unique qualities that characterize any people, one must examine the unique qualities of its language. The very existence of a specific language is an external sign of the singular station of a specific people. Such a language unites the members of the group internally and distinguishes them from all others groups speaking their own languages. The English are those whose mother tongue is English; the French are those who speak French, and so on. Thus each national group is distinguished from every other as each communicates within its own distinct circle, in its own particular language. Yet beyond this unifying and differentiating fact of communication, we must also consider the significance of the special linguistic qualities of each language that accompany its functional operation as a language. These qualities reflect the unique national "spirit" and influence the essence of the entire national culture, particularly its literature — the living store of memory that is passed from one generation to the next as it bears the content of its national culture.

Occasionally, those thinkers who guided the creation of Hebrew culture in Eretz Israel attempted to describe the unique qualities of the Hebrew language. Of course, these were subjective impressions; some are quite convincing, but none can be verified in scientific terms. They are important for our purpose insofar as they reflect the cultural consciousness of the national elite. They attributed a constitutive and distinguishing status to the unique characteristics of the Hebrew language as these were reflected in the national literature, establishing common spiritual themes for all members of the society. Against this background, it is easier to understand the importance attached to the revival of Hebrew as the everyday, spoken language of Eretz Israel, as the language of instruction and research in all educational institutions, and as the language of all genres of literature. It would be no exaggeration to state that the revival of the Hebrew language was considered Zionism's most important national cultural endeavor. Consummate attention was paid to this enterprise, both as a tool and as an inherent component of culture. In the national consciousness of the pioneers of the Yishuv, who were also those who revived the Hebrew language, it was Hebrew speech that imbued their social and settlement activity with a national Jewish character, while it was settlement that created the population that was to speak Hebrew. Thus linguistic consciousness *capitalized* on all aspects of material and cultural life, set them apart and forged them into the culture of the people. Anything that was produced or done in Hebrew, anything that functioned through Hebrew thought and speech became *Hebrew* in its own right: *Hebrew* settlement, *Hebrew* labor, *Hebrew* economy (with *Hebrew* cows and chickens!), *Hebrew* transport, *Hebrew* literature, *Hebrew* education.

So it was that Hebrew as an ideology (*ivriut*) became an intrinsic cultural value. An effort was made to speak *correct* Hebrew, not only grammatically, but also stylistically — to the point of engaging in purple prose. In addition to providing relevant information in a factual and precise manner, typical agents of Hebrew culture also conveyed to each other a sense that they were proud Hebrews speaking Hebrew for its own sake, allowing their language to make its mark on all their discourse. Linguistic correctness came to be seen as an "added value" in terms of cultural and national identity.

The task of modernizing the Hebrew language was approached in the same spirit. Hebrew was to be expanded but without introducing foreign elements — not only by refraining as far as possible from using foreign words within the flow of Hebrew speech, but also by avoiding the use of foreign forms of expression. The creation of new words was seen as an art of *procreation* made on the basis of the traditional linguistic pool, of realizing the potential inherent in the characteristics of the language. The most impressive achievement was the development of a modern Hebrew language whose speakers could express any facet of modern culture and yet were able to read and understand the ancient sources without difficulty.

Naturally this approach to language was expressed most effectively in literary creativity. The revival of modern Hebrew literature was organically linked to the revival of the Hebrew language, not merely in the sense that the language was the tool of literature, but also in the sense that Hebrew literature took on the role of expressing the unique character of Hebrew as its identifying "added value" and its central and significant strata. Of course, the aspiration to achieve linguistic virtuosity is a qualitative feature of any literary creation of a high artistic level. In modern Hebrew literature, however, the conscious awareness of linguistic values was expressed in a systematic effort to develop Hebrew versions of all the existing genres of world literature. There was a demand that Hebrew be full, comprehensive and self-sustaining, meeting all literary cultural needs and standing up to comparison with any national literature, in terms of scope and function and in terms of unique identity.

This part of the discussion can be summarized by stating that the renewal of Hebrew language and literature during the Yishuv period was the feature of Hebrew culture that best identified and distinguished the national culture of the Jewish people. This body of creativity was the most impressive achievement of Hebrew culture to be inherited by future generations. The Yishuv created a living, national language with the functional capability equal to that of any cultivated national language. Hebrew literature produced a full range of genres and forged a system of communication capable of documenting cultural activity in the fields of science, technology, thought, family and social life, politics, morality and matters of the spirit.

There is a parallel between the status and function of the arts which arose in Eretz Israel and the emergence of Hebrew language and literature. Art, too, expressed the aspiration to contribute to the revival of the people as it returned to normal national life. Aware of the artistic dynamism and achievements in European culture at the beginning of the century, as well as the absence of any independent artistic tradition within the Jewish people, Hebrew artists strove to adapt the arts and to be artistically innovative so as to present art as a valid form of Jewish expression. Their goal was to ensure that now there would be Jewish art worthy of the name, and equal to other cultures. This led to a dialectic tension between two complementary-contradictory aspirations: to achieve a high level of artistic quality according to universal (i.e. European) artistic standards, while at the same time ensuring due expression of the Jewish people's national uniqueness, exactly as did the national art forms of other nations. The difficulty in combining these two aspirations was a result of the artistic richness of the European models by comparison to the poverty of the models rooted in Jewish tradition. The solution was found in the creation of original *autonomous* models created by adapting European forms to themes and subjects related to the emerging new society — landscapes, immigrants, pioneers, the local Arab populations, the historical markers to be found in the landscape, the ancient symbols derived from traditional literature. In this way art, too, contributed to the creation of the particular experience in the reconstruction of Eretz Israel, and in so doing generated its own new subjects and models.

All this indicates that the painting, sculpture, music, dance, theater and cinema created in Eretz Israel were distinguished by the aspiration to raise values of national revival in the emotive and associative consciousness, to register these values and to transmit them to the next generation. This was their *Hebraic stamp*. Though the language of art is not verbal, analogies and complements to Hebrew were found in these art forms through sight, sound, rhythm, and physical movement and gesture. It was a deliberate effort to use these art forms to symbolize ancient landscapes and Middle Eastern or Biblical vistas, even as they were emblematic of the modern national awakening. The essential character of the Land of Israel, the experience of the eastern milieu and of ancient times, the Biblical figures and formative historical events also acted as a junction for memories, emotions and representations identified with the Hebrew language as rooted in Biblical literature. Thus the language of the arts could also be termed *Hebrew*. To this must be added the fact that the performing arts, particularly theater, dance and music, were loyal to old Hebrew texts and emphasized their significance. Consequently, it was only natural that the founders of the Yishuv related to the arts that emerged in Eretz Israel as *Hebrew* arts.

Which came first? Did linguistic, literary and artistic creativity precede the emergence of social reality and mores, or did social reality and mores generate linguistic, literary and artistic creativity? It would appear that some of the features that characterized Hebrew culture in the Land of Israel — and, indeed, some of the difficulties that encumbered this culture — resulted from the fact that linguistic and literary creativity preceded the emergence of the society that had need of such sources. A language was renewed in order to serve a future society; literature undertook a mission whose essential feature was the expression of the present from the perspective of a vision which, it was hoped, would be realized in the future. Such an endeavor demanded spiritual and cultural change on the part of the individuals who immigrated to Eretz Israel in order "to build it and be rebuilt in it." Literature was needed to express personal and social change, to document its travails, doubts and failures, and yet to portray its vision.

Alongside the renewal of modern Hebrew language and literature, a "transition of values" took place in Eretz Israel from an exilic society and ethos to the society and ethos of a people living in its own land, bearing full responsibility for all its material and spiritual needs. The expansion and enrichment of language reflected this change for the individual, and literature did so through its affirmation of the national mission. It was an engaged literature that expressed the consciousness of the elites in Yishuv society, and in so doing emphasized another facet of the significance of the terms *Hebrew* and *Hebraic*. For the national and social ethos, *Hebrew* and *Hebraic* meant identification with the values of Zionist realization: reclaiming the land, making the desert bloom, establishing a defense force, building social and political institutions and education systems (schools and youth movements) that were charged with the task of generating the transvaluation of values in Jewish society and with shaping the figure of the new Jew — the figure of the Hebrew persona.

The question that arises in this context is: What were the value-based content, norms, and symbols that shaped this new socio-cultural reality? The answer can be found by examining the new forms of settlement created in Eretz Israel — Hebrew villages (the collective and communal settlements) and Hebrew cities (Tel Aviv, Haifa, and the New Hebrew Jerusalem as differentiated from the Old City). In terms of social ethos, the telling aspects can be observed mainly in rural settlements: the *moshava*, *kibbutz*, *kvutza* and *moshav*, though even in the Hebrew cities movement-based frameworks were established to facilitate the implementation of egalitarian and cooperative socio-cultural values. These frameworks were seen as having a value in their own right for the realization of social justice, but also as the most suitable means for Zionist realization in the country as a whole.

The fundamental values of national and social Zionist realization in-cluded individual commitment to the public good, self-labor, cooperative effort, and mutual assistance. From the standpoint of Zionist realization, labor as a value made the greatest impression on the socio-cultural reality of the Hebrew Yishuv. This value embodied all the other values since it was related to existence itself; it was essential to devote oneself to this value and struggle for its realization, both in terms of personal adaptation of the immigrants to a way of life they had not known in exile, and in terms of the demand that Jewish society recognize the priority of "Hebrew labor." Accordingly, the main task of pioneering Zionism was the "conquest of labor" (*kibbush ha'avoda*) in the individual and public sense. Labor came to be seen as an anvil on which to forge the individual and collective transvaluation of values in the shift from exilic to Hebraic rootedness.

In order to round out the description of the Hebrew culture created in Eretz Israel during the Yishuv period, the commitment to the creation of Hebrew "civilization," rather than merely "culture" must be emphasized again. Zionist fulfillment, achieved through the return of the Jewish people to normal national life, implied the creation of a Hebrew civilization. It was this perspective that led to the emphasis on *labor* as the focal personal, societal and national value, and to the demand that culture, too, be the spiritual outcome of a working life. In this way the material and instrumental infrastructure of civilization — politics, organization and management, technology, economics and the military — would all be imbued with Hebraic cultural values and significance. All these elements were necessary for their concrete utility, but no less than this they were needed as the embodiment of spiritual and moral values in the transformation from exilic ethereal spirituality to worldly spirituality: a spirituality that seeks to be realized.

From the outset, therefore, there was a correlation between the Hebrew ethos of realization and the aspiration to establish a prospering national civilization. One should not, however, overlook the problematic nature of idealizing the creation of material values for a society rooted in traditional Jewish religious culture (in the case of religious Zionism) or a society with a modern, nationalist idealist culture. First, there is a fundamental and internal tension between the autonomous values of material civilization per se (the desire for political power and utility, the drive for exploitation and manipulation in human and social relations) and the values derived from moral and spiritual ideals. Second, in the context of Hebrew culture, a problem of assimilation arose. The creation of a material civilization for a nation returning from exile to its homeland required virtual enslavement to external sources of material support and the imitation of aspects of western civilization — a civilization to which Jews as individuals had contributed a great deal and, yet, in national terms, belonged not to the Jews but to their host nations.

Zionism assumed that the problem of assimilation inherent in the acculturation of Jews to modern Western civilization could be overcome by acquiring a civilization that would serve all the national needs of the Jewish people. However, the tension between the aspiration for selfhood and the desire to borrow and mimic the cultural content of other nations could not be balanced by such a process of acquisition, nor by giving Hebrew names to foreign acquisitions, nor yet by dealing with them in

251

the Hebrew language. It is useful to recall that the difference between the content of civilization and the content of culture is a relative, not an absolute one. Along with science, technology and organizational and management structures, *foreign* cultural values were also absorbed: social, political, moral and esthetic values that influenced the style of life. Of course, these values also greatly influenced the language despite efforts to avoid foreign linguistic influence.

While the problem did not go unnoticed, it would be fair to say that most of the leading elites who identified with Hebrew culture during the Yishuv period were not overly concerned with the issue. They assumed that national independence — political and social — would guarantee the autonomous character of national life. The content created would be that of a free people at liberty to forge its own values. From the perspective of the elites, the most important aspect was a civilization created by the nation itself for which its people were responsible, whose needs the nation met rather than being responsive to the needs of others on whom the nation was dependent. Such a civilization would protect its identity from threat even if foreign models and patterns were borrowed or mimicked. But Hebrew culture encompassed a variety of ideological streams, some of which adopted critical positions. Moreover, the Land of Israel was also home to Jewish movements that sought to create — and indeed created — a Jewish culture whose content was at extreme variance with Hebrew culture. Two such movements were, for example, the ultra-Orthodox culture which tended to close itself off from modern civilization while consuming its products, and the non-nationalist secular culture which evinced a conscious interest in assimilation.

Criticism of Hebrew culture came particularly from Religious Zionism and Spiritual Zionism; both movements claimed that a mundane, secular national culture would not be able to resist the trend toward assimilation, even in Eretz Israel. Their position was that the autonomous content of Jewish identity had been and remained traditional and religious in character, or at least based on Jewish *heritage*. Accordingly, linguistic, literary and artistic Hebraisms and the values associated with social and national realization alone would not be able to resist the pressures of an imported European secular culture. Only the force of Jewish heritage could preserve the continuity of national consciousness and autonomous identity.

This brings us to the focal point of the weaknesses inherent in Hebrew culture in Eretz Israel. On one hand, there was the question of the relationship between Hebrew culture and the Jewish heritage created from the Biblical period through the modern Hebrew period. On the other hand, there was a parallel question regarding the ability of the new culture to meet individual and social (familial-communal) needs and expectations which are met by religious traditions in all cultures, and are therefore their essential core — familial-communal morality and mores, festivals, symbols and ceremonies that translate identifying beliefs and philosophies into a way of life. These two questions are closely linked insofar as both relate to the ambivalent attitude toward Jewish religion and tradition among the founding elites of Hebrew culture.

Their attitude was, indeed, ambivalent. Part and parcel of the "Negation of the Exile" was a negation of the cultural and religious products created in the Diaspora. This negation reflected a desire to break with the halahkic and rabbinic tradition represented by the Talmud — in spiritual, intellectual and academic terms — and by the *Shulḥan Arukh* — as a directive for practical behavior. Yet, as discussed above, these elites also aspired to maintain the historic continuity of national consciousness, an identity with the Jewish people and a sense of belonging to it. Most members of the founding elites that created the culture of Eretz Israel were themselves from religious homes and had been educated in an exilic tradition. The religious culture against which they rebelled was their native culture; it served as the seed-bed for their later absorption of modern non-Jewish culture and their subsequent participation in the creation of modern Hebrew culture. Ironically, a predisposition to be influenced by the tradition as it had been expressed in their formative education, memories, and social behavior was particularly evident in their literary activity. Early life experience may explain why many of these writers did not sense the void inherent in the Hebrew culture they were creating in Eretz Israel. Through literary expression, the void was filled by memories of childhood and adolescence. Typically, in Eretz Israel, modern literary works took the place of liturgical texts traditionally associated with the Jewish festivals. Liturgical content was lived through literary descriptions that attributed national and secular significance to the nostalgic memories of religious life. The underlying question, of course, was whether the same method could be used to fill the void for the younger generation, born in Eretz Israel, who had no such memories in common. It was a particularly acute question since the very existence and relevance of a culture depend on the manner in which it is transmitted from one generation to the next.

The awareness of this problem created the arena for an increasingly fierce debate between two approaches. The more radical Hebraic school of thought focused its concerns on how to transmit values and knowledge about Eretz Israel, Hebrew, the Bible, history and modern Hebrew litera- ture, utterly rejecting religious and traditional themes. The opposing school of thought believed that some contact with the entire spectrum of traditional content also had to be maintained, even if this was sometimes achieved through a radical process of national and humanist reinterpretation. When one evaluates the residual influence of these schools on current lifestyles, it is clear that even the school of Spiritual Zionism was unable to prevent a break with the tradition. In most cases, traditional and religious themes did not come across in the actual lifestyles of everyday reality because they were limited to sporadic references in literature and in the curricula that documented the history of the Jewish people.

Bialik attempted to create a cultural alternative to tradition, particularly for the Sabbath and festivals. However, he was unable to establish an organized community around such an alternative, nor did he found a formal spiritual movement. The only Hebrew alternative to Jewish tradition that took hold on a communal basis was found in the rural labor settlements, and in the youth movements that educated toward such a way of life. The highly institutionalized communal frameworks of the kibbutz, *kvutza* and *moshav* felt a powerful need to develop their own festival tradition. Cooperative communal life would be barren without a quasi-religious tradition that shaped a way of life imbued with spiritual significance. Consequently, alternatives were developed for ceremonies for the Sabbath, the Jewish festivals and personal lifecycle events. These alternatives encompassed traditional elements reinterpreted through the prism of modern Hebrew literature, as well as content that related to nature, national and historic memory, social values and folklore.

Whatever affinity to religious tradition was maintained in this alternative was most apparent in structure and ritual, which were also employed to convey ideological messages. The most outstanding and well-known example is the Passover Seder. The religious ritual of the tradition extended through the festive meal and the reading of the Haggadah. An effort was made to replicate the structure of the traditional Haggadah; indeed, while much of the text was new, some traditional passages were used. The kibbutz Haggadah continued to relate the story of the Exodus, with an emphasis on its implications for the current historical events of the Jewish people: the Exodus from slavery to freedom, and from Exile to homeland. At Shavuot, the alternative tradition ignored the rabbinic theme of the "Giving of the Torah," retaining the original Biblical intent of the festival: pilgrimage, the offering of the first fruits, and thanksgiving for return to the promised Land. At Sukkot, the traditional symbol of the sukkah was preserved along with the expression of joy at a harvest festival. An ideological theme emphasized the connection between the redemption of Israel and the redemption of humanity as a whole. Hanukkah was celebrated as a festival that represented Zionist fulfillment: the miracle of the cruse of oil interpreted as a symbol of eternal Jewish national hope, and the original story of the Maccabean revolt retold as a struggle for national liberation, more emphatically than it appeared in rabbinic tradition. At Purim, continuity was reflected mainly in terms of folklore — costumes and theatrical performances relating to the Book of Esther.

Thus elements of an on-going tradition were certainly present — yet the changes were substantive and profound. The transformation was evident, above all, in terms of the emancipated, non-halakhic style in which traditional patterns were cast. These patterns were not treated as binding or normative commandments but as customs that could be shaped and interpreted at will by each community. There was also great freedom in the selection and interpretation of content. The Hebraic alternative to the traditions for Sabbath and festivals emphasized nature and agriculture at the expense of expressions of religious faith. The intention was to convey an unmediated experience of settling on the soil and in the landscapes of the homeland. National historic themes were also adapted to the present, focusing on the redemption of the people in its own land. It goes without saying that the redeemer of the people was no longer seen as God, but as the people itself, leaving slavery for freedom on its own initiative and through its own strength. The Sabbath was celebrated as a social value — the laborer's rest from his toil; its religious significance was neither retained nor mentioned. Of course, the traditional religious liturgy was not suited to these interpretations of the Sabbath and festivals; therefore, at most, certain more appropriate passages were quoted. The literary sequence was new, drawing on modern Hebrew literature and the contemporary arts — music, dance and theater. The old vessels of tradition were restored and filled with content that was, for the most part, new.

In evaluating continuity and discontinuity, it is evident that the latter outweighed the former, particularly in the transmission of tradition to the generation born in Eretz Israel, a generation no longer able to identify traditions even when they were found in modern Hebrew literature. The break was especially profound with regard to the unambiguous religious themes that formed the foundation of the tradition. For example, no convincing *Hebraic* alternative could be crafted for festivals such as Rosh Ha-shanah and Yom Kippur which have a limited national and social aspect and are mainly religious in nature, or for the days of national mourning associated with the destruction of the Temple. Consequently, these festivals were largely ignored, though there was an awareness that this was extremely problematic given their central place in the national psyche. The same phenomenon could be clearly seen when teaching the Bible. Passages of overtly "religious" significance were ignored, and the traditional relationship of the Bible to the Oral Law was abandoned. Thus an image emerged of the *Hebrew* Bible in Eretz Israel that differed dramatically from the traditional Jewish image of the Bible.

To conclude, it can be said that the Hebrew culture fashioned in Eretz Israel was unsuccessful in devising a meaningful sense of continuity with the traditional religious heritage of the Jewish people. Was it more successful in meeting the need for cultural environment in familial and communal life? Was the new convention for the festivals and holidays successful in becoming institutionalized and functioning as a tradition? Could the new tradition imbue daily life with its content? Was a new mode developed that could shape and reflect interpersonal relations in the family and community? Was a new and unifying code of behavior forged for dialogue between members of the nation? Did forms of expression emerge which could articulate the experiences of individuals in their lifecycle events — birth, marriage, mourning, bereavement, physical and mental torment? A review of the research and *belles lettres* that accompanied the creation of Hebrew culture reveals a multitude of expectations as well as a mass of doubts and disappointments about the way these questions were addressed. Writers and thinkers who took part in this act of cultural creation complained of the lacunae that emerged, yet believed that these would gradually be corrected: a culture could not be built in a single generation.

The process called for commitment and engagement on the part of the public. An examination of the writings of those who saw themselves as responsible for the creation of the new tradition and its introduction into communal life (the members of cultural committees, of every type and on every level) shows that while the public sensed a lack, it did not display a high level of willingness to commit itself to independent activity. The free-thinking public preferred passive, uninvolved programs performed by professional artists rather than active participation in ceremonies and symbols that would express their own thoughts and feelings. The implication is that the new tradition failed to create an institutionalized alternative to the authority inherent in religious commandments which relate directly to all members of the community. The absence of a binding, commanding and directive authority was perceived as a shortcoming by the ruling cultural elite; however, its attempts to overcome this weakness proved unsuccessful. Apparently secular culture was unable to create an alternative authority to religion in aspects relating to everyday life; indeed, such authority would be incompatible with the emphasis on free-thinking as a formative cultural value. Bialik, it will be remembered, spoke of the need for a "new Halakhah," yet even he made no attempt to create one, much less to make such a Halakhah operational in the community at large.

The sense that the achievements of Hebrew culture in Eretz Israel were inadequate and left a void in terms of the continuity and rootedness of cultural consciousness, in terms of shaping a lifestyle for families and communities, and in terms of individuals confronting their existential problems, grew progressively throughout the entire Yishuv period, becoming deeper and more intense as Zionism neared its goal of completing the pioneering stage and preparing for statehood. Once settling the Land of Israel was no longer perceived as the primary pioneering act that granted national significance to the way of life of the settler; once agriculture lost its romantic and quasi-religious significance as an expression of becoming one with the soil, nature and landscape and became a commercial, technological industry; once the revival of the Hebrew language was complete and the act of speaking Hebrew no longer projected an "added value" of nationally significant creativity — the void was laid bare and it became obvious that the Hebrew alternative to tradition developed in the Land of Israel had lost its significance and validity, and was waning even before it managed to be fully established as a tradition. The process became apparent first in the cities and later in the rural settlements.

Thus it can be seen that despite the tremendous achievement of forging a vibrant, integrated, modern language that nonetheless is linked to the literary roots of all its generations, the scope of Hebrew culture in Eretz Israel was too restricted — and what it derived from its own sources too tenuous in proportion to what it drew upon from external sources to create an authentic and autonomous presence. Further creativity would require reshaping original models in order to define objectives and locate sources in the Jewish heritage and "general" Western heritage so as to enable the possibility of merging these sources in the development of an autonomous national culture. This "crossroad" was already visible during the decade preceding the establishment of the State of Israel.

The transformation that took place after the establishment of the State was more far reaching, however, than could have been anticipated during the early years when a deliberate effort was made to blend diverse immigrant communities on the narrow basis of Hebrew culture and the "melting pot" policy. In effect, this policy was an obsessive leveling in which all the limitations, weaknesses and gaps of Hebrew culture were revealed. It became evident that Hebrew culture had failed to create sufficient space or depth to bridge the gaps between the various segments of the veteran Yishuv, or to enable the social and cultural absorption of mass immigration. Nor was this culture capable of creating the complex nexus that was needed between the segments of the Jewish people living in their own state and those segments which continued to live in the Diaspora. It proved impossible to

257

continue the melting pot approach, and accordingly the policy failed and collapsed. No new cultural ideology emerged to replace it, but it became clear that in practical terms what had been termed "Hebrew" or "Eretz Israel" culture — in keeping with the name of the language and land, and which had been viewed as the basis of national unity — was now moribund. The era of what henceforth would be termed "Israeli" culture — in keeping with the name of the state — had begun.

The transitions and challenges that followed the establishment of the State of Israel can be summarized as follows:

1. Hebrew culture was a direct expression of only part of the Jewish population in Eretz Israel during the Yishuv period. Alongside this culture there existed other Jewish sub-cultures of a parallel or adversarial nature. After the establishment of the state, all these cultures became part of a common political framework, and this demanded a different style of discourse on both the social and the cultural levels. This partnership of sub-cultures required greater accord than had existed previously, and it emerged on the basis of political and social pragmatism that were, in retrospect, to have numerous ramifications for the values and moral positions of all the parties involved in the process. Yet alongside this accord, there was a growing struggle to influence the shape of a public cultural milieu for the new state.

2. The mass immigration of Jews from different countries of origin doubled the size of the Jewish population within the first few years of the state and brought with it diverse heritages and traditions, some of which had previously existed in the Land of Israel during the Yishuv period without having a meaningful influence, while others were entirely new. Though the crisis of being uprooted from their country of origin, settling anew in the homeland, and the impact of the melting pot policy of the state's early years repressed the traditions of the immigrants, those traditions did not disappear. On the contrary, the fact that they took root in the homeland was demonstrated a generation later by the rehabilitation of those very traditions even as they were adapted to modern socio-political realities. The current picture reveals a multifaceted mosaic of Jewish sub-cultures, admittedly with significant gaps and disconnections that still exist among the diverse heritages. None of these traditions is complete within itself, and none is autonomous.

3. During the Yishuv period, the Land of Israel was first ruled by the Ottoman Empire, and then subject to the British Mandate. The dominant external sources were first French and German, and subsequently English; in all cases, it was the European national cultures that influenced local culture. It was the European cultures that projected the same national ethos

that had provided the stimulus and background for Zionism. Following the establishment of the State, European influence was replaced by the American model. The new cultural messages related to nationalism and national autonomy as well as socioeconomic stratification, patterns of social ethos, socialization processes and everyday life.

4. In the wake of the Second World War, the entire Western world underwent a transition from modernism to postmodernism. With its tremendous achievements in science, technology and economics, and the no less astonishing spiritual and moral cost, the United States led the technological and sociocultural revolution that is embodied in the term "postmodernism." The establishment of Israel coincided with this period, but there was a certain delay in applying the American model, which was due mainly to the economic difficulties of the fledgling state. Currently, however, Israel is facing the full range of postmodernist challenges in all spheres of civilization and culture.

5. With the establishment of Israel, there was a growing awareness that a new definition was needed to deal with the tenor of relations between the national "center" and the Jews of the Diaspora. This meant that the base of Zionist activity had to be broadened from its exclusive concentration on immigration to Israel and education toward immigration. In order to meet the challenge, Jewish society in Israel was obliged to develop a common cultural language with Jewish communities abroad that were beset by ambivalent identities while coping with the crisis of assimilation.

To confront these challenges while maintaining its cultural distinctiveness, the State of Israel must be more firmly anchored in its Jewish sources, for only these sources can draw the divided people into a circle of communication that maintains their particular autonomy and direct resources to a culture possessed of a unique, identifying value system. Israel must be completely open to all segments of the people and to Western culture (American and European). At the same time, Israel must absorb the scientific and technological advantages of the postmodern era while moderating its destructive socio-cultural and moral costs. If a balanced formula can be found to forge a multifaceted, diverse and complex culture open to internal and external dialogue, it will certainly be a tense synthesis of different heritages, progressing along a force-field of contradictory ideological streams. Such a dialogue might enable the definition of basic values in the desired culture, pointing both to sources and avenues of development. However, no theoretician has yet been able to present the model for such a culture or to characterize its "vision." The existing streams will each propose their own models drawn from sources discussed earlier; but the synthesis of these models, if indeed it emerges, will be the product of a creative struggle.

The struggle is already underway. What we now see as the content of the culture we call "Israeli" is in fact, the emergence of a number of sub-cultures. In terms of content, tendencies, and objectives, the differences and contradictions between these sub-cultures are greater than their common denominator. The basis for national unity inherent in these sub-cultures may be defined as the historic memory by which they are each linked to the Jewish people, the Hebrew language as a standard national tongue, the bond to Eretz Israel, Zionist nationalism, various modalities of affinity to traditional values and sources that express a link to the people, and civic loyalty to the State of Israel. Will these be sufficient to overcome polarized conflict, to deepen roots, fill voids, bridge gaps and forge a multifaceted and autonomous culture within the unifying framework of national discourse? Only time will tell.

Glossary

Aggadah — narrative, lore. The portion of rabbinic tradition complementary to halakhah (law), comprising stories, legends, parables, theological musings, and wisdom.

Aliyah — "going up," specifically, immigration to the Land of Israel.

Batlan — "idler," specifically, in traditional east-European Jewish society, a person not in regular employment and available to participate in a quorum for religious services.

Beit Midrash — House of Study, a study-hall where Jews (primarily male adults and adolescent youths) engage in study of traditional Jewish texts.

Derekh Eretz — "way of the world": proper worldly conduct and respect, worldly occupation, secular learning, the realm of secular activities and the norms governing them.

Eretz Israel — "Land of Israel" as Jewish religious-national or secular-national ideal and reality, homeland of the Jewish people.

Gemara — "learning," especially Talmud, more specifically the later stratum of the Talmud superadded to the Mishnah, and considered the chief staple of advanced traditional Jewish studies.

Haggadah (pl. *haggadot*) — "story-telling," the book or script of the home ceremony of Passover eve centering on the recitation of the Exodus narrative. Traditionally a rather standard, fixed text, in modern times one of the staples of the Jewish cultural renewal has been the proliferation of hundreds of different creative elaborations of the Haggadah to express the outlooks of the many varieties of modern Jewish experience.

Hagshamah — "realization," especially the realization of ideals (such as the Zionist ideal) into practical patterns of life. Examples range from the creation of Jewish life in a single household to the creation of the Yishuv and State of Israel.

Halakhah — "Law," especially traditional Jewish religious law.

Halutz (pl. *Halutzim*) — "pioneer," referring to the young Zionist settlers in the Land of Israel, especially in the period 1900-1933, creating a new way of life based on agricultural work, revival of Hebrew, and communal structures such as the Kibbutz.

Haskalah — "Enlightenment," specifically, the Jewish Enlightenment movement in Germany and eastern Europe from the mid-18th century through the late-19th century.

Heder — "room," Jewish primary school, especially for young boys, generally devoted exclusively to traditional Jewish subjects.

Hevruta — fellowship, particularly small, intimate fellowship for purpose of Jewish study, prayer, and celebration.

Hibbat Zion (= *Hovevei Zion*) — the proto-Zionist movement in Eastern Europe in the 1880s–1890s.

Humash — the Five Books of Moses.

Jüdische Wissenschaft — "Science of Judaism," the historical scholarship of Judaism generally; specifically, the movement of Jewish historical scholarship that began in Germany in the early 19th century and flourished through the early 20th century.

Kibbutz — "collective," an agricultural community, especially one organized on socialist principles, developed in early Zionism.

Knesset Israel — "community of Israel."

Maskil — "enlightened," a follower, adherent or propagator of the Jewish Enlightenment (Haskalah).

Midrash — "exegesis" (< *darash*, "to seek out"), interpretation of Scripture, particularly derivation of rabbinic teachings from the Biblical text.

Mishnah — the traditional short code of rabbinic law (composed ~ 200 C.E.), basis of the Talmud.

Mitzvah (pl. *Mitzvot*) — "commandment," (narrowly) any of the actions included as "commanded" in the traditional corpus of Jewish law, (broadly) any action deemed praiseworthy in a Jewish value orientation, "good deed."

Mohel — "circumciser," a Jewish religious functionary trained specifically to perform ritual circumcision.

Musar — "morals," Jewish moral teaching generally, or more specifically a school of Jewish moral-centered teaching founded by Israel Salanter (19th century).

Oleh (pl. *olim*) — immigrants to Israel, those who "make Aliyah."

Shekhinah — "Divine Presence."

Shelilat ha-Golah — "Negation of the Exile," a seminal attitude in Zionism that was critical of (1) the fact of Jews living in Exile (outside the Land of Israel), and (2) the negative characteristics of Diaspora Jewish life (economic backwardness and poverty, religious obscurantism, or whatever the critic chooses to regard as "negative" in Diaspora Jewish experience).

Talmud — the corpus of traditional Jewish law, comprising Mishnah and the free-ranging discussion on it (Gemara), inclusive of Halakhah and Aggadah, staple and basis of all later traditional Jewish learning, compiled ~ 450 C.E.

Torah — "instruction," (broadly) Jewish learning as such; the whole corpus of Jewish learning; especially Jewish Law. (narrowly) the foundational texts of Jewish learning, especially the Five Books of Moses (Written Torah) or the basic corpus of rabbinic law (Oral Torah).

Yeshiva — "sitting," a traditional school of Jewish learning, especially for youths and adults.

Yishuv — "settlement," specifically the totality of Jewish settlement in the Land of Israel, especially prior to 1948, together with their governing and institutional structures.

Bibliography

Foreword: Jewish Culture and Modernity

Ettinger, Shmuel, *The History of the Jewish People in Modern Times* (Hebrew). Tel Aviv: Devir, 1969.

Frank, Daniel and Oliver Leaman, eds. *History of Jewish Philosophy.* London & New York: Routledge, 1997.

Guttmann, Julius, *Philosophies of Judaism* (tr. David Wolf Silverman). New York: Holt, Rinehart & Winston, 1964.

Katz, Jacob, *Out of the Ghetto: the social background of Jewish emancipation 1770–1870.* New York: Schocken, 1973.

Kaufmann, Yehezkel, *Exile and Alienation* (Hebrew). Tel Aviv: Devir, 1960.

Sachar, Howard Morley, *The Course of Modern Jewish History.* New York: Dell, 1977.

Schweid, Eliezer, *Jewish Thought in the 19th Century.* Tel Aviv: Kibbutz Me'uhad, 1978.

— *Jewish Thought in the 20th Century.* Atlanta: Scholars Press, 1992.

Chapter One: Culture as Concept and Ideal

Buber, Martin, "Judaism and Civilization" in *At the Turning: Three Addresses on Judaism.* New York: Farrar, Straus & Young, 1951.

Cassirer, Ernst, *The Philosophy of Enlightenment.* Boston: Beacon Press, 1955.

Dawson, Christopher, *Religion and Culture.* London: Sheed and Ward, 1948.

Eliot, T.S., *Notes Towards the Definition of Culture.* New York: Harcourt Brace, 1949.

Gay, Peter, *The Enlightenment: The Rise of Modern Paganism.* London: Wildwood House, 1973.

— *The Enlightenment: The Science of Freedom* London: Wildwood House, 1973

Geertz, Clifford, *Interpretation of Cultures.* New York: Basic Books, 1973.

Kroeber, A.L, *Culture: A Critical Review of Concepts and Definitions.* Cambridge, Massachusetts: Peabody Museum of Archaeology and Ethnology, 1952.

Rotenstreich, Nathan, *Humanism in the Contemporary Era.* The Hague: Mouton & Co., 1963.

Chapter Three: Internalizing the Cultural Ideal

Feiner, Shmuel, *The Jewish Enlightenment.* Philadelphia: University of Pennsylvania Press, 2003.

Katz, Jacob, *Out of the Ghetto: The social background of Jewish emancipation 1770–1870.* New York: Schocken, 1973.

Kaufmann, Yehezkel, *Exile and Alienation (Hebrew)*: Volume 2, Chapters 1–2.
Meyer, Michael, *Response to Modernity: A History of the Reform Movement in Judaism*. New York: Oxford University Press, 1988.
Schweid, Eliezer, *Between Orthodoxy and Religious Humanism* (Hebrew). Jerusalem: Van Leer Institute, 1977.
Shmueli, Efrayim, *Seven Jewish Cultures* (Hebrew), Chapter 10. Tel Aviv: Yaḥdav, 1980.

Chapter Four: The Underlying Philosophy of Jewish Enlightenment

Altmann, Alexander, *Moses Mendelssohn, a biographical study*. Birmingham: University of Alabama Press, 1973.
Arkush, Allan, *Moses Mendelssohn and the Enlightenment*. Albany: State University of New York Press, 1994.
Cohen, Arthur, *The Natural and Supernatural Jew*, Chapters 1–3. New York: Pantheon Books, 1962.
Mendelssohn, Moses, *Jerusalem* (translated by Allan Arkush). Hanover, NH: Brandeis University Press, 1983.
Shohat, Azriel, *Beginnings of the Haskalah among German Jewry* (Hebrew). Jerusalem: Bialik Institute, 1961.
Wessely, Naphtali, *Words of Peace and Truth* (Hebrew). Berlin: Jüdische Freyschule, 1782.

Chapter Five: The Meaning of Being a Jewish-Hebrew Maskil

Eliav, Mordecai, *Jewish Education in Germany in the Time of Emancipation* (Hebrew). Jerusalem, 1960.
Kaufmann, Yehezkel, *Exile and Alienation*, Volume 1, Chapter 10.
Lessing, Gotthold, Ephraim, *Nathan the Wise* (Tr. Ellen Frothingham). New York: H. Holt & Company, 1867.

Chapters Six & Seven: Crossroads: From Haskalah to Science of Judaism

Cohen, A., *The Natural and Supernatural Jew*, Chapter 1, Section IV.
Gooch, G.P., *History and Historians in the Nineteenth Century*. Boston: Beacon Press, 1959.
Mendes-Flohr, Paul, ed., *Modern Jewish Studies: Historical and Philosophical Perspectives* (Hebrew). Jerusalem: Zalman Shazar Institute, 1979.
Meyer, Michael, ed., *Ideas of Jewish History*, pp. 141–241. Detroit: Wayne State University Press, 1974.

Chapters Eight & Nine: A Modern Guide to the Perplexed; Science of Judaism

Cohen, Arthur, *The Natural and Supernatural Jew*, pages 29–39.
Krochmal, Nachman, *The Guide of the Perplexed of the Time* (Hebrew), Introduction by S. Rawidowicz, in *The Writings of Nachman Krochmal*. London & Waltham: Ararat, 1961.

Rotenstreich, Nathan, *Jews and German Philosophy: The polemics of emancipation*. New York: Schocken, 1984.
Schorsch, Ismar, *From Text to Context: The Turn to History in Modern Judaism*. Waltham: Brandeis University Press, 1994.

Chapter Ten: Reform Judaism and Historical Positivism

Davis, Moshe, *The Emergence of Conservative Judaism: The historical school in 19th century America*. Philadelphia: Jewish Publication Society, 1963.
Ellenson, David, *After Emancipation: Jewish Religious Responses to Modernity*. Cincinnati: Hebrew Union College Press, 2004.
Gillman, Neil, *Conservative Judaism: The New Century*. New York: Behrman House, 1993.
Hirsch, Samson Raphael, *The Nineteen Letters of Ben Uziel*. Jerusalem: Feldheim, 1995.
Horwitz, Rivka, ed., *Zacharia Frankel and the Beginnings of Positive Historical Judaism* (Hebrew). Jerusalem: Zalman Shazar Institute, 1984.
Meyer, Michael, *Response to Modernity: A History of the Reform Movement in Judaism*. New York: Oxford University Press, 1988.
Meyer, Michael, ed. *Ideas of Jewish History*, pp. 217–244.
Plaut, W. Gunther, *The Rise of Reform Judaism*. New York: World Union for Progressive Judaism, 1963.
— *The Growth of Reform Judaism*. New York: World Union for Progressive Judaism, 1965.
Rudavsky, David, *Modern Jewish Religious Movements: A History of Emancipation and Adjustment*. New York: Behrman House, 1979.

Chapter Eleven: Critique of Science of Judaism

Glatzer, Nahum N., *Franz Rosenzweig: His Life and Thought*, Chapter II: "Renaissance of Jewish Learning and Living." New York: Schocken, 1975.
Hertzberg, Arthur, *The Zionist Idea*, Chapters 2–5. New York: Meridian, 1960.
Scholem, Gershom "Thoughts on the Science of Judaism" in *Devarim be-Go* (Hebrew). Tel Aviv: Am Oved, 1975.
Schweid, Eliezer, *Jewish Thought in the 20th Century*, Chapter 5.

Chapter Twelve: Accelerated Change and Revolution

Frankel, Jonathan, *Prophecy and Politics*. New York: Cambridge University Press, 1981.
Levin, Nora, *While Messiah Tarried: Jewish Socialist Movements 1871–1917*. New York: Schocken, 1977.
Mendelssohn, Ezra, ed., *Essential Papers on Jews and the Left*. New York: New York University Press, 1997.
Silber, Michael K. "The Emergence of Ultra-Orthodoxy" in *The Uses of Tradition* (Jack Wertheimer, ed.). New York: Jewish Theological Seminary, 1992.
Vital, David, *Zionism: The Formative Years*. Clarendon & New York: Oxford University Press, 1982.
Wistrich, Robert S., *Socialism and the Jews*. Rutherford, NJ: Fairleigh Dickinson University Press, 1982.

Chapter Thirteen: Vision of Political Zionism

Birnbaum, Nathan, "Der Zionismus als Kultur Bewegung" in *Ausgewählte Schriften,* Vol. I, pp. 67–83. Czernowitz: Birnbaum & Kohut, 1910.

Halpern, Ben, *The Idea of the Jewish State.* Cambridge: Harvard University Press, 1969.

Herzl, Theodor, *The Jewish State.* London: Pordes, 1967.

Jabotinsky, Zev, *Nation and Society* (Hebrew). Jerusalem, 1940.

Klausner, Joseph, *Judaism and Humanism* (Hebrew). Warsaw, 1905.

Laqueur, Walter, *A History of Zionism.* New York: Schocken, 1972.

Reinharz, Yehuda and Anita Shapira, eds., *Essential Papers on Zionism.* New York: New York University Press, 1996.

Sachar, Howard Morley, *A History of Israel: From the Rise of Zionism to Our Time.* New York: Knopf, 2007.

Shimoni, Gideon, *The Zionist Ideology,* Part II, Chapter 3. Hanover, NH: Brandeis University Press, 1995.

Chapter Fourteen: Pioneering Culture of Labor Zionism

Buber, Martin, *Paths in Utopia.* Boston: Beacon Press, 1958.

Katzenelson, Berl, *Revolution and Roots* (Hebrew). Tel Aviv: Yaron Golan, 1996.

Shimoni, Gideon, *The Zionist Ideology,* Chapter 5.

Chapter Sixteen: Alienation from Religion and Tradition

Canaani, David, *The Second Aliyan and Its Relation to Religion and Tradition* (Hebrew). Tel Aviv: Sifriyat ha-Poalim, 1977.

Govrin, Nurit, *The Brenner Affair* (Hebrew). Jerusalem: Itzhak Ben-Zvi Foundation, 1985.

Mintz, Alan, *Banished from Their Father's Table: Loss of Faith and Hebrew Autobiography.* Bloomington: Indiana University Press, 1989.

Chapter Seventeen: The Jewish Folk Culture of Eretz Israel

Berdyczewski, M. J., *Sinai und Garizim über den Ursprung der israelitischen Religion : Forschungen zum Hexateuch auf Grund rabbinischer Quellen (Sinai and Gerizim: On the Origin of the Israelite Religion: researches on the Hexateuch as the basis of rabbinic sources).* Berlin: Morgenland, 1926

Hertzberg, Arthur, *The Zionist Idea,* Chapter 5.

Lilker, Shalom, *Kibbutz Judaism: A New Tradition in the Making.* London: Cornwall Books, 1982.

Chapter Eighteen: Judaism as Totality of National Historic Culture

Ahad Ha-Am, *Nationalism and the Jewish Ethic: Basic Writings of Ahad Ha-Am* (ed. Hans Kohn). New York: Schocken, 1962. Contains "The Wrong Way," "The Jewish State and the Jewish Problem," "Pinsker and Political Zionism," "Supremacy of Reason," other essays.

— *Selected Essays* (ed. Leon Simon). Philadelphia: Jewish Publication Society, 1936. Contains: "Sacred and Profane," "Past and Future," "Priest and Prophet," "Imitation and Assimilation," "Slavery in Freedom," "The Transvaluation of Values," "The Spiritual Revival," "Moses," other essays.

Gottschalk, Yehiel Alfred, *Ahad Ha-Am and the Jewish National Spirit* (Hebrew). Jerusalem: Sifriya Tziyonit, 1992.

Simon, Leon, *Ahad Ha-Am, Asher Ginzberg: A Biography*. Philadelphia: Jewish Publication Society, 1960.

Zipperstein, Steven, *Elusive Prophet: Ahad Ha'Am and the Origins of Zionism*. Berkeley: University of California Press, 1993.

Chapter Nineteen: Sanctity and the Jewish National Movement

Bialik, Hayyim Nahman, *All the Works of Ch. N. Bialik* (Hebrew). Tel Aviv: Devir, 1962.

— *The Book of Legends* (tr. William Braude). New York: Schocken, 1992.

— *Complete Poetic Works of Hayyim Nahman Bialik* (English, ed. Efros). New York: Histadruth Ivrith of America, 1948.

— *The Hebrew Book: An Essay* (tr. Minnie Halkin). Jerusalem: Bialik Institute, 1951.

— *Revealment and Concealment: Five Essays.* Jerusalem: Ibis, 2000.

— *Selected Poems* (ed. Aberbach). New York: Overlook Duckworth, 2004.

Burnshaw, Carmi, Spicehandler, eds., *The Modern Hebrew Poem Itself.* New York: Schocken, 1966.

Feinstein, Sara, *Sunshine, Blossoms and Blood: H.N. Bialik in His Time.* University Press of America, 2005.

Chapter Twenty: The Dimension of Sanctity in Pioneering Labor Zionism

Buber, Martin, *Eclipse of God.* New York: Harper, 1957.

— *Hasidism and Modern Man.* New York: Horizon, 1958.

— *Israel and the World: Essays in a Time of Crisis.* New York: Schocken, 1948.

— *On Judaism.* New York: Schocken, 1967.

— *On Zion: The History of an Idea.* New York: Schocken, 1973.

— *The First Buber: Youthful Zionist Writings of Martin Buber* (ed. Gilya G. Schmidt). Syracuse: Syracuse University Press, 1999.

— *The Knowledge of Man: Selected essays.* New York: Harper & Row, 1965.

— *The Martin Buber Reader: Essential Writings* (ed. Biemann). New York: Palgrave Macmillan, 2002.

Friedman, Maurice, *Martin Buber: The Life of Dialogue.* Chicago: University of Chicago Press, 1976.

— *Martin Buber's Life and Work* (3 volumes). New York: Dutton, 1983.

Gordon, A.D., *Selected Essays* (tr. Frances Burnce). New York: League for Labor Palestine, 1938.

Rose, Herbert H., *The Life and Thought of A.D. Gordon: Pioneer, Philosopher and Prophet of Modern Israel.* New York: Bloch, 1964.

Shimoni, Gideon, *The Zionist Ideology,* Chapter 5.

Chapter Twenty One: Orthodox Zionist Culture — Sanctifying Modernity

Aviad, Yishayahu (Oskar Wolfsberg), *Zionism: Chapters on its Essence, Vision and Reality* (Hebrew). Jerusalem: Histadrut / Mosad ha-Rav Kook, 1946.

Ish Shalom, B. & Sh. Rosenberg, eds., *The World of Rav Kook's Thought: Avichai Sponsored Conference*. Jerusalem: Avichai, 1991.

Katz, Jacob, "The Forerunners of Zionism" in Reinharz, ed. *Essential Papers on Zionism*, 1996.

Kook, Abraham Isaac, *The Essential Writings of Abraham Isaac Kook* **(ed. Ben Zion Bokser).** New York: Amity House, 1988.

Schwartz, Dov, *The Theology of the Religious Zionist Movement* (Hebrew). Tel Aviv: Am Oved, 1996.

Schweid, Eliezer, *Democracy and Halakhah (a monograph on Haim Hirschensohn)*. Lanham: University Press of America, 1994.

Chapter Twenty Two: Judaism as a Culture in the Diaspora

Goldsmith, Emanuel S., Mel Scult and Robert Meitzer, eds., *The American Judaism of Mordecai M. Kaplan*. Detroit: Wayne State University Press, 1990.

Kaplan, Mordecai M., *Dynamic Judaism*. New York: Schocken, 1985.

— *Judaism as a Civilization*. New York: Macmillan, 1934.

Mintz, Alan, ed., *Hebrew in America : perspectives and prospects*. Detroit: Wayne State University Press, 1993.

Scult, Mel, *Judaism Faces the Twentieth Century: A Biography of Mordecai M. Kaplan*. Detroit: Wayne State University Press, 1993.

Chapter Twenty Three: The Secular Jewish Culture of Yiddish

Dubnow, Simon (Koppel S. Pinson, ed.), *Nationalism and History: Essays on Old and New Judaism*. New York: Atheneum, 1970.

Howe, Irving, *World of Our Fathers*. New York: Harcourt Brace, 1976.

Howe, Irving and Eliezer Greenberg, eds., *A Treasury of Yiddish Stories*. New York: Viking, 1954.

Hundert, Gershon David, editor-in-chief, *The YIVO Encyclopedia of Jews in Eastern Europe*. New Haven: Yale University Press, 2008.

Lansky, Aaron, *Outwitting History: The amazing adventures of a man who rescued a million Yiddish books*. Chapel Hill: Algonquin Books, 2004.

Liptzin, Sol, *The Flowering of Yiddish Literature*. New York: T. Yoseloff, 1963.

— *A History of Yiddish Literature*. New York: Jonathan David, 1972.

Index

internalizing secular while remaining
  religious, 19, 20, 25
Jewish morality, 152, 166, 171, 262
"Jewish personality," 240
  right to be Jewish, 153
  suppression of identity of, 15–16, 17
  universally Jewish, 160
  wishing to join the dominant class,
    xiv, 5, 10, 11, 81–82
  See also Jewish culture; Jewish na-
    tionalism
Joseph II (kaiser), 24
Joshua, 142
Judah Loewe Ben Bezalel. *See* "Maharal" of
  Prague
Judah, Rabbi, 66
Judaism, xi, 49
  "authentic" (rational) Judaism, 76,
    87
  based on dogmas, 154
  as basis for a contemporary world
    culture, viii, xi–xii. *See also* Jewish
    culture
  cultural sources of Judaism, 123
  as a culture in the Diaspora, 226–36
  as a culture vs. as a religion, 73
  as ethical monotheism, 87
  expressed in contemporary life, 74
  "Germanizing of," 96
  holiness as the core experience, 201
  influence on secular culture, 17
  as means of identity, 147
  a national historic culture, 146–72
  as a national religion, 83
  as a national spirit, 66
  pagan influence, 87
  post-Biblical Judaism, 98
  rabbinic Judaism, 33
  rabbis compared to Catholic Church
    priests, 132
  reflected in literature, 74
  Reform Movement, 85–94
  role of morality in, 167–68
  "Science of Judaism," 39, 66, 68, 69–70,
    103, 210, 241
    and Berdyczewski, 141
    and Bialik, 175
    and the cultural ideal of the
      Enlightenment, 95–100
    as a descendent of Enlighten-
      ment, 98
    Jüdische Wissenschaft, xii, 35, 36,
      71, 210, 262
    needing to recognize importance
      of Hebrew literature, 183

research in Judaism as a culture,
  71–84
transition from Haskalah to
  science of Judaism, 35–36
Wissenschaft des Judentums
  [Science of Judaism], 71, 210
as a supra-natural culture, 138
as a total life experience, 230
transition from religion to a national
  culture. *See also* Jewish nationalism,
  Jewish National Movement
as word of God, xii
See also Conservative Judaism; Hasidism; Modern Orthodox Judaism;
  Neo-Orthodox Judaism; Neo-Orthodox Movement; Orthodox Judaism;
  Positive-Historical (Conservative)
  Movement; Reform Judaism; ultra-
  Orthodox Judaism
"Judaizing" national values, 107
Judges, 142
Jüdische Wissenschaft, xii, 35, 36, 71, 210, 262
  See also Science of Judaism movement;
  Wissenschaft des Judentums [Science
  of Judaism]
Judismo (Judeo-Arabic jargon), 16
justice, 8, 54, 67, 163, 166, 167, 170–71, 203
  absolute justice, 185
  partial justice, 219
  social justice, 118, 144, 250
  and truth, 84, 168–69, 170–71, 218–20
justification, ethical, 233

K
kabbalah, 62, 97, 98, 207, 221
  kabbalistic mysticism, 220
  kabbalistic-pantheistic theory, 218
Kant, Immanuel, 87
Kaplan, Mordecai, 172, 227–36, 242
  and Ahad Ha-Am, 227–28, 231–32, 234
  and Bialik, 227–28
kashrut, 214
kibbush ha'avoda [conquest of labor], 251
kibbutz/kibbutzim, vii, 131, 250, 254, 261, 262
  kibbutz ha-Dati Movement [Orthodox
    kibbutzim], 214, 231
  secular kibbutzim, 214
Kingdom of God, 208
Kingdom of God, The (Buber), 211
Klausner, Joseph, 113–14
Knesset Israel, 136, 137, 262
knowledge
  knowledge must be scientific, 9
  knowledge of the truth, 55
  objective knowledge, 9

philosophy examining all knowledge,
40–42
self-knowledge, 40
Torat ha-Adam [Human Knowledge/
Law], 21, 22, 37, 70, 91
Torat ha-Elohim [Divine Knowledge/
Law], 21, 24
true knowledge, 218
of truth, 218
use of the word "Torah" to embrace
knowledge, 21 (note)
value of, 9
Kohelet Musar ["Tribune of Morals"] (periodical), 19
Kook, Abraham, 111, 112, 214, 217–23,
224–25
kosher and non-kosher, 28
Krochmal, Avraham, 131
Krochmal, Nachman, ix, 43–70, 71, 72, 75,
86, 87, 91, 168, 174, 218
Kulturkampf, 111–12
Kurzweil, Baruch, 171
kvutza, 250, 254

L
labor
Buber's views on, 206, 209
and Eretz Israel, 121, 250–51
importance of, 197–99, 202, 205, 211
labor as a secularized equivalent of
worshipping, 118
Labor Israel, 144
manual labor, 117–18
social significance of, 204
societal character of, 202–3
See also Culture of Labor
Labor Battalions. *See* "Gedud ha-Avodah"
Labor Movement
in Eretz Israel, 193–211
Jewish Labor Movement, 238, 239
pioneering culture, 115–22, 130, 193–
211, 214, 257
See also Hebrew Labor Movement;
Jewish Labor Movement
Labor Zionism, 214
sanctity and, 193–211
Ladino jargon, 16
Land of Israel. *See* Israel, Land of
language
analysis of Bialik's use of, 187
Arabic language, 24–25
of art, 249
as basis for both civilization and
culture, 13
as basis for European culture, 15

changes in showing impact of history,
47–48
as expression of national spirit, 246
Haskalah movement stressing the
learning of, 26–27
importance of to Bialik, 175–76
Jews creating a national language,
108–10
Jews using language of the environment, 16
key way to distinguish and define a
culture, 243–44
name of culture and language different
from name of the land, 244–45
natural language, 204, 205
negation of languages of the Diaspora,
243
opening access to Jewish culture in
non-Judaic languages, 20–21
rejection of dual languages, 160–61
as spiritual potential, 204
as a unifier, 39
See also Arabic language; Aramaic
language; German language;
grammar; Hebrew language;
Judismo (Judeo-Arabic jargon);
Ladino jargon; Latin language;
philology; Yiddish jargon
lashon [tongue], 243
Latin language, 68
"law of God," 22–23, 25, 37, 38, 70, 91
See also Torat ha-Elohim [Divine Know-
ledge/Law]
"law of man," 21–22, 23, 24, 29
See also Torat ha-Adam [Human Know-
ledge/Law]
laws, 54
Mishpat Ivri [Jewish law], 163–64
learned scholar [*talmid ḥakham*], 5
learning
Jewish learning, 21 (note), 87, 89, 93,
262
value of, 9, 31, 45, 53, 261
See also education; Gemara; knowledge
legislation, 54, 58
Lehi, 114
Leibowitz, Yeshayahu, 171
"Levadi" ["Alone"] (Bialik), 175
Leviticus 19:2, 201
liberalism, 95, 227
"Lifnei Aron ha-Sefarim" ["Facing the Bookcase"] (Bialik), 175, 189
Lilienblum, Moses Leib, 99, 106, 146, 212
linguistic ethos. *See* language

Made in the USA
Lexington, KY
29 March 2013